GAUL IN

HELVETII Tribal names

| 0 | 50 | 100 |

| 0 | 50 | 100 | 150 | 200 | 250 |

D0467397

GERMANS

UBII

SUEBI

CHERUSCI

GERMANY

ES

Rhine

Danube

Danube

DACIANS

HARUDES

ETII

DUNI

A l p s

G a u l

Cisalpine

Po

Po

Aquileia

Northern Italy

I l l y r i c u m

Tiber

ITALY

Rome

THE BATTLE
FOR GAUL

JULIUS CAESAR
THE BATTLE FOR GAUL

A new translation by
ANNE & PETER WISEMAN
with illustrations selected by
BARRY CUNLIFFE

David R. Godine, Publisher
Boston

First U.S. edition published in 1980 by
DAVID R. GODINE, *Publisher*, Inc.
306 Dartmouth Street
Boston, Massachusetts 02116

Library of Congress Cataloging in Publication Data
Caesar, C   Julius.
The Battle for Gaul.
Translation of De bello Gallico.
1. Gaul – History – 58 BC – 511 AD. I. Wiseman, Anne.
II. Wiseman, Peter, 1940–   III. Title.
DC62.C2813 1980 936.4 79–54955
ISBN 0–87923–306–0

Designed and produced by Russel Sharp Ltd,
66 Woodbridge Road, Guildford, Surrey, GU1 4RD, England.

Designer: Patrick Yapp
Picture Researcher: Caroline Lucas

Typesetter: SX Composing Ltd, England
Printer: Dai Nippon Printing Co. Ltd, Hong Kong

FRONTISPIECE: Julius Caesar, from the bust in
the Vatican Museum. The ancestral busts in the
reception-hall of the Julii family included those
of ten consuls.

CONTENTS

COLOR PLATES

NOTE: *The page numbers given are those opposite the plates.*

INTRODUCTION

CAESAR

Gaius Iulius Caesar was a Roman aristocrat, a patrician whose family claimed descent from the legendary kings of Alba Longa, and through them from Aeneas of Troy, whose mother was the goddess Venus and whose son Iulus originated the family name.

The Roman Republic that his ancestors had served was an oligarchy, its ruling class motivated by a competitive lust for glory; each senator advanced as far as he was able through a sequence of annual magistracies in which the two senior posts – the praetorship and the consulship – carried *imperium*, the legal right to command an army. There above all, in victory and conquest, lay the Roman statesman's goal – the almost superhuman glory of the triumph, when for one intoxicating day he was the equal of the gods, and ever after the inscribed monuments of his achievement, paid for by the spoils of war, kept his name and reputation alive in the eyes of his fellow-citizens. Major commands naturally fell to the consuls, and since there were only two each year, out of an annual senatorial intake of 15 or 20, the consulship was a prize only the noble, the lucky, or the unusually gifted could hope to win.

Caesar was born in 100 BC, the sixth consulship of the great but humbly born Gaius Marius (his uncle by marriage), who had put to shame the incompetent aristocrats of his day by saving Italy from the threatened invasion of the Cimbri and the Teutoni. Marius's triumph over these Germanic peoples – whose victories inflicted on earlier Roman commanders echo ominously in the background of the *Commentaries* – had taken place a few months before Caesar's birth.

The ancestral busts in the reception-hall of the Iulii included ten consuls, but eight of those had been in the dim days of the fifth century BC; and there was only one with a triumphal garland, Caesar's great-great-great-great-grandfather, victor in a forgotten campaign near Brindisi in 267 BC. The marriage connection with Marius was worth more to the family than its own record, and may be the reason for its revival, marked by the Julian consuls (Caesar's uncle and two of his cousins) of 91, 90, and 64 BC. Caesar himself was faithful to Marius's memory throughout his career, dangerous though that was in a generation of political discord and civil war when Marius's name was the symbol of a 'popular' political movement hostile to the traditionally conservative oligarchy. There was even a time, during Sulla's dictatorship in 82 BC, when Caesar was in hiding with a price on his head.

By the time he had made his way to the praetorship, in 62 BC, Caesar was known to the ruling oligarchy as a dangerously able and ambitious man.

They deprived him of a triumph after his praetorian command (in Spain in 61–60), and did their best to prevent him from being elected consul; but he held the consulship in 59 BC, and forced through, in the teeth of furious conservative opposition, a legislative programme of which they profoundly disapproved.

He was able to do this thanks to the support of Gnaeus Pompeius, 'Pompey the Great'. Caesar thus owed to Pompey the consular command by which his ambitions could be fulfilled – and in another sense, it was because of Pompey that those ambitions were so vast.

Only five years older than Caesar, Pompey had already won no fewer than three triumphs. His honorific nickname likened him, not unjustly, to Alexander the Great; his last campaign, against king Mithridates in the East, had more than doubled the income of the Roman treasury and added three new provinces to the empire of Rome. After Pompey, anyone who aspired to be *princeps civitatis*, the leading figure in the Republic, had to do much more than just win an ordinary triumph. The price of glory had gone sharply up.

It was for this reason that Caesar, as consul, got a special law pushed through giving him an exceptional five-year command (later extended for a further five years in 55 BC). His province was Cisalpine Gaul and Illyricum – that is, roughly north Italy and the Adriatic coast of Jugoslavia. It gave him the chance of conquest either in the Balkans, against the growing power of the Dacian Burebista, or in Gaul, where the Sequani, with their German master Ariovistus, were harassing the Aedui, allies of Rome. In the end, it was in Gaul that the crisis came, with the migration of the Helvetii. The Senate, on the proposal of Pompey, added to Caesar's province the territory of Transalpine Gaul (roughly Provence), which had been taken over by Rome 60 years earlier to protect the land route to Spain. This is 'the Province' for whose protection Caesar shows himself so anxious. But not even he could pretend that his campaigns were just defensive: they were aimed at conquest, at the expansion of the dominion of Rome and the establishment of Caesar's own glory.

The greater the command, however, the longer the absence from Rome. Caesar was lucky in that his responsibilities included holding assizes in north Italy (Cisalpine Gaul), which brought him closer to Rome than any other provincial commander could be. But it was in the city itself that he needed to have his achievements publicised, his reputation kept alive. There were – as Ariovistus reminded him – plenty of political enemies who would stop at nothing to end his career, and whose influence it was essential to resist.

In this, Caesar had the great advantage of being a man of letters as well as a man of war. One of the foremost political orators of his day, he had also written tragedy (*Oedipus*, in his youth) and poetry (*The Journey*, on his way to Spain); his two books *On Analogy*, an important and influential work of linguistic theory (dedicated to Cicero) were actually written in Gaul, while en route from the assizes to his army. It was a talent that enabled him to be, as the Romans said, his own herald.

Pompey's campaigns had been written up by Theophanes of Mytilene, the general's confidential adviser, and by a certain Voltacilius Pitholaus. But the first of these was a Greek, the second a freed slave; the great man himself was not at ease with the pen. Other generals had written auto-biography – notably Quintus Catulus, Marius's aristocratic colleague in the Cimbric campaign – but only after the event, for retrospective self-justification. What Caesar did was something new. The commander-in-chief himself recorded his campaigns, and had the record published year by year.

It is sometimes argued that Caesar's seven books of *Commentaries* on the Gallic War were written all at once in 51 or 50 BC, or else that, though written year by year, they were all published together after Book VII was completed. But Caesar needed the Roman reading public to have his achievements constantly in mind. Each book is complete in itself, and we may much more plausibly imagine Caesar writing them quickly each winter, and having them copied and distributed to make their impact in Rome each spring.

The *Commentaries* must be carefully distinguished from Caesar's despatches to the Senate, which are referred to at the end of Books II, IV, and VII. (A few such despatches, from other commanders, survive in the collection of Cicero's correspondence.) In Latin, *commentarius* has a quite specific meaning. It translates the Greek *hypomnema*, and means something like '*aide-mémoire*', a memorandum or narrative sketch of the historical material that could be written up into a full-scale history with all the literary and rhetorical elaboration Greek and Roman readers expected.

Caesar was a purist in the use of language, and the uncluttered factual style required of a *commentarius* suited him very well. But he must have been aware that his commentaries on the Gallic War were more than just sketches for other men to work up. Aulus Hirtius added Book VIII after Caesar's death, to link the narrative with the Civil War commentaries: in his prefatory letter he says quite rightly that Caesar was not, as his title implies, offering other historians the chance of writing up the Gallic War, but rather denying them that chance for ever. That was certainly how it struck Cicero, whose comment (in a dialogue published in 46 BC) may serve as a summing-up:

> The *Commentaries* are splendid: bare, straight and handsome, stripped of rhetorical ornament like an athlete of his clothes. He intended to provide material for others to use in the writing of history; but though he may have gratified some fools who will want to use their curling-irons on it, he has frightened off all the men of sense from putting pen to paper. For there is nothing in a history more attractive than clean and lucid brevity.

Caesar got his conquest, and his glory. But to get his triumph, and the pre-eminent position in the Republic to which he felt his achievements entitled him, he had to cross the Rubicon. By leading his army in 49 BC across the boundary of his province and into Italy, Caesar declared civil war on Pompey and the Republic. There followed five seasons of bitter fighting, the unprecedented Dictatorship for life, and finally, on the Ides of March 44 BC, below Pompey's statue, the bloody daggers of the 'honourable men'.

GAUL

'Celts' and 'Gauls' were names frequently used by Greek and Roman writers to describe the barbarian peoples who occupied much of northwestern Europe. The words were largely interchangeable and covered a multitude of tribes of different ethnic origin and varying customs. Yet the generalization is a useful one. Archaeological research has shown that by the fifth century BC large parts of Europe from Britain to Romania and from northern Italy to Belgium shared many cultural elements in common. This does not mean that we are dealing with a Celtic nation but simply that by the processes of trade and exchange, by folk movement and by convergent evolution, the barbarian communities of Europe had developed a degree of cultural similarity. It was this that impressed the classical observers when they wrote of 'Celts or Gauls'.

The fourth and third centuries BC were a time of migration. From somewhere in eastern France and southern Germany – the home of a spectacular aristocratic culture in the sixth and fifth centuries – migratory waves of warriors spread out in all directions across the face of Europe. The Roman historian Livy believed the reason for the exodus to be overpopulation in their homeland. This may well have been an important factor. Another reason was probably that the conspicuous consumption of the aristocracy over a number of decades, burying, for example, objects of enormous value with the dead, outran the productive capacity of the community. At any event the aristocratic society collapsed in a fury of folk movement.

Tens of thousands of migrants spread through the Alpine passes into the fertile Po valley, and when that land was saturated they crossed the Appenines to terrorize first Etruria and then Rome, actually destroying the city in c. 390 BC. Other bands passed eastwards along the Danube into Transdanubia (modern Hungary). Some settled in Romania, others pressed on through Illyria and Thrace (Yugoslavia and Bulgaria) and in 279 BC a horde of warriors attacked the sacred oracle at Delphi. A few years later, driven back from Greece and Macedonia, thousands of men, women, and children crossed into Asia finally settling in central Turkey.

The second and first centuries BC saw the Celts in retreat. Driven north as the classical world of the Macedonians and Romans gained strength they were forced to settle in the Danube valley and beyond the Alps where they were soon to come under pressure from their barbarian neighbours. The Dacians of Romania pushed westwards forcing them from Hungary while the tribes of northern Europe, loosely referred to as the Germans, thrust down from the north. Occasionally these pressures built up to such an extent that they exploded in folk movement, as for example in the late second century BC when two northern tribes, the Cimbri and the Teutoni, moved south terrorizing Gaul and striking fear into the hearts of the Romans when they beat successive Roman armies on the borders of Italy. The menace was successfully dealt with by the Roman general Marius but the vivid memory of the near disaster remained. Caesar made good use of it by playing up the 'German' threat. His assessment of the Gaulish political scene – Gaul would have to become Roman or it would be overrun by Germans – was probably a gross exaggeration but as a justification for his Gaulish campaigns it would have convinced many who remembered the panic of 50 years before.

By the beginning of the first century BC one of the principal concentrations of Celtic peoples lay in the territory spreading from southern Germany, through France, to Britain. They were a population in a state of flux. Pressure on land was still intense and the migratory movements of the previous centuries were far from over. Indeed Ariovistus's negotiations for land and the decision of the Helvetii to migrate westwards provide fully documented examples of the fluid nature of barbarian settlement: Caesar's detailed analysis of the preparations of the Helvetii offers a unique insight into the causes and mechanisms of Celtic migration.

There has been a tendency to view the Gauls of Caesar's time as a nation – it is an attitude that might appeal to modern French politicians but is historically and archaeologically unacceptable. Indeed Caesar himself, in his famous opening lines, was at pains to point out the variety he observed among the Gauls, but even his threefold division belies the complexity of the situation. It is more realistic to visualize France at this time divided into a series of roughly concentric zones spreading outwards from Marseilles at the mouth of the Rhône. Those nearest the core were economically and socially more developed than those on the periphery.

Massilia (Marseilles) – the Greek trading colony founded about 600 BC – provided the Mediterranean coast of France with an urban model that was gradually accepted by neighbouring communities. The native hill towns of Enseérune, Cayla, and Entremont had, by the second century BC, adopted many of the elements of classical urbanization while the sophistication of the temple architecture of Roquepertuse owes much to classical ideas. This is hardly surprising for not only had the influence of the Greek traders long been manifest but as soon as Rome acquired interests in Spain, southern France became an important corridor along which successive Roman armies passed. Thus when the Saluvii attacked the territory of Massilia in 125 BC Rome was bound to act. The Saluvii were defeated in 124, their capital of Entremont was taken and a new Roman colony set up in the valley below at Aquae Sextiae (Aix-en-Provence). The conversion of southern Gaul into a Roman province gave a considerable impetus to trade. Already the Rhône valley had served as an axis along which luxury goods had been transported to the chieftains of the Côte d'Or as far back as the sixth century. In all probability this trade continued, though on a diminished scale after the migration had begun, and with the foundation of the Province it would have intensified once more. The control of the route and the safeguarding of Roman economic interests were important considerations that lay behind the successive Roman campaigns in the Rhône valley.

Control of the Rhône route was important to Rome for the direct access that it gave to the markets and production centres of central and northern Europe. So too was the command of the Garonne, which flows into the Atlantic. This was one of the traditional routes by which metals, and in particular tin, were brought to the Mediterranean from Brittany and Britain.

Those native communities who occupied territories on the fringe of the

Province were naturally influenced by the Roman presence and by Roman market economy. They would necessarily have become the middlemen through whose land trade to the more remote areas had to pass. There would have been financial benefits but more far reaching were the social changes that ensued. Caesar provides us with the relevant evidence in respect of three tribes, all significantly on the fringe of the Province, the Aedui, Arverni, and Helvetii. All three had, by this time, evolved social systems appropriate to primitive states: they were ruled by annually elected magistrates answerable to councils and they had developed codes of public laws. That this change, from tribal society to early state, was comparatively recent is shown by the strict regulations designed to prevent reversion – anyone who aspired to kingship (i.e. tried to overthrow the state and establish his personal authority) could be punished by death. This had happened to the Arvernian, Celtillus, the father of Vercingetorix (VII 4) and it was the charge levied at Orgetorix, the Helvetian noble (I 2–4). Indeed it could be argued that Vercingetorix himself, in establishing his reputation as a freedom fighter against Rome (against the will of his own people) was also planning to make a bid for kingship.

The evidence provided by Caesar, taken together with an assessment of Gaulish coinage, shows that the early state system was already in force among the Helvetii, Sequani, Aedui, Arverni, and Bituriges Cubi and may well also have been developing among the Lingones, Lemovices, and Pictones. In other words a great block of territory stretching around the fringes of the Roman Province, from the Alps to the Atlantic, was controlled by stable governments of the type with which Rome could easily deal. Treaties of friendship promising mutual support were already established: thus these people were of no immediate concern to Caesar. Beyond, however, were tribes whose political organization was more archaic. The Aquitanian tribes, close to the Province and hemmed in by the Pyrenees and the Atlantic seem to have posed little problem but to the north the situation was more uncertain. The Carnutes and Senones, between the Seine and the Loire, were still ruled by kings and at this stage the centre of the ancient druidic faith lay in the land of the Carnutes. It may have been an unwillingness to disturb the religious susceptibilities of the Gauls that persuaded Caesar to stay clear of their territory until their opposition left him no option but to intervene. The power of the Druids was considerable: potentially, they could have united Gaul against the Romans but it is possible that, with the evolution of the archaic state among the central and southern tribes, their power was already waning by Caesar's time.

Farther north still were even more primitive tribes, the Belgae and the tribes of Aremorica and Normandy, forming a broad arc of hostility to Rome, and beyond them, across the sea, were the equally primitive Britons. All these tribes were still largely untouched, as Caesar says, by the enervating luxuries of Mediterranean life. They were ruled by kings and their social systems were such that prowess and prestige could be attained only by acts of valour in battle. For this reason intertribal warfare was common and the young men were brought up to be courageous fighters. The most distant group, the tribes that Caesar calls Germans, who lived beyond the Rhine, were even more primitive.

This then was the situation when Caesar entered Gaul in 58 BC. His immediate concern was to deal with the Helvetii and Ariovistus. These encounters were a useful prelude: they provided experience for his army and a means of establishing himself in the eyes of the Gallic politicians. The next year he was ready for the real business – the subjugation of the primitive tribes of the northern arc.

It probably took longer than he had anticipated (from 57 until 53) to finally establish Roman superiority, and even then it needed several acts of the most brutal genocide before resistance was quelled. The rebellion of 52 seems to have been unexpected, indeed it could be interpreted as an aberration, the one-off act of an individual in search of personal glory. At any event Caesar quickly dealt with it: that he needed only one further year in the field to tie up loose ends is a measure of his success and reflects on the superficial nature of pan-Gallic resistance once Vercingetorix had been removed.

Caesar's conquests have fascinated generations of readers. As a folk hero he is immortalized in the hundreds of 'Caesar's Camps' that litter the French and British countryside – the name assigned indiscriminately to earthworks of all dates – but serious attempts to trace the topography of the campaigns did not begin until just over a hundred years ago. Between 1860 and 1865 Napoleon III sponsored an expedition, led by Colonel Stoffel, to discover and excavate the forts and battlefields of the Gallic wars located in France. The results were, by any standards, spectacularly successful and were lavishly published by Napoleon III in his *Histoire de Jules César* in 1865. Although the debate as to the precise location of specific sites has continued since then, the starting point has always been Napoleon III's publication.

More recently the growing use of air photography in France has brought to light much new evidence. Particularly impressive is the magnificent work of Roger Agache in northern France, which has added several new Roman camps to the map, and of René Goguey in the region of Alesia – work that has both confirmed and extended the interpretations of Colonel Stoffel.

Of the natives against whom Caesar battled much is now known as the result of innumerable excavations in all parts of France and southern Britain. Bibracte, the *oppidum* of the Aedui on Mt. Beuvray, was examined last century (and incidently desperately needs reinvestigation using modern techniques); hundreds of Belgic cemeteries have been excavated in northern France and the Low Countries and just before the last war Sir Mortimer Wheeler organized a campaign to explore the native fortifications of Normandy and Brittany.

From many of these sources we have chosen material to illustrate this new translation. We hope we have shown that far from being static the study of Caesar's military genius and of the people he conquered is a rapidly developing enquiry. Each year brings much that is new.

Barry Cunliffe and Peter Wiseman

TRANSLATORS' NOTE

Expressions of distance have been left in Roman measurements: the Roman foot was 296 mm, the passus 1.48 m, the Roman mile 1.48 km or about 1665 yards. So when Caesar says '20 miles', he means just over 19 English miles.

We have made no attempt to find English equivalents for Roman military formations or the titles of Roman officers. A cohort consisted of 480 infantry, a legion consisted of ten cohorts. There were six centurions to each cohort, each in charge of a century of 80 men; each legion had six military tribunes (*tribuni militum*), who were employed in general staff duties. The legates (*legati*) were deputy commanders chosen by the commander-in-chief, in this case Caesar; they were of senatorial rank, and normally in command of a legion each. Caesar's quaestor, a junior senator, was in charge of financial matters, but also sometimes employed as a legionary commander.

We have deliberately left the word *oppidum* (plural *oppida*) untranslated. 'Town', 'fortified town', or even 'stronghold' would give the wrong impression; to understand what an *oppidum* was, the reader must refer to the illustrations.

As for place-names, we have used modern equivalents where they are familiar (Kent, Paris, etc), and left the ancient names where they are not (Alesia, Uxellodunum, etc), in the hope that the reader's recognition of at least some of the geography will outweigh the inconsistency. Where we use 'the Province' or 'the Roman province' without further specification, the reference is to what the Romans called 'further Gaul' – France south and east of the Massif Central; the 'nearer' province of Gaul, corresponding to Italy north of a line roughly from Pisa to Rimini, appears as 'northern Italy' in our translation. Where it is essential to distinguish between the two provinces, we have reluctantly used the transliterations 'Transalpine' and 'Cisalpine'.

Finally, except in the eighth book (which was written by Hirtius), we have allowed Caesar to speak of himself as 'I'. In the Latin he refers to himself in the third person, but in English this convention seems unnecessarily mannered.

The extant manuscripts of the *Commentaries*, none of which is older than the ninth century, fall into two main groups known as α and β, of which the former is regarded as providing in general a more authentic text. The edition of the text most conveniently available to British and American readers is that of R. Du Pontet in the Oxford Classical Texts series (O.U.P. 1900, frequently reprinted), who – like most editors – follows the α tradition wherever possible. We have used the Oxford text as the basis of our translation, adopting other readings – from the β tradition or modern emendations – only where Du Pontet leaves a corrupt text, marked by †, or where we found his reading either unintelligible or for some other reason unlikely to represent what Caesar wrote. The places where we differ from the Oxford text are listed below.

		Oxford text	**This translation**	**Authority**
I	51.2	Triboces	Tribocos	β MSS
	53.1	quinque	XV	Rice Holmes
	54.1	Ubi . . . [senserunt]	ubi . . . senserunt	All MSS
II	2.1	interiorem	ulteriorem	β MSS
	30.2	vallo pedum in circuitu quindecim milium	vallo pedum XII in circuitu V milium	Rice Holmes
III	6.2	interficiunt	intercipiunt	Lange
	13.3	transtra pedalibus	transtra ex pedalibus	β MSS
	13.6	scopulis	copulis	Platinus
	20.1	Mallius	Manlius	Some β MSS
	24.5	timidiores	timoris	Stephanus
IV	3.3	et † paulo quam sunt eiusdem generis et ceteris humaniores†	ii paulo, quamquam sunt eiusdem generis, sunt ceteris humaniores	Ukert
	15.1	Mosae	Mosellae	Cluverius
	25.6	† ex proximis primis†	ex proximis	Hotomannus
V	25.3	† inimicis iam multis palam ex civitate et eis auctoribus eum † interfecerunt	inimaci palam multis ex civitate auctoribus interfecerunt	β MSS
	34.2	† numero	studio	Davies, Heller
	53.6	[quaestore]	legato	β MSS
VI	7.6	in consilio	consulto	Hecker
	14.1	militiae vacationem omniumque rerum habent immunitatem	omit	Meusel
	22.2	qui † cum †	quique	β MSS
	29.3	Volcatium	Volcacium	Dittenberger
VII	4.6	Andos	Andes	Glareanus
	19.2	† saltus †	semitas	Fleischer
	20.3	† se ipsum †	se ipse sine	Bentley
	45.7	qui	ne	β MSS
	47.1	† concionatus †	continuo	von Göler
	50.2	† pacatum †	pacatorum	Georges
	55.9	[aut adductos inopia ex provincia expellere]	aut adductos inopia in provinciam expellere	Nicasius
	74.1	† eius discessu †	omit	Oudendorp
	75.2	† Ambluaretis †	Ambivaretis	Glück
	75.3	† Senonibus †	Suessionibus	Glareanus
	87.3	† una XL †	una XI	Ciacconius
	90.6	Ambibaretos	Ambivaretos	Glück
VIII	pref. 2	comparantibus	competentibus	Bernhardy
	24.3	† incolae illorum †	Illyriorum	Frigell
	52.2	maiore et commendatiore	maior ei commendatio	Kraffert
	52.5	† iusserunt †	evicerunt	Jurin, Madvig

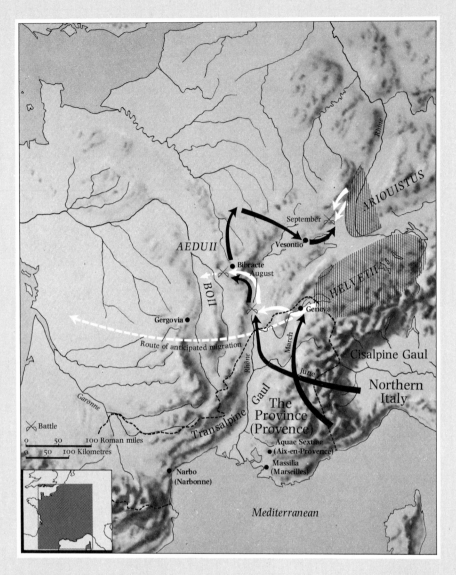

The campaign of 58 BC was fought on the fringes of the known world. Southern France had been subjected to classical influences for centuries after the foundation of the Greek trading town of Massilia (Marseilles) in about 600 BC. The coastal strip between Italy and Spain, vital to Rome's interests, was annexed in 123 BC after the native tribe, the Saluvii, were decisively beaten and the Romans founded the town of Aquae Sextiae (Aix-en-Provence). The new territory – the Province – was the springboard for Roman involvement in Gaul. Friendly tribes on the border, like the Aedui, were encouraged and rewarded while recalcitrant tribes were punished. In 121 the territory of the Allobroges, in the Rhône valley as far north as Geneva, was annexed: a few years later a colony was founded at Narbonne – not long after the territory around Toulouse was absorbed. Transalpine Gaul was of great economic importance to Rome – Cicero could write 'all Gaul is filled with traders, is full of Roman citizens', an exaggeration no doubt but when the stability of Gaul was threatened by the migration of the Helvetii and by the political manoeuvrings of Ariovistus, Caesar was provided with an admirable excuse to move his armies deep into uncharted territory.

BOOK I · 58 BC

1 The Helvetic campaign

Gaul as a whole consists of three separate parts; one is inhabited by the 1
Belgae, another by the Aquitani and the third by the people we call Gauls,
though in their own language they are called Celts. In language, customs
and laws these three peoples are quite distinct. The Celts are separated from
the Aquitani by the river Garonne, and from the Belgae by the Marne and
the Seine.

Of all these peoples the toughest are the Belgae. They are the farthest away
from the culture and civilized ways of the Roman province, and merchants,
bringing those things that tend to make men soft, very seldom reach them;
moreover, they are very close to the Germans across the Rhine and are continually at war with them. For the same reason, it is the Helvetii who are the
bravest of all the other Gauls because they have almost daily skirmishes with
the Germans, either keeping them out of Helvetian territory or else starting
hostilities on German land themselves.

The part of the country that the Celts occupy faces north; it starts at the
river Rhône and is bounded by the Garonne, the Atlantic, and the territory
of the Belgae, and where the Sequani and the Helvetii are, it reaches the
river Rhine. The area occupied by the Belgae, which faces northeast, starts
at the northernmost boundary of the Celts and extends to the lower Rhine.
Aquitania starts at the Garonne and stretches to the Pyrenees and the section
of Atlantic coast nearest to Spain; this part faces northwest.

By far the richest and most distinguished man among the Helvetii was one 2
Orgetorix. He wanted to become king, so during the consulship of Marcus
Messalla and Marcus Pupius Piso he started a conspiracy among the nobles
of the tribe and persuaded the people to move out of their territory, taking
all their forces with them. His argument was that it would be easy for them,
the bravest of the Gauls, to get control of the whole country. And it had the
greater effect on them because the Helvetii are hemmed in on all sides by
natural barriers: on one side there is the Rhine, very broad and deep, separating Helvetian territory from the Germans, on the other the vast Jura range,
separating them from the Sequani, while on the third, Lake Geneva and the
Rhône form the boundary between them and the Roman province.

These geographical features meant that they could not range over a wide
area and had greater difficulty in making war on neighbouring tribes. Since
the Helvetii enjoyed fighting, they bitterly resented the restriction. They considered that the territory they had did not match the size of their population
or its reputation for bravery in war; it was too small, being some 240 miles
long and 180 miles wide.

3   Prompted by these considerations and swayed by Orgetorix's influence, they decided to make the necessary preparations for their migration – buying up as many draught animals and wagons as they could, sowing as much land as possible to have an adequate supply of grain for the journey, and securing peace and friendly relations with the neighbouring tribes. They thought that two years would be enough for completing these preparations, and they passed a law declaring that they would set out in the third. Orgetorix was chosen to see to all this and he took it upon himself to make the formal visits to the neighbouring states. In the course of his mission, he persuaded a Sequanian called Casticus – whose father Catamantaloedis had for many years been king of the Sequani, and had been given the title 'Friend of the Roman people' by the Senate – to seize the royal power that his father had previously held. Similarly, he persuaded the Aeduan Dumnorix – whose

The Aedui, who occupied the territory around Autun in the valley of the Saône, were of great significance to Rome. They were a comparatively stable pro-Roman enclave on the fringe of Roman territory – a buffer against the less friendly tribes of the north. Caesar (*left*) carefully cultivated the friendship of the Aeduan leaders, who gained prestige for themselves and for their tribe through their friendship with Rome. A powerful tribe like the Aedui could dictate to lesser tribes who remained subservient to them. In this way the tentacles of Rome spread deep into Gaul. Thus the political aspirations of Aeduan leaders like Dumnorix (*right*) were of direct concern to Rome.

brother Diviciacus at that time held the chief magistracy in the tribe and enjoyed the widest support of his people – to attempt the same thing, and he gave him his own daughter in marriage.

    He assured them that what he suggested was very easy for them to do, because he himself was going to get control of his own tribe. There was no doubt, he said, that the Helvetii were the most powerful tribe in the whole of Gaul; he would use his own resources and army to establish them in their kingdoms. They were won over by his persuasion, and the three exchanged an oath of loyalty, hoping that when each had seized royal power they would be able to get control of the whole of Gaul through the great power and strength of their three nations.

4   But the conspiracy was reported to the Helvetii by an informer. Following their custom, they compelled Orgetorix to stand trial in chains. If he were found guilty, the automatic punishment would be death by burning. So on

the day appointed for the trial, he assembled his entire household (about 10,000 people) at the scene and brought all his dependants and debtors there too, of whom there was a vast number. Through them he was able to escape having to stand trial. This provoked the people; they tried to gain their right by armed force, and the magistrates were collecting large numbers of men from the countryside when Orgetorix died. One cannot help suspecting, as the Helvetii believe, that he took his own life.

After the death of Orgetorix, the Helvetii did not abandon their attempts 5 to move out of their territory as they had determined to do. When they eventually thought they were ready to start the migration, they set fire to all their *oppida*, about 12 altogether, and to some 400 villages and the individual buildings that remained. They burned all the grain, except for what they intended to take with them. This ruled out any hope of returning home and made them more ready to face all the dangers ahead. They told everyone to take from home three months' supply of flour for his own use.

They persuaded their neighbours the Raurici, the Tulingi, and the Latovici to adopt the same policy and to set fire to their *oppida* and villages before setting off with them. The Boii, who had lived on the other side of the Rhine but had crossed into Norican territory and attacked the town of Noreia, became their allies and went with them.

There were really just two routes by which the Helvetii could leave their 6 country. One was through the territory of the Sequani; it was a difficult route, going between the Jura range and the river Rhône, so narrow that wagons could hardly get along it in single file, and the high mountain range overhanging the road made it easy for a handful of men to block it. The other route lay through the Roman province; this was much easier and quicker, because the river Rhône, which flows between the territory of the Helvetii and the recently subdued Allobroges, can be forded at several points.

The frontier town of the Allobroges closest to Helvetian territory is Geneva, and a bridge there links the two countries. Because the Allobroges appeared still unreconciled to Rome, the Helvetii thought they could persuade them to give them passage through their land; if not, they would force them to do so. With all preparations for their departure complete, they fixed the day on which all should assemble on the bank of the Rhône; it was the 28th of March in the consulship of Lucius Piso and Aulus Gabinius.

When I received the report that the Helvetii were attempting to march 7 through our province, I hurriedly left Rome for Transalpine Gaul, and, travelling with all possible speed, reached the area around Geneva. There was one legion in Transalpine Gaul, so I gave orders for as many troops as possible to be raised from the entire province, and the bridge at Geneva to be destroyed.

Hearing of my arrival, the Helvetii sent an embassy of their most distinguished citizens, led by Nammeius and Verucloetius, with instructions to say that their intention was to pass through the Province without doing any damage, simply because they had no alternative route. They asked me to agree to their doing so. But I remembered that the consul Lucius Cassius had been killed by these Helvetii, and his army routed and sent under the yoke. So I thought no concession should be made.

8   It was my opinion that given the chance to pass through our province, these people, hostile as they were, would not refrain from violence and destruction. But as I needed a breathing space for mustering the troops I had ordered, I told the envoys that I would take time to consider their request. If they wanted to raise the matter again, they should come back on the 13th of April.

In the meantime, using the legion that I had with me and the troops who had been levied from the Province, I constructed a wall 16 feet high and a trench 19 miles long from Lake Geneva, which flows into the Rhône, to the Jura range, which marks the boundary between the Sequani and the Helvetii. When this earthwork was finished, I put fortified redoubts complete with garrisons along it, so that if the Helvetii defied me and tried to cross, it would be easier for me to stop them.

When the day we had agreed on arrived, their envoys returned. I told them that it was impossible for me, following the custom and precedent of the Roman people, to allow anyone to march through the Province, and I made it clear that if they attempted to force their way through, I should stop them. Thwarted in this, the Helvetii tried to break through, sometimes by day but more often by night; they lashed boats together and made numerous rafts, or they forded the river at its shallowest points. But they were foiled by the fortified earthworks and by the swift reaction and the weapons of my soldiers, and they abandoned these attempts.

9   There remained only the road through the territory of the Sequani, which could not be used without their consent because it was so narrow. When the Helvetii acted on their own, they did not succeed in persuading the Sequani, so they sent spokesmen to the Aeduan Dumnorix, hoping that if he pleaded their cause they would get what they asked of the Sequani.

Dumnorix was popular and generous and so had great influence with the Sequani; he was a friend of the Helvetii because his wife, the daughter of Orgetorix, was one of them. His ambition was to be king, he was eager for political change and wanted to have as many tribes as possible bound to him by ties of gratitude. So he undertook the task, succeeded in persuading the Sequani to let the Helvetii pass through their territory, and arranged that they should exchange hostages. The Sequani agreed not to hinder the Helvetii on their march; the Helvetii undertook to pass through without violence or destruction.

10   The reports reaching me were that the Helvetii intended to travel through the territories of the Sequani and the Aedui into the country of the Santones, which is not far from that of the Tolosates, a tribe in the Roman province.

I realized that if this happened it would be very dangerous for the Province; it would mean warlike people, enemies of Rome, bordering on rich farmlands that had no natural defences. For that reason I put my legate Titus Labienus in charge of the fortifications I had built. I myself travelled as fast as I could to northern Italy, where I raised two new legions; I sent for the three legions that were in winter quarters near Aquileia, and with these five legions marched back to Transalpine Gaul by the shortest route, over the Alps.

There the Ceutrones, the Graioceli, and the Caturiges seized some commanding heights and tried to hinder my army on the march; we drove them

By Caesar's time the Roman army had been refined to a peak of efficiency. The turning point was in the last decade of the second century BC when the Roman general Marius, facing the barbarian hordes of Cimbri and Teutoni who were threatening Italy, reformed the army. Before then it had been composed largely of citizens who served when called, now it was a highly professional body of full-time soldiers. Roman armies owed their allegiance to their generals and Caesar was a brilliant leader much loved by his men. Morale was high, not least because Caesar had virtually doubled his soldiers' pay. Moreover the promise of new territories to conquer meant there would be booty to distribute.

Above: marble relief from the altar of Domitius Ahenobarbus (115–100 BC) showing Roman soldiers. The Roman general Ahenobarbus campaigned in the Rhône valley half a century before Caesar and annexed the territory of the Allobroges.

off in several engagements. I reached the territory of the Vocontii in the Transalpine province on the seventh day after leaving Ocelum, the last town in northern Italy. From there I led my army into the territory of the Allobroges, and thence into that of the Segusiavi, the first tribe outside the Province on the far side of the Rhône.

The Helvetii had already led their forces through the pass in the country of **11** the Sequani and had reached that of the Aedui and were pillaging it. Since the Aedui could not defend themselves or their property from them, they sent envoys to me to ask for help.

They pointed out that they had always been loyal to Rome and so it was not right that their land was being laid waste, their children led off into slavery, and their *oppida* taken by storm under the very eyes of my army. At the same time, the Ambarri, kinsmen and allies of the Aedui, informed me that their fields had been pillaged and they were finding it difficult to fend off the violent attacks of the enemy from their *oppida*. Similarly the Allobroges, who had villages and property across the Rhône, fled to me and indicated that there was now nothing left to them but the bare soil of their land.

Prompted by these complaints, I decided that I must not delay; if I did, everything that our allies owned would be destroyed, and the Helvetii would get through to the country of the Santones.

12   There is a river called the Saône, which flows through the territory of the Aedui and the Sequani into the Rhône. The current is so unbelievably slow that it is impossible to say, just by looking at it, in which direction it is flowing. The Helvetii crossed it with rafts and boats.

When I discovered, from patrols, that they had already got three-quarters of their forces across the river, but that about a quarter of them were still on the near side, I set out from camp soon after midnight with three legions and came to that section of their troops that had not yet crossed. They were hampered by baggage and not expecting our attack. We killed a large number, and the rest turned to flight and hid in the nearby woods.

Helvetia as a whole is divided into four cantons; this particular one, called the Tigurini, had, within our fathers' lifetime, marched out alone from their country, killed the consul Lucius Cassius and sent his army under the yoke. So, whether by chance or by the design of the gods, this section of the Helvetii, which had inflicted such a notorious defeat on the Roman people, was the first to pay the penalty for it. In this I avenged not only the wrongs suffered by our state, but also personal ones as well, because in the same battle in which Cassius died, the Tigurini had killed the legate Lucius Piso, grandfather of my father-in-law of the same name.

13   After this battle, I had a bridge built over the Saône and took my army across it so that I could pursue the remaining Helvetian troops. They were thrown into confusion by my sudden arrival – they realized that the operation of crossing the river, which they themselves had taken 20 days and a great deal of trouble to complete, I had carried out in one. They sent envoys to me led by Divico, who had been the leader of the Helvetii in the war against Cassius.

These are the proposals he put to me: if the Roman people made peace with the Helvetii, they would go and settle in whatever area I specified for them; but if I persisted, and continued making war on them, I should remember the traditional valour of the Helvetii and the earlier disaster suffered by the Romans. As for the fact that I had made a surprise attack on a single canton, when those who had already crossed the river could not come to their assistance, I should not exaggerate my own ability or despise theirs. What they had learned from their fathers and ancestors was to fight like men rather than resort to trickery or guile. So, he said, I should not act in a way that would make the place where we stood famous in history because of a disaster to the Romans and the destruction of their army.

14   My reply was this. 'I remember the incidents to which your envoys have referred; they make me all the more determined, because I bitterly resent

what the Roman people, who had done nothing at all to deserve it, suffered at that time. If the Romans had been conscious of having done you wrong, it would have been easy for them to take precautions. But we were deceived; we were not aware of having done anything to cause us to fear, and are not given to groundless apprehension.

But even if I were willing to forget the wrongs inflicted recently – that you have defied me and tried to force your way through our province, and that you have harassed the Aedui and the Ambarri and the Allobroges – the fact that you are boasting so insolently of your victory, marvelling that for so long I have endured your outrages without retaliating, leads to the same conclusion. When the gods wish to take vengeance on humans for their crimes, they usually grant them, for a time, considerable success and quite a lengthy period of impunity, so that when their fortunes are reversed they will feel it more bitterly.

But even so, if you give me hostages as security that you will do what you promise to, and if you give satisfaction to the Aedui and the Allobroges, too, for the wrongs you have inflicted on them and their allies, I will make peace with you.'

Divico replied that it was the long-established practice of the Helvetii to take hostages, not to give them, and the Roman people could bear witness to that. And with that reply, he left.

Next day the Helvetii moved their camp. I did the same. My entire cavalry, 15 about 4,000 men, raised from the whole Province and from the Aedui and their allies, I sent ahead to see which regions the enemy were marching for. They pursued the enemy rearguard too eagerly and joined battle with the Helvetian calvalry on unfavourable ground, with the result that a few of our men were killed.

This engagement raised the spirits of the Helvetii, because they had driven off such a great number of our cavalry with only 500 of their own. They became bolder, halting quite often and challenging our men to fight with their rearguard. I kept my men from fighting; I had enough to do for the time being stopping the enemy looting and foraging and ravaging the country. For about 15 days they marched on, with the gap between the enemy rear and our vanguard not more than five or six miles.

In the meantime I was daily demanding from the Aedui the grain they had 16 formally promised me. For because of the cold – Gaul is, as I have said before, a northern country – the crops in the fields were not yet ripe and there wasn't even an adequate supply of fodder either. It was less practicable for me to use the supply of grain I had brought in boats on the Saône because the Helvetii had moved away from the river and I didn't want to lose contact with them.

The Aedui kept putting me off from one day to the next, saying the grain was being collected, was being transported, was even on hand. But when I realized that I was being put off rather too long, and we were almost at the day when I must issue corn to the men, I summoned their chiefs.

There were a great many of them in my camp. Diviciacus was among them, and so was Liscus, who held the highest office of state, called Vergobret by the Aedui. (This annually elected magistrate has power of life and death over his countrymen.) Not mincing my words, I accused them of being no help to me at such a critical time, with the enemy so close and grain impossible to buy or harvest from the fields. And I pointed out that since it was largely their entreaties that had induced me to undertake the war, I particularly resented being let down by them.

17   Eventually Liscus was moved by my words and produced information that he had previously kept quiet about. He said there were among the Aedui some men who had very great influence over the people and who, though private individuals, had more power than the magistrates themselves. These people were using seditious and criminal talk to intimidate the mass of the people from bringing in the grain that was due.

Their line of argument, he said, was that if the Aedui themselves could no longer gain supremacy in Gaul, it was better to be under the power of other Gauls rather than Romans; for there was no doubt that if the Romans defeated the Helvetii, they would proceed to rob the Aedui and the rest of Gaul of their freedom. Liscus also revealed that these same people were reporting our plans and all that happened in our camp to the enemy, and he himself was unable to stop them. What is more, he was well aware of the extent of the danger he put himself in by reporting all this to me, and that was why he had kept quiet as long as he could. Now, however, he had felt obliged to speak out.

18   After hearing Liscus's words, I realized that it was Diviciacus's brother, Dumnorix, who was being referred to. However, I didn't want the matter to be discussed with so many people present, and so I quickly dismissed the meeting, but kept Liscus behind. When he was on his own, I questioned him about what he had said at the meeting, and he answered more freely and more confidently.

Other people, secretly questioned, confirmed the truth of his statements. The individual referred to was Dumnorix, a man of supreme daring, a great favourite with the people because of his generosity, and eager for political change. I gathered that for several years he had bought the right of collecting river tolls and all the other Aeduan taxes at a low price, simply because, when he put in a bid, no one dared to bid against him for the right. By this he had increased his personal fortune and had acquired great resources that could be used for bribery. He always had about him a large number of cavalry, kept at his own expense.

He had wide reaching power not only in his own country but also among neighbouring tribes. To confirm this influence he had arranged a marriage between his mother and a very powerful and distinguished citizen of the Bituriges. He himself had a Helvetian wife, and his halfsister and other female relatives were married into various other tribes. Because of his marriage he was an ardent supporter of the Helvetii and had personal reasons for hating the Romans, and me in particular; when we arrived, his power had diminished and his brother Diviciacus had regained his former position of influence and distinction. If we Romans suffered defeat, Dumnorix confidently expected the help of the Helvetii to make him king; but if Rome had control, he had no hope of becoming king or of retaining what influence he had.

I discovered something else in the course of my inquiries; Dumnorix was in command of the cavalry sent to assist me by the Aedui, and in our cavalry defeat a few days earlier, it was Dumnorix and his men who had been responsible for starting the flight that had made the rest of our cavalry panic.

Such were the reports I received, and indisputable facts confirmed these **19** suspicions: it was Dumnorix who had secured for the Helvetii passage through the territory of the Sequani, arranged the exchange of hostages between them, and done all this not only without instructions from me or his own tribe but even without their knowledge; and he was now being accused by the chief magistrate of the Aedui. So I considered I had sufficient ground for punishing him myself or else for ordering his own people to do so.

But there was one objection to all this. I had got to know his brother Diviciacus as an earnest supporter of the Roman people, extremely loyal to me personally, remarkably trustworthy, and a fair and moderate man, and I was afraid of offending him if I punished Dumnorix. And so before attempting anything, I summoned Diviciacus and spoke with him.

I sent away the ordinary interpreters and used instead my close friend Gaius Valerius Procillus, a leading man in the Province and one in whom I had absolute confidence. I reminded Diviciacus of what had been said in his presence about Dumnorix in the meeting with the chiefs, and at the same time I revealed what various individuals had reported to me about him. I begged him not to take offence but to agree that I personally should hear the case against his brother and decide on the punishment, or else instruct his government to do so.

Diviciacus burst into tears. He embraced me and started to beg me not to **20** be too harsh in dealing with his brother. 'I know it's all true,' he said, 'and no one is more grieved by it than I am, especially because it was through me that Dumnorix grew powerful, at a time when I had very great influence at home and in the rest of Gaul while he, being young, had very little. He is now using the resources and strength I gave him, not only to weaken my influence but almost to destroy me.

But I am moved both by love for my brother and by the thought of what people will say. If you deal harshly with my brother, everyone will think that it was my idea, since I am such a friend of yours. If that happened, the whole of Gaul would turn against me.'

He did not stop at that but, weeping, continued to make his pleas. I took his right hand and, reassuring him, asked him to stop. I made it clear that I had such a high regard for him that because of his wishes and entreaties, I would overlook the crime against Rome and my own resentment.

I sent for Dumnorix, and in the presence of his brother, made clear to him what it was I objected to in his behaviour; I told him what I had learned for myself and what complaints his own countrymen had made against him. I warned him not to do anything in future to make me suspect him; his past deeds I forgave him only for the sake of his brother, Diviciacus. I set men to keep a watch on Dumnorix so that I should know what he was doing and with whom he was in contact.

On the same day, I learned from patrols that the enemy had halted eight **21** miles from our camp. I sent out a party of men to reconnoitre the hill and the way up it on the farther side; they reported back that it was straightforward. I explained my plan to Labienus, my deputy commander, and gave him instructions to leave soon after midnight with two legions and with the men who had done the reconnaissance as his guides, and to climb to the ridge of the hill. About an hour or so later I marched towards the enemy along the same route that they themselves had used, sending all my cavalry in front. I sent ahead with patrols Publius Considius, who was reckoned to be a first-rate soldier and had served in the army of Lucius Sulla and, later, of Marcus Crassus.

22   At dawn, Labienus was in control of the hill top and I myself was no more than a mile and a half away from the enemy camp; the enemy, as I discovered afterwards from prisoners, had no idea of my approach nor of Labienus's. Considius came galloping up to me and said that the hill I had intended Labienus to occupy was in enemy hands; he knew this from their Gallic weapons and crests. I withdrew my own troops to high ground nearby and formed them up ready to fight.

    My instructions to Labienus had been not to engage in fighting unless my troops could be seen close to the enemy camp, so that we could launch our attack from all sides simultaneously. So having seized the hill, he was waiting for my troops and deliberately not engaging the enemy. Eventually, quite late in the day, I discovered from patrols that the hill was in our hands, and the Helvetii had moved camp. Considius, I was told, had panicked and had reported that he had seen what in fact he had not. That day I followed the enemy at the usual distance, and pitched camp three miles from theirs.

23   In two days' time the distribution of corn to the men would be due, and as I was no more than 18 miles from Bibracte, by far the largest and richest *oppidum* of the Aedui, I decided next day that we should do something about the grain supply. So I stopped following the Helvetii and marched for Bibracte.

    This was reported to the enemy by some deserters of Lucius Aemilius, the commander of our Gallic cavalry. Either the Helvetii thought that the Romans were terrified and so were no longer pursuing them, the more so because on the previous day we had not engaged in battle even though we had controlled the high ground; or else they were confident that they could cut us off from our grain supplies. Either way, they changed their plan, altered the direction of their march, and started to pursue our rearguard and harass it.

24   When I saw what they were doing, I withdrew my troops to a nearby hill and sent the cavalry to withstand the enemy's attack. In the meantime I drew up the four veteran legions in three lines halfway up the hill. I gave orders that the two legions recently levied in northern Italy and all the auxiliary troops should be posted on the summit, and that the whole hillside should be covered with men. Meanwhile I gave instructions that the packs and baggage should be collected together in one place, which was to be fortified by the men who were in position on the higher ground.

    The Helvetii pursued us with all their wagons. They collected their baggage together in one place, then lining up in very close order, they drove our

The Roman soldier of Caesar's time was well armed. He carried two javelins or throwing spears and may occasionally (as above) have had a thrusting spear as well but this would have been rather old fashioned. The javelin had a killing range of about 30 metres. For close fighting he used a short sword with double-edged blade for slashing and thrusting. His dagger was also useful if the sword was lost or broken in the heat of the battle. For protection he carried a tough shield large enough to cover the body. His body armour consisted of a leather jacket, a kind of sporran and a metal helmet. *Above:* relief from Magonza, Italy.

cavalry back, formed a phalanx, and moved up towards our front line. I had all the officers' horses, beginning with my own, taken out of sight so that the 25 danger would be the same for everyone, and no-one would have any hope of escape. I encouraged my troops, then joined battle.

Because they were hurling their javelins down from the higher ground, they easily broke through the enemy's phalanx, and when that disintegrated, they charged them with drawn swords. It was a great handicap for the Gauls as they fought that several of their shields could be pierced and pinned together by a single javelin, which they could not wrench out because the iron head would bend; and with the left arm encumbered it was not possible for them to fight properly, so that many, after tugging frequently on their shield arms, preferred to let go their shields and fight unprotected.

At last, exhausted by their wounds, they began to retreat, withdrawing towards a hill that was about a mile away. They gained this hill and our men were moving towards them when the Boii and the Tulingi, who, with a force of some 15,000 men, completed the enemy's column and protected their rearguard, marched up and, attacking on our exposed right flank, surrounded us.

The Helvetii, who had retreated to the hill, saw all this and began to press forward once more and to renew the battle. We advanced in a double front, the first and second lines to oppose those whom we had already defeated and

26 driven back, the third to hold out against those who were coming afresh. So the battle, long and fiercely fought, was in two directions. When they could no longer withstand our charges, one section withdrew, as they had begun to do, to the hill, and the other made for their wagons and baggage. Although the fighting lasted from early afternoon until evening, in this entire engagement, we saw not a single one of them running away. Around their baggage pile the fighting went on well into the night; they had made a barricade of their wagons and kept hurling weapons down on our men as they came up, and there were some low down between the wheels of the wagons, who were causing casualties among our men by hurling spears and javelins up at them.

After a long struggle, my men took possession of their camp and baggage, and the daughter of Orgetorix and one of his sons were captured there.

About 130,000 of the enemy survived that battle; they marched without stopping for the whole of that night and three days later reached the territory of the Lingones. We could not pursue them because we took three days to see to our wounded and to bury our dead. I sent messengers to the Lingones with a letter telling them not to give the Helvetii grain or any other assistance, because if they did so I should regard them exactly as I did the Helvetii. At the end of the three days, I started in pursuit with all my forces.

27 The Helvetii were now without supplies of any kind and so were compelled to send envoys to me to discuss their surrender. These envoys met me on the march. They flung themselves at my feet and using the language of suppliants they begged, in tears, for peace. I ordered that the Helvetian army should stay where it was and await my arrival. My order was obeyed, and when I got there I demanded from them hostages, their weapons, and the slaves who had deserted to their side.

Night came on while all these were being searched for and collected together, and about 6,000 men from the canton called Verbigenus left the camp of the Helvetii in the early hours of darkness and made their way towards the Rhine and the territory of the Germans. Either they were stricken with panic in case they were going to be put to death once they had handed over their weapons, or else they were led on by the hope of getting away safely, thinking that, as the number of prisoners was so vast, their own flight could be concealed or escape notice entirely.

28 When I discovered this, I sent orders to the tribes through whose lands the fugitives had gone, to hunt them out and bring them back unless they wanted me to think them involved in the escape too. They were brought back and I dealt with them as enemies.

I accepted the surrender of all the rest after they had complied with my terms and handed over their hostages, their weapons, and the deserters. The Helvetii, the Tulingi, and the Latovici were told to return to the territories from which they had started their migration, and because all their produce was lost and they had nothing at home to stave off starvation, I ordered the Allobroges to supply them with grain.

I instructed the Helvetii to rebuild themselves the *oppida* and villages they had burnt. My chief motive in this was that I did not want the area that the Helvetii had left to stay uninhabited in case its fertility should induce the

Germans from across the Rhine to leave their own territory, move into that which belonged to the Helvetii, and so become neighbours of the Roman province and of the Allobroges.

I allowed the Boii to be settled in the territory of the Aedui, who asked for this arrangement because the Boii were known to be outstanding in valour. The Aedui gave them land, and later gave them the same legal and civil rights and privileges as they themselves enjoyed.

Some documents, written in Greek script, were discovered in the Helvetian 29 camp and brought to me. They contained a list of the names of all those capable of bearing arms who had set out on the migration; in the same way, the old men, women and children were listed, separately. The grand total was 368,000, made up of 263,000 Helvetii, 36,000 Tulingi, 14,000 Latovici, 23,000 Raurici and 32,000 Boii. About 92,000 of these were capable of bearing arms. When, on my instructions, a census was taken of those who returned to their homes, the number was found to be 110,000.

2 Ariovistus

At the conclusion of the campaign against the Helvetii, leading men of the 30 tribes from practically the whole of Gaul came to me to offer formal congratulations on behalf of their peoples. They realized, they said, that in the campaign I had been punishing the Helvetii for the wrongs they had done the Roman people in the past; but even so, the outcome had been just as beneficial to Gaul as it was to Rome, because the Helvetii had been thriving in their own country when they left it with the express aim of making war on and getting control of the whole of Gaul; their intention had been to choose from the whole country a place that would be the most convenient and fertile for themselves to settle in, and to make the rest of the tribes pay tribute to them.

The spokesmen asked to be allowed, with my sanction, to name a day for a council of the whole of Gaul, for they had requests that they would like to submit to me when general agreement had been reached on them. I gave permission and they fixed a day for their council. They agreed among themselves on oath that no individual would disclose its proceedings except on instructions from the entire council.

When this council had concluded its business, the same chiefs as before 31 came back to me and begged to be allowed to have private discussions with me, in secret, on a matter that concerned their own personal safety as well as that of the whole country. I granted their request, whereupon they all flung themselves at my feet weeping. They were just as anxious, they said, not to have their words disclosed as they were to gain what they were asking for, because if anything did leak out, they knew that they would suffer the cruellest punishment for it.

Then the Aeduan Diviciacus, speaking on behalf of them all, told the following story. In the whole of Gaul there were two factions, one led by the Aedui, the other by the Arverni. For many years they struggled fiercely between themselves for supremacy until eventually the Arverni and the Sequani sent for German mercenaries; about 15,000 came across the Rhine in the first contingent. But after those uncivilized savages had developed a liking for the good land and the high standard of living enjoyed by the Gauls, more came across, until by now there were some 120,000 of them in Gaul.

The Aedui and their dependent tribes had been involved in armed conflict against these Germans more than once, but they had suffered a disastrous defeat and had lost all their nobles, their entire council, and all their cavalry. They had previously been the most powerful people in Gaul because of their own valour and their ties of hospitality and friendship with the Roman people; but they were broken by these disastrous defeats. They were compelled to hand over to the Sequani as hostages their leading men and to bind their tribe by an oath that they would not try to get their hostages back or ask the Romans for help, but would submit for ever to being under the power and control of the Sequani.

'I am the only individual in the whole Aeduan tribe,' said Diviciacus, 'who could not be induced to swear that oath or give my children to be hostages. That was why I fled from my country and went to the Senate in Rome to ask for help – because I was the only one not prevented by the oath or by the hostages.'

However, things had turned out worse for the victorious Sequani than for the vanquished Aedui: Ariovistus, the king of the Germans, had settled in their territory and had seized a third of their land, the best in the whole of Gaul; now he was telling the Sequani to move out of another third because a few months before, 24,000 of the Harudes had come over to him and he had to find land for them to settle in.

Within a few years, Diviciacus went on, all the Gauls would be driven from their lands and all the Germans would come across the Rhine, for there was really no comparison between the land in Gaul and that in Germany or between the ways of life of the two peoples. As for Ariovistus, after inflicting a single defeat on the armies of the Gauls at the battle of Admagetobriga, he was behaving like a cruel and arrogant tyrant, demanding as hostages the children of all their distinguished citizens and inflicting on them every kind of torture if everything was not done exactly according to his will and pleasure. He was a savage, given to rages and without self-control; it was impossible to endure his tyranny any longer.

'Unless we have assistance from you, Caesar, and the Roman people,' he said, 'all the Gauls will have to do what the Helvetii did – move out of their native territory and seek another home in land far away from the Germans, taking their chance with whatever might befall them.

If Ariovistus should hear all this, he will most certainly inflict the most terrible punishment on all the hostages he has in his power. But you, Caesar, through your own prestige and that of your victorious army or just the very name of Rome, can prevent still greater numbers of Germans being brought across the Rhine and protect all Gaul from the outrages of Ariovistus.'

32   So Diviciacus ended his speech and with much weeping all those present began to beg help from me; I noticed, however, that the sole exceptions were the Sequani, who did not act like the rest but hung their heads and gazed gloomily at the ground. I was surprised and asked them why. They made no reply, remaining silent and dejected. When I had repeated my question

several times but still failed to get a single word out of them, Diviciacus, the Aeduan, spoke for them.

'The plight of the Sequani is more wretched and more serious than that of the rest of us, because they alone do not dare, even in secret, to voice their complaints or to beg for help, and even though Ariovistus is far away, they dread his cruelty as if he were actually here. The rest of us have at any rate a chance of fleeing beyond his reach, but they have admitted him inside their territory and all their *oppida* are in his power, so they must endure all his atrocities.'

When I had heard all this, I spoke a few words of encouragement to the 33
Gauls and promised I would take care of the matter. I told them I had great hopes that because of my authority and the kindness I had shown him in the past, Ariovistus would stop behaving in such an outrageous way. When I had finished my speech I dismissed the meeting.

Now in addition to the information just received, there were many other considerations that led me to believe that I must think carefully about this problem and take action on it. First, I could see that the Aedui, who had so often been given the title of 'Brothers and Kinsmen' in the Roman Senate, were now held enslaved, a subject people of the Germans, and I was aware that Aeduan hostages were in the hands of Ariovistus and the Sequani; I thought this was an absolute disgrace both to me and to the state, considering the greatness of Rome's empire.

Then too I saw that it was dangerous for Rome to have the Germans gradually getting into the habit of crossing the Rhine and coming into Gaul in vast numbers. Once they had occupied the whole of Gaul I did not imagine that such a fierce uncivilized people would refrain from moving out, as the Cimbri and Teutoni had done before them, into the Province and then pressing on into Italy, especially as there was only the river Rhône separating our province from the territory of the Sequani.

I came to the conclusion that I must deal with these matters without delay. The behaviour of Ariovistus himself had become so highhanded and arrogant as to be intolerable.

I decided therefore to send envoys to Ariovistus asking him to choose a 34
place for a conference somewhere halfway between the two of us, for I wanted to discuss with him matters of state, of the utmost importance to us both.

This was the answer he gave to my delegation: 'If I wanted anything from Caesar, I should go to him; if he wants anything from me, he ought to come to me. I would not dare to venture without an army into those parts of Gaul Caesar controls, and I cannot bring my army together into one place without the considerable trouble involved in getting provisions for them. Moreover I cannot imagine what business either Caesar or the Romans as a whole, for that matter, can have in the part of Gaul that is mine because I won it in war.'

When his reply reached me, I sent a second set of envoys to deliver this 35
message to him: 'Although you enjoy the great privilege, conferred by me personally and by the Roman people, of being given the title of "King and

Friend" by the Senate during my consulship, you show your gratitude to me and the Roman people for this by refusing my invitation to a conference and by making out that matters that affect us both need be of no concern to you.

Since that is your attitude, here are the demands I make of you. First, that you should not bring any more large numbers of men across the Rhine into Gaul. Second, that you should hand back the Aeduan hostages whom you hold and authorise the Sequani to give back the hostages they hold. Third, that you should not harass the Aedui or make war on them or their allies.

If you meet these demands, you will enjoy for ever the goodwill and friendship of me and of the Roman people. If you reject them, then I shall act in accordance with the decrees passed by the senate in the consulship of Marcus Messalla and Marcus Piso, directing whoever is responsible for the province of Gaul to protect the Aedui and the other allies of Rome, in so far as that is consistent with the interests of our state. I shall certainly not allow the outrages you have committed against the Aedui to go unpunished.'

36   Ariovistus replied that in war it was the accepted rule that the conquerors should impose their will on the conquered. Certainly the Romans were in the habit of ruling those they had conquered not according to the will of anyone else but according to their own judgment. If he did not tell the Romans how to exercise their rights, they should not stop him exercising his.

The Aedui, he said, now paid tribute to him because they had risked a war, fought him, and been defeated. I was doing him a great wrong, because my coming meant his revenues were reduced. He was not going to give the Aedui their hostages back, but if they kept to their agreement and paid him the tribute annually, he would not make war on them and their allies unless he was provoked; if they did not, the title 'Brothers of the Roman people' would do them little good.

As to my declaration that I should not allow his outrages against the Aedui to go unpunished, no one, he said, had engaged in war with him

❦

The spectacular results of the Roman military machine in Gaul were indeed a remarkable achievement but we must remember that by this time Rome was a powerful, and reasonably united, state with many centuries of practice in military matters gained through campaigns of conquest. Decades of warfare in Spain had taught them the strengths and weaknesses of barbarian peoples while victories in North Africa, Greece and Asia Minor against the Carthaginians and the Macedonian kings had introduced Roman generals to the need for flexibility in fighting technique. Armed with such a variety of experience, the Romans found that the Gauls of France presented a not insuperable problem.

Rome had had long experience of Gaulish fighting methods. In 390 BC a vast Gaulish horde had swept down through Italy and had caught Rome unawares, destroying the city. It took more than 50 years to drive the marauding bands northwards back into the Po valley, where they had settled, and for a further one and a half centuries these hostile and warlike peoples were a thorn in Rome's flesh. Caesar's conquest of Gaul would have been seen by some as the ultimate response to the Gaulish threat.

The Forum (right), heart of ancient Rome, showing the ruins of the Temple of Saturn. The building, which housed the state treasury and the offices of the quaestors, was traditionally founded in 497 BC. It was rebuilt two years after Caesar's death, and again restored in the fourth century AD.

without being destroyed. He challenged me to attack whenever I wished; I should discover, he said, what the valour of his Germans could do, for they had never been defeated, they were superbly trained fighters, and for 14 years had never sheltered beneath a roof.   37

At the very time when this message was being delivered to me, envoys came also from the Aedui and the Treveri. The Aedui complained that the Harudes, who had recently been brought across into Gaul, were ravaging their territory; even though they had given hostages, they had not been able to buy peace from Ariovistus. The Treveri reported that 100 clans of the Suebi, with the brothers Nasua and Cimberius as their leaders, had camped on the bank of the Rhine and were trying to get across.

This information was extremely disturbing. I realized I had to act quickly. If this new band of Suebi joined up with Ariovistus's existing troops, it would be more difficult to resist them. And so I lost no time in making arrangements about grain supplies, and then marched with all possible speed towards Ariovistus.

After three days on the march I received a report that Ariovistus was   **38** moving with all his troops to seize Besançon, the largest *oppidum* of the Sequani, and had completed three days' march from his own territory.

I considered that I must strive to the utmost to prevent him taking the place, for in it there was a plentiful supply of military stores. It also had such good natural defences that it would offer a fine opportunity of prolonging the campaign: the river Doubs, winding round in a near-perfect circle, surrounds almost the entire *oppidum*, and the gap left by the river, no more than 1,600 feet wide, is closed by a high hill in such a way that on each side the lower slopes come right down to the river bank. A wall encloses this hill, making it into a citadel and linking it with the *oppidum*.

It was for this place that I headed, marching at speed by night as well as day. I occupied it, and posted a garrison there.

We delayed for a few days near Besançon to see to grain supplies and other **39** provisions, and during this time our men questioned the Gauls and merchants there. They described the Germans, mentioning their enormous physique, their unbelievable valour, and extraordinary military training.

The Gaulish warrior sculpture from Vachères in southern France symbolizes the noble Gaul seen through the eyes of a sculptor well versed in classical techniques. The warrior is shown with his oval Celtic shield and wearing chain mail – an unusual, but not unknown, form of defensive armour among the Celtic peoples. Celtic warfare had changed considerably since the Celts first invaded Italy in 390 BC. Early Celtic warfare was an uncontrolled affair – violent and savage onslaughts launched amid a colossal din, the individual warriors displaying great feats of valour or retreating in abject panic when things went badly for them. By Caesar's time they had learnt much: Roman armies had after all been marching across southern France en route to Spain for several centuries and for 60 years or so the tribes of southern France had directly experienced the Roman military machine. Celtic chariots so prominent in accounts of early battles were now a thing of the past, except in Britain (IV 24, 32). Instead troops of well-schooled cavalry provided the native armies with their mobility in action. The Gauls were rapidly updating their fighting skills when Caesar struck.

The Gauls said that often when they had encountered the Germans they had not been able to endure even the expression on their faces or the glare of their eyes.

As a result of this kind of talk, the whole army was suddenly seized with such a panic that the judgment and nerve of all were seriously undermined.

It began with the military tribunes, the prefects of the auxiliary troops, and the other officers who had followed me from Rome to cultivate my friendship and had little military experience. They began to beg me for permission to leave, each individual giving a different urgent reason for his departure.

There were those who were shamed into staying with me, to avoid being thought cowards, but they could not control the expressions on their faces or, on occasion, stop themselves weeping; lurking in their tents, they lamented their own fate or joined their friends in bemoaning the danger they were all in.

All over the camp wills were being made and sealed. Gradually even those who had considerable experience of army life, soldiers and centurions and cavalry officers, began to be unsettled by the talk and panic of the others. Some of them, wishing to seem less frightened than they were, said that it was not the enemy they feared but the narrow route to be negotiated and the enormous forests which lay between us and Ariovistus, or else the difficulties of maintaining adequate grain supply. Some even told me that when I gave the order for striking camp and advancing, the men would not obey, and would be too frightened to advance.

40   Now that I knew how things stood, I called a meeting and summoned to it the centurions of all grades. I reprimanded them severely for thinking that it was their business to ask questions or even think about where they were being taken or why.

'During my consulship,' I said, 'Ariovistus was very eager in his desire to have the friendship of the Roman people. Why then should anyone think that he will be so rash as to fail in his obligation to us? I for my part am convinced that when he realizes what I am asking of him, and sees the fairness of my terms, he will not reject my goodwill or that of the Roman people.

But suppose he is driven on by some mad frenzy and makes war on us, what of it? You have nothing to fear. Why do you not trust your own courage and my competence? There was danger from this enemy in our fathers' time; then, the Cimbri and the Teutoni were defeated by Gaius Marius, and the army quite clearly deserved just as much praise for the victory as the general himself did.

And there was also danger from them recently in Italy, during the revolt of the slaves, though they had some advantage from the training and discipline they had learned from us. You can see from that what a good thing it is to be resolute. For a long time, quite without justification, our men feared these slaves while they were unarmed, but later we defeated them, although they had weapons and had won victories.

Finally, these Germans are the same people whom the Helvetii have often fought and on most occasions defeated, not only in their own territory but also on German soil; but the Helvetii could not match up to our army.

If any of you are worried by the defeat and flight of the Gauls, you will discover, if you go into the matter, that the Gauls had become exhausted by the length of the campaign. For many months Ariovistus had kept to his camp or the marshes, denying them the chance of fighting him; when he suddenly attacked them they had already given up hope of a battle with him and had scattered. It was by cunning and strategy that he defeated them, not courage. Against untrained native troops there was a place for methods like that, but not even Ariovistus expects that our armies can be taken by them.

As for those who are disguising their own cowardice with excuses about the grain supply and the narrowness of the route we must take, they are being presumptuous: it seems they have no confidence in my ability as commander-in-chief, or else they are telling me what I should be doing. These matters are my concern. Grain is being supplied by the Sequani, the Leuci and the Lingones, and the crops in the fields are now ripe; as for our route, you will soon be able to judge for yourselves.

I am not in the slightest bothered by statements that my soldiers will not obey the command to advance. I know that in every instance of an army not obeying the command, it has been either because things have been bungled and the commander's luck has run out, or because some crime has been uncovered and his dishonesty revealed. My own integrity has been evident all my life, and the sort of luck I have was clear in my campaign against the Helvetii.

And so I shall do tonight something I had intended to postpone to a later date. I shall strike camp in the early hours so that I can see as soon as possible whether your shame and sense of duty are stronger than your fear. If no one else follows me I shall still march, with just the Tenth legion. I have no doubts at all about the men of the Tenth, and I shall make them my bodyguard.' (I had always shown particular favour to this legion, trusting completely in its valour.)

The end of my speech saw a remarkable change of heart in them all. They 41 were inspired with a great eagerness and enthusiasm for going into action.

First of all the military tribunes of the Tenth, on behalf of their men, thanked me for my high opinion of them, and assured me that they were absolutely ready for action. Then the other legions persuaded their military tribunes and senior centurions to explain their conduct to me. They had never felt any doubts or fears, they said, nor had they thought that they should make decisions about the conduct of the campaign; that was for me as commander-in-chief. I accepted their explanations.

I trusted Diviciacus more than any other Gaul; he studied the route and reported that if I made a detour of more than fifty miles, I could take my army through open country. I set out in the early hours, as I had said I would. We marched continuously, and on the seventh day I was informed by patrols that Ariovistus's troops were about 24 miles away from us.

When Ariovistus learned of our arrival, he sent envoys to me, saying that 42 now I had come closer, he could comply with my earlier request for a conference, since he felt he could do so without danger.

I did not reject his offer. I thought he was now coming to his senses because he was of his own accord agreeing to do what he had previously refused when I had asked him. I was becoming very hopeful that, in return for my great kindness towards him and that of the Roman people, he would stop being so obstinate when he realized what it was that I was asking of him. We fixed that the meeting should take place five days from then.

In the meantime messengers went frequently to and fro between us, and Ariovistus demanded that I should not take any infantry to the conference. He said he was afraid that he would be tricked and surrounded by them, and he suggested that we should each go to the conference with cavalry only, otherwise he would not go at all.

I did not want some such excuse to lead to the cancellation of the meeting but I did not dare to entrust my personal safety to Gallic cavalry. So I decided that the best solution to the problem was to take away all the horses from the Gallic cavalry and mount the legionaries of the Tenth on them; I had absolute confidence in them, and they would provide the most devoted body-guard if I should need one. While this was being done, a legionary from the Tenth said something quite witty. 'Caesar is better than his word; he said he'd have the Tenth legion as his bodyguard and now he's knighting us.'

43   About halfway between our two camps there was quite a high mound of earth standing in a wide plain. We met there, as agreed, for our conference. I positioned my mounted legion 200 paces from the mound. Ariovistus's cavalry halted too, the same distance away. He stipulated that we should confer from horseback, and that each of us should bring ten men as an escort.

When we came to the spot, I started my speech by recalling my own and the Senate's acts of kindness towards him. The Senate had given him the titles 'King' and 'Friend', and he had received most generous presents. I told him that few people had enjoyed such privileges, which were usually granted only in return for important services to Rome; he on the other hand had no proper right to enter the Senate and no reasonable grounds for making any request, but had gained those benefits only because of goodwill and gener-osity on the part of me and the Senate.

I pointed out that our alliance with the Aedui was of long standing and based on a just foundation; the Senate had frequently passed decrees honour-ing them, and their tribe had always been supreme in the whole of Gaul, even before they sought our friendship. I told him it was the practice of the Romans to want their friends and allies to grow in influence, importance, and esteem, and certainly not to lose any they already had. It was intolerable, I said, that we should allow them to be robbed of what they had when they became our friends.

I then repeated the demands I had made before through my envoys, namely, that he should not make war on the Aedui or their allies, that he should give back the hostages, and finally that, if it was impossible for him to send any of the Germans back home, at least he should not allow any more to cross the Rhine.

44   Ariovistus said very little in reply to these demands of mine, but a great deal about his own merits. He had crossed the Rhine, he claimed, not of his

own accord but at the invitation of the Gauls who had sent for him. Even then it had been because he had good reason to expect rich rewards that he had left his home and his relatives. The land he was occupying in Gaul had been granted him by the Gauls themselves, their hostages had been freely given, and the tribute he was exacting was merely that which any victor imposes on the vanquished by right of war.

It was not he who had started hostilities, but the Gauls; all the tribes of Gaul had come to attack him and had directed their troops against him; all these forces he had defeated and routed in a single engagement. If they wanted to make a second attempt, he was ready to fight again; but if peace was what they wanted, it was unjust of them to refuse to pay the tribute they had willingly paid until then.

'As for the friendship of the Roman people,' he went on, 'it should be a distinction and a protection to me, not a disadvantage, or so I expected when I sought it. If I lose the tribute because of Rome, and have to give up those who have surrendered to me, I shall be just as ready to renounce the friendship of the people of Rome as I was to gain it. And the great numbers of Germans I am bringing across the Rhine are to protect me, not to attack the Gauls; the fact that it was only after being invited that I came, and only in self-defence that I fought, proves this.

I was in Gaul before your people were, Caesar. Until now the Roman army never left the boundaries of the Roman province of Gaul. What do you mean by coming into lands that belong to me? This part of Gaul is my province, just as the other is yours. If I invaded your territory, it would be right for you to object; in exactly the same way it is wrong that you are interfering with me in a matter that falls entirely within my rights.

You say that the Aedui had been given the title "Brothers" by the Senate; I am not such a barbarian or so out of touch with affairs as not to know that during your recent war with the Allobroges, the Aedui gave Rome no assistance, nor received any from Rome in their own quarrels with me and with the Sequani. I can only suspect that this friendship is a sham and that your reason for keeping an army in Gaul is to crush me. Unless you take yourself and your army away from this region, I shall regard you not as a friend but as an enemy.

Indeed, if I killed you, my action would be to the liking of many nobles and leading men in Rome. I know this as a fact, because they have told me through their agents; by killing you I could gain the friendship and gratitude of them all. But if you take yourself off and give me undisputed possession of Gaul, you will be well rewarded; any wars that you want fighting, I will finish off for you, without any exertion or risk on your part.'

I explained at length why it was impossible for me to abandon my intention. I told him that it was not my practice nor the practice of the Roman people to abandon loyal allies, and that in my opinion Gaul did not belong to him any more than it belonged to Rome. When Quintus Fabius Maximus defeated the Arverni, and the Ruteni, the Roman people pardoned them. We did not annex their land or demand tribute from them.

If sovereignty in Gaul was to be decided by asking who had been there

45

longest, then the claim of the Roman people was most just; and if the judgment of the Senate was to be upheld, the country ought to be free, because the Senate had agreed that although Gaul had been defeated in war, it should still be governed by its own laws.

46   While the conference was proceeding along these lines, it was reported to me that Ariovistus's cavalry were coming nearer to the mound, riding up to our men and throwing stones and javelins at them. I ended the discussion and returned to my men. I told them not to throw a single javelin back in reply. Of course I saw that there would be no risk to my picked legionaries in an engagement with cavalry, but even so, I thought it better not to take any action; I did not want it said, after the enemy had been defeated, that I had gone back on my word and ambushed them during a conference.

But after news got out in our ranks of how arrogantly Ariovistus had behaved during the conference, telling us Romans to get out of the whole of Gaul, and of how his cavalry had interrupted the conference with their attack on our men, my army was inspired with much greater enthusiasm and eagerness for battle.

47   Next day, Ariovistus sent envoys to me to say that he wanted to continue with me the discussions we had started but not completed. He asked me to decide on a day for another personal exchange of views or, if that did not suit me, to send one of my officers to him.

I could see no good reason for a personal interview, especially as on the previous day the German king had not been able to stop his troops hurling javelins at our men. I considered that it would be very risky to send one of my officers to him; I should be sending him to face a set of savages. My best plan seemed to be to send Gaius Valerius Procillus, a very well-educated young man of exceptional courage, whose father Gaius Valerius Caburus had been granted Roman citizenship by Gaius Valerius Flaccus. Procillus was trustworthy and knew the Gallic language which Ariovistus, from long practice, now spoke fluently, and the Germans could have no reason to do him any harm.

I sent with him Marcus Mettius, who was bound to Ariovistus by ties of hospitality. Their instructions were to find out what Ariovistus had to say, and to report back to me. But when Ariovistus saw them in his camp, he shouted out in front of his army, 'Why are you here? Have you come to spy?' They tried to speak but he stopped them and had them put in chains.

48   On the same day, he moved his camp forward and took up a position at the foot of a hill some six miles from our camp. The following day he led his troops past it and camped two miles beyond us, intending to cut us off from the grain and supplies being brought up from the Sequani and the Aedui.

For five consecutive days I led my men out in front of our camp and kept them in battle formation, so that Ariovistus would have an opportunity of fighting if that was what he wanted. But although he engaged in cavalry skirmishes each day, all this time he kept his main forces inside his camp.

There was a particular type of fighting in which the Germans had been trained. Their force of 6,000 cavalrymen went into battle supported by an equal number of infantry; these foot-soldiers were outstandingly brave and nimble, and each had been selected from the whole army by a cavalryman for his personal protection. The cavalry would fall back on their support, and in a crisis the infantry would run up to help. They would surround any cavalryman who had been wounded and fallen from his horse. Through training they had become so swift of foot that if it came to a long advance or a rapid retreat, they could keep up by running, clinging to the horses' manes.

I realized that he was not going to come out of his camp. So, in order that **49** I should not be cut off from my supplies any longer, I selected a good site for a camp some 600 paces beyond the enemy's position and marched there with my army in a three-line battle formation. I ordered the first and second lines to stand by under arms; the third line was told to fortify the camp.

As I have already stated, the site was about 600 paces from Ariovistus, and he sent about 16,000 light-armed troops and all his cavalry to frighten my men and stop them fortifying the camp. However, I had decided on my plan and kept to it. I ordered the first two lines to drive the enemy off, while the third completed the fortification. When the camp was fortified, I left two legions in it with some of the auxiliaries and took the other four legions back to the larger camp.

The next day I followed my usual routine and led out my troops from both **50** camps. I advanced a little beyond the larger camp, formed my men in a battle line and gave the enemy an opportunity of fighting. It was clear to me that they were not going to come out even then, so about noon I led my army back into camp. Then at last Ariovistus sent a section of his troops to attack our smaller camp. The battle went on until evening, keenly fought on both sides. At sunset he and his men withdrew to their camp. There had been many casualties on both sides.

I questioned prisoners to find out why Ariovistus would not fight a pitched battle. Apparently it is customary among the Germans for their matrons to draw lots and use other sorts of divination to decide whether or not it is advisable to engage in battle; on this occasion they had declared that the Germans were not destined to win if they fought before the new moon.

Next day, leaving what seemed to me to be adequate garrisons in both **51** camps, I formed up all my auxiliary troops in front of the smaller camp in full view of the enemy. My legionary soldiers were weak in numbers by comparison with the Germans, so I wanted to use the auxiliaries to give a show of strength. Then, with the legions drawn up for battle in three lines, I marched right up to the enemy camp.

Now at last the Germans were forced to bring out their troops. They formed them up, by tribes, at regular intervals – Harudes, Marcomani, Triboci, Vangiones, Nemetes, Sedusii, and Suebi. Then behind their line they arranged their carts and wagons, to rule out any hopes they might have of escaping by flight. On this barrier they placed their women, who, weeping and with hands outstretched, implored their menfolk as they went into battle not to let them become slaves to the Romans.

I placed each of my five legates in command of a legion, and my quaestor

52 at the head of the remaining one, so that each individual soldier would know there was in his legion a senior officer to witness his courage in action. I myself began the engagement from our right wing because I had noticed that that was the weakest part of the enemy line.

When the signal was given, our troops made such a spirited charge at the enemy, and they rushed forward at us with such speed and suddenness, that there was no time for us to hurl our javelins at them. These were jettisoned, and the fighting was with swords at close quarters. The Germans, however, quickly adopted their usual phalanx formation and withstood our sword thrusts. Many of our men actually jumped onto the wall of shields, wrenched the shields from the enemy's hands and stabbed down at them from above.

On the left, the German battle line was routed, but on the right, with sheer weight of numbers, they were pressing our men hard. Young Publius Crassus, who was in command of the cavalry and therefore able to move about more easily than the officers who were fighting in the line, saw what was happening and sent the third line up to help our troops in difficulties.

53 So the battle swung once more in our favour.

The enemy all turned and fled, not stopping until they came to the Rhine, about 15 miles away. There a very few of them, trusting to their strength, did their best to swim across, or found boats and so saved themselves. Ariovistus was one of these; he came across a small vessel moored to the bank and escaped in that. All the rest were overtaken by our cavalry and killed.

Ariovistus had two wives both of whom died in that rout. One of them, a Suebian by birth, he had brought with him from Germany; the other, a Norican, had been sent by her brother King Voccio to Gaul where Ariovistus married her. Of his two daughters one was killed, the other taken prisoner.

While I was with the cavalry pursuing the enemy, we came upon Gaius Valerius Procillus; he was fettered with three chains and being dragged along by his guards in their flight. This meeting certainly gave me as much pleasure as the victory itself. For as well as being the worthiest man in the whole Province Procillus was a personal friend of mine, and there were ties of hospitality between us. Now I had seen him snatched from the hands of our enemies and restored to me; providence had kept him safe and so had not detracted from our pleasure and rejoicing.

Procillus told how three times he had been present when the Germans had decided by lots whether to burn him to death at once or keep him for a later occasion. It was thanks to the lots that he was safe. Marcus Mettius was found too and brought back to me.

54 When news of the battle reached the other side of the Rhine, the Suebi, who had come as far as the banks of the river, began to turn back home. The tribes living near the Rhine realized what a panic they were in and pursued them, killing great numbers of them.

In the space of a single summer I had completed two important campaigns. I led my army to winter quarters in the territory of the Sequani slightly earlier than the season required. Leaving Labienus in command, I set off for northern Italy to hold the assizes there.

The wise men of Gaul who, with their various skills, together made up the class of society known as the Druids (VI 13, 14), maintained and taught the store of society's accumulated knowledge. Awareness of the seasons and the need to divide accurately the year so that the festivals could be honoured and the gods appeased was one of the Druids' functions.

This remarkable bronze calendar found at Coligny near Bourg dates to the late first century BC and is the oldest and most extensive example of writing in the Celtic language. It was divided into 16 columns representing 62 lunar months (with two additional intercalary months) making up a 19-year cycle. The months are subdivided into light and dark halves and the days are individually numbered. Some days and months are marked 'good' (MAT) and 'not good' (ANM), indicating when it was auspicious to begin a new venture.

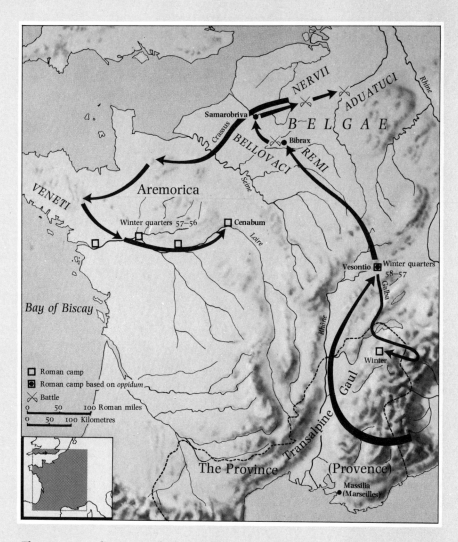

The campaign of 57 BC was the logical follow-up to the successes of the previous year. Caesar's scouts and informants would have provided him with a detailed knowledge of the geography and the peoples of Gaul. He would have been well aware of the natural limits of the country – the river Rhine to the northeast and the sea to the north-west and west. He also knew of the warlike Belgic tribes who occupied the territory north of the river Seine. By this stage it is clear that Caesar had decided on total con-quest. His first move was inevitable – a thrust northward to demonstrate the might of Rome among the Belgae, who had not yet directly experienced the Roman army. But hand in hand with the show of strength Caesar played at diplomacy. The native tribes would have heard how beneficial friendship to Rome could be – the added prestige of Roman patronage could bring them power over weaker neighbours and the assurance of Roman support should other tribes threaten their supremacy. The Remi were quick to grasp this reality and Caesar made good use of their friendship.

While Caesar was occupied among the Belgae, Crassus was given the task of dealing with the maritime tribes of Normandy and Brittany, who appear readily to have submitted. The encirclement of Gaul was thus complete. But Caesar evidently recognized that his task was not finished: for this reason the legions were kept in the north, probably along the Loire, throughout the winter.

42

BOOK II · 57 BC

1 The Belgic campaign

While I was in northern Italy for the winter, as I have already indicated,   1
frequent rumours reached me, confirmed by dispatches from Labienus, that
all the Belgae were conspiring against Rome and exchanging hostages.

The Belgae, as I explained, occupy a third of the whole land of Gaul. The
reasons for their conspiracy were these. First, they were afraid that if all the
rest of Gaul were subdued, our army would proceed to invade their country.
Second, they were being urged by certain of the other Gauls; some of these
did not take any more kindly to having a Roman army wintering in their
country and establishing itself there, than they had to the prolonged presence of the Germans, and others were eager for a change of overlords,
simply because they were fickle and fond of change. There was also the fact
that in Gaul royal power was commonly seized by those powerful individuals
who had the means of hiring mercenaries; realization that this would be
more difficult to do if the Romans had control of the country prompted yet
others to support the conspiracy.

These reports and dispatches alarmed me. I raised two new legions in   2
north Italy, and at the start of the summer I sent them across the Alps into
Gaul under the command of my legate, Quintus Pedius. As soon as fodder
became plentiful, I went to join the army myself.

I assigned to the Senones and the other Gauls whose land bordered that
of the Belgae, the task of finding out what was going on among them, and
keeping me informed about it. All the reports I received from them were consistent: troops were being raised and an army concentrated into one place.
It was then clear to me that I must take the initiative and move towards
them. I made arrangements about the grain supply, struck camp, and in
about two weeks reached the borders of Belgic territory.

I had marched more quickly than anyone imagined possible, so my   3
arrival was unexpected. The Remi, the Belgic tribe nearest to the rest of
Gaul, sent to me Iccius and Andecomborius, the two leading men of their
tribe, as envoys. They had been ordered to say that they placed themselves
and all their possessions under the power and protection of Rome; they had
not gone along with the other Belgic tribes in conspiring against Rome, and
were ready now to give hostages, obey my orders, withdraw from their
oppida, and supply grain and any other assistance I required. They told me
that all the rest of the Belgae were ready armed and that the Germans on
this side of the Rhine had joined them; all these tribes were now filled with
such fierce determination that they themselves had not been able to dis-
suade even the Suessiones from joining the conspiracy, though they were

their own close kinsmen, sharing the same rights and customs and under the same command and authority as themselves.

4   I asked the Remi for more detailed information about the tribes that were ready armed, their numbers and military strength. This is what I discovered. Most of the Belgae were of German origin; they had crossed the Rhine long ago, driven out the Gauls they found living there and settled in that part of Gaul because its soil was fertile. A generation ago, when all the rest of Gaul was overrun by the Cimbri and Teutoni, the Belgae were the only ones who stopped them invading their territory. And so, because they remembered this earlier achievement, they had great pride and a sense of superiority in their military ability. About their numbers the Remi said they had precise information; they were related by kinship and intermarriage and knew from the general council of the Belgae how many men each tribe had promised for the war. The strongest of all, in valour, prestige, and population were the Bellovaci, who could provide 100,000 troops and had promised from these a contingent of 60,000 picked men; they demanded for themselves the supreme command of the campaign.

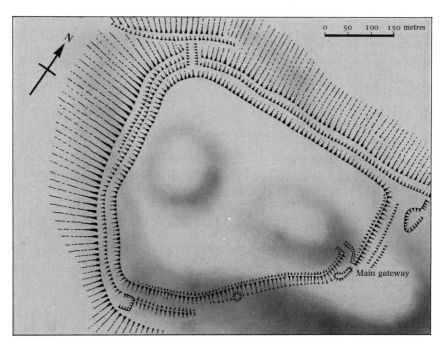

The tribes of the north built or refurbished a number of fortified sites to counter Roman attack. A typical example is Le Petit Celland near Avranches, in Normandy, one of the forts of the Venelli. It consists of a naturally strong promontory strengthened by a rampart and ditch enclosing about 48 acres. The gate, always a point of weakness in a defensive circuit, was carefully planned so that any attacker would find himself virtually surrounded by earthworks as he tried to reach the gate. Suitably manned, these earthworks would have created a death-trap.

Le Petit Celland was partially excavated by Sir Mortimer Wheeler in 1938. He found that the ramparts were laced with timbers nailed together in a manner described by Caesar (VII 23). Nineteen Gaulish coins of Caesar's time were recovered.

The Suessiones had very extensive and fertile territory, bordering on that of the Remi themselves. Within living memory their king had been one Diviciacus, the most powerful ruler in the whole of Gaul, who had control not only over a large area of this region but also of Britain. Their present king however was Galba, and because of his integrity and good sense he had been entrusted, by general consent, with the supreme command. He had 12 *oppida* and promised to provide 50,000 troops. This was the number promised by the Nervii too, who lived in the most remote area and were considered by the Belgae themselves to be the fiercest.

Some 15,000 men had been promised by the Atrebates, 10,000 by the Ambiani, 25,000 by the Morini, 7,000 by the Menapii, 10,000 by the Caleti, 10,000 jointly by the Veliocasses and the Viromandui, and 19,000 by the Aduatuci. The Remi said they believed the so-called German tribes – the Condrusi, the Eburones, the Caeroesi, and the Paemani – could provide about 40,000 men.

I spoke to the Remi in gracious and reassuring terms, telling them that the   5 whole of their council should assemble at my headquarters, and the children of their leading men be brought to me as hostages. They carried out all my instructions carefully and punctually. I then spoke very seriously to Diviciacus the Aeduan, explaining how important it was for Rome and for the safety of us both that the various enemy contingents should be kept separate, so that we should not have to fight such an enormous force all at once. This could be achieved, I said, if the Aedui took their forces into the territory of the Bellovaci and started devastating the land there. I sent him away with instructions to do just that.

I realized that the Belgae had concentrated all their forces and were moving towards me. When I learned from the Remi and the patrols I had sent out that they were now quite close, I quickly took my army across the river Aisne, which is very close to the borders of the Remi, and pitched camp there. This meant that one side of my camp was defended by the banks of the river, which also provided me with protection from the rear and allowed supplies from the Remi and the other tribes to be brought up to me without risk. There was a bridge over the river and I placed a guard on it; on the other bank I left six cohorts under the command of the legate Quintus Titurius Sabinus. I gave instructions that the camp was to be fortified with a rampart 12 feet high and a ditch 18 feet wide.

Eight miles away from this camp was an *oppidum* of the Remi called   6 Bibrax. As soon as they reached it, the Belgae launched a vigorous attack on it, and the garrison there had great difficulty holding out that day.

The Gauls and the Belgae use the same method of attacking such places. They begin by surrounding its entire wall with a large number of men and hurling stones at it from all sides. When this has stripped the wall of its defenders, they hold up their shields to provide a protective shell, set fire to the gates, and begin to undermine the wall.

This method of attack could easily be used on that occasion because when their enormous force of men began to hurl stones and javelins, it was impossible for anyone to stand his ground on the wall. When nightfall put

By the time of Caesar's conquest most of the tribes of Gaul were minting their own distinctive coins. The distribution patterns made by chance finds of these coins helps to locate the area occupied by the tribes.

The coins illustrated here are of the Remi, the tribe on whose support Caesar relied particularly in the campaign of 57 BC. The Remi occupied that part of France in which Reims is now situated.

an end to the attack, Iccius, a very influential Reman nobleman, sent a message to me. (He had been one of the envoys who came to me to ask for peace; now he was in command of the *oppidum*.) He said that he could not hold out any longer unless he got help.

7   Just after midnight I sent some Numidian and Cretan archers and some Balearic slingers to help Iccius, using as their guides the same men who had brought his message to me. Their arrival had a significant effect: it gave the Remi some hope of defending their *oppidum* and made them keen to fight back; it made the enemy give up hope of capturing the place. So they stayed near the *oppidum* for a short while, ravaging the fields of the Remi and setting fire to all the villages and isolated buildings they could reach. Then they marched with all their men towards our camp. They set up their own camp less than two miles away from us; from the smoke and flames of their fires we could tell that their camp extended over some eight miles or more.

8   Because of the size of the enemy's force and their great reputation for valour, I decided at first to avoid a general engagement. But every day we engaged in cavalry skirmishes and I tested the extent of the enemy's fighting spirit and the morale of our men; I found that our men were just as good as theirs.

The ground in front of the camp happened to be ideal for drawing up an army in battle line, for the hill on which our camp stood rose slightly above the level ground and was just wide enough facing the enemy to take my legions in their battle formation. On each flank there was a sharp drop and in front a slight ridge that sloped down gradually to the level ground. On either side of the hill I had a trench dug for about 400 paces at right angles to the fighting line, and at the ends of the two trenches I placed redoubts and artillery. When I formed my army up to fight, I did not want the enemy with their superior numbers to be able to encircle my men from the flanks while they were fighting.

This done, I left the two recently recruited legions in the camp so that they could be brought out to help if necessary. The other six legions I drew up in fighting formation in front, facing the enemy. The Belgae too had marched their troops out of camp and drawn them up for battle.

Between the two armies there was a small marsh. The enemy were 9 waiting to see if our men would cross it, and our troops stood at the ready to attack them, if they made the first move to cross, when they were at a disadvantage. Meanwhile a cavalry skirmish was going on in the space between their infantry line and ours.

Neither side attempted to cross the marsh and so after some success in the cavalry action, I took my men back into camp. The enemy immediately marched from their position to the river Aisne which was behind our camp, as I explained. They found a ford and tried to take a section of their forces across, with the intention, if they could, of storming the guard post which my legate Quintus Titurius Sabinus commanded, and destroying the bridge. If those operations failed, they meant to ravage the country of the Remi, which was extremely important to us for our campaign, and to cut us off from our supplies.

Sabinus reported this to me. I crossed the bridge with all my cavalry, the 10 light-armed Numidians, slingers and archers, and marched against the Belgae. Fierce fighting ensued. My men attacked and killed a great many of the Belgae; they were trying to cross the river and so were hampered in their attempts to fight back. Others boldly attempted to cross over the dead bodies of their comrades, but we drove these men back with a shower of javelins. Our cavalry surrounded those who had managed to cross earlier and killed them.

The Belgae now realized they had been wrong to hope they could take Bibrax and cross the Aisne. They saw that we were not going to advance to fight on unfavourable ground. Moreover their own grain supplies were beginning to run out. So they summoned a council of war at which they decided that the best plan was for everyone to return home; they would rally and join forces again to defend the first tribe among them to have their territory invaded by the Roman army. In that way they would have the advantage of fighting on their own ground rather than in foreign territory, and they would have their own supplies of grain to use. They had discovered too that Diviciacus and the Aedui were approaching the territory of the Bellovaci, which meant that the Bellovaci could not be persuaded to stay any longer but wanted to go to help their own people. This, added to the other arguments, led them to make their decision.

Having agreed on this plan, they left their camp a little before midnight 11 with a great deal of noise and confusion, without any proper order or discipline. Each man wanted to be at the front to get home quickly, with the result that their departure was just like a rout.

My scouts immediately reported this to me. However, I kept my army and cavalry in camp, because I was afraid of a possible ambush, not yet knowing exactly why the Belgae were leaving. But at dawn, when the reports of my patrols confirmed what I had been told, I sent forward my entire cavalry under the command of the legates Quintus Pedius and Lucius Aurunculcius Cotta to delay the enemy rearguard. I told the legate Titus Labienus to follow in support with three legions.

The troops attacked the rearguard and pursued them for many miles, killing great numbers of them as they fled. For while those whom we had reached at the extreme rear of the enemy column stood firm and bravely resisted our men's attacks, those in front thought they were a long way from the danger and did not need to keep any order. There were no officers to control them, so when they heard the shouting, they broke ranks and tried to escape. The result was that, without any risk, our men killed as many of them as the hours of daylight allowed. At sunset they had to stop, and they returned to camp in accordance with instructions.

12 The next day, before the enemy could recover from their panic and the effects of their flight, I led my army into the country of the Suessiones, neighbours of the Remi, and by a forced march we came to the *oppidum* of Noviodunum. I had heard that it was without people to defend it, so I attempted to storm it as soon as we arrived. However this proved impossible; even though there were only a few defenders, the *oppidum* was protected by a wide ditch and high wall. We fortified our camp and began to bring up protective sheds and make the necessary preparations for a siege.

In the meantime, however, the next night, the whole throng of Suessiones returning from their flight crowded into the *oppidum*. We quickly brought the sheds up to the walls, shovelled earth into the ditch, and erected siege-towers. The size of these works, which had never been seen or heard of in Gaul before, and the speed with which we were acting, alarmed the enemy, and they sent envoys to me to ask for terms of surrender.

13 The Remi begged that I should spare them and this I agreed to do. They gave me as hostages some of their leading men, including the two sons of King Galba himself, and they handed over all the weapons in the *oppidum*. I then finally accepted the surrender of the Suessiones, and led my army into the territory of the Bellovaci.

These people had taken all their belongings and retired to the *oppidum* of Bratuspantium. When we were about five miles from the place, all the older

❧

Wealth could be hoarded in several ways in the Celtic world. Coins, particularly gold coins, were by Caesar's time widely used, but among some tribes in the more remote areas the number of one's cattle still provided the simplest and most readily recognizable means of displaying wealth and status.

Another way of consolidating wealth was in the form of elaborately decorated gold torcs like these examples from Ipswich in Suffolk. The sheer quantity of precious metal and the quality of the craftsmanship involved in their decoration must have made them objects of enormous value. The Ipswich hoard produced six torcs. While they may have belonged to a single individual, it is possible that they were once housed in a shrine, perhaps the spoils of war or a communal offering, melted down and fashioned into a form appropriate for a god.

The coins shown here are those of the Suessiones (*above left*); the Nervii (*above right*); the Veneti (*below left*); and (*below right*) one depicting Commius, king of the Atrebates.

men came out. With hands outstretched they began to cry out that they were putting themselves at my mercy and under my authority, and were not offering any armed resistance. Later, when we came up to the *oppidum* and were pitching our camp close to it, the women and children came onto the wall; with hands outstretched as was their custom, they too begged us for peace.

Diviciacus spoke in support of them. (After the retreat of the Belgae he **14** had disbanded his Aeduan troops and returned to us.) He pointed out that the Bellovaci had always enjoyed the protection and friendship of the Aeduan people, and had broken off their association with them, and made war on the Romans, only because they had been driven to do so by their chiefs, who told them that I had reduced the Aedui to slavery and was making them suffer every kind of insult and humiliation.

The men responsible for that policy had fled to Britain when they had realized what a disaster they had brought upon their country. Not only the Bellovaci, he said, but also on their behalf the Aedui, begged me to show my usual mercy and forbearance towards them. If I did, I should be enhancing the prestige of the Aedui among all the Belgae, on whose help and resources they always relied in any wars they became involved in.

Out of respect for Diviciacus and the Aedui, I said I would receive the **15** Bellovaci into my protection and would spare their lives. However, I demanded 600 hostages from them, since the tribe had great authority among the Belgae and the largest population. When the hostages had been handed over and all the weapons in the *oppidum* collected, I left to march into the territory of the Ambiani, who immediately surrendered unconditionally.

2 The battle with the Nervii

Beyond the boundaries of the Ambiani, lived the Nervii. I made inquiries about them, their character, and customs, and this is what I discovered. Traders were not given access to their country; they did not allow wine and other luxuries to be imported because they considered that things of that kind softened men's spirits and weakened their courage. They were fierce and courageous, and they bitterly denounced the rest of the Belgae for having thrown away their traditional courage by surrendering to the Romans. They were emphatic that they were not going to send envoys or accept peace on any terms.

The gradual spread of coinage among the Celtic tribes of Gaul and Britain did not necessarily mean that a regular money economy was in practice. The idea of coinage was probably first introduced by Celtic mercenaries returning from wars in the Mediterranean with their spoil in the form of Greek coins. These small objects of recognizable value were a convenient medium for making gifts or paying tribute – essential patterns of behaviour in Celtic society. Soon the concept was adopted by local kings and later, with the decline in kingship among the more civilized Gauls, by the tribe.

Increased contact with the Mediterranean world and the intensified trade that followed from it, led to the development of market centres and it was this more advanced form of economic system that encouraged the moneyers to mint coins of lesser value in silver and bronze to facilitate small-scale transactions.

16   When we had marched through their territory for three days, I discovered from prisoners that the river Sambre was only ten miles away from our camp and that on the far side of it all the Nervian forces had taken up position, waiting for us to arrive. The Atrebates and the Viromandui, neighbouring tribes whom they had persuaded to join them in the risks of war, were with them. I was told that they were also waiting for the forces of the Aduatuci, who were already on the way. Their women folk and those considered to be too old or too young to fight had been thrust into a place where marshes made it impossible for an army to approach them.

17   On receiving this information, I sent out patrols with some centurions to choose a good site for a camp. A large number of the Belgae who had surrendered and other Gauls were following, marching with us. Some of these, as I later discovered from prisoners, having noted the marching routine of my army during those days, went by night and told the Nervii that between one legion and the next we had a long baggage train, and so when the first legion reached camp, the rest would be a long way behind; it would be quite easy to attack it while the men were still carrying their heavy packs. Once the first legion had been routed and the baggage train plundered, the rest would not dare to make a stand against them.

The plan proposed by these informers was favoured by a tactic of the Nervii developed long ago because their cavalry was almost non-existent – indeed to this day they pay no attention to that arm, preferring to rely entirely on their infantry forces – and they had to find a way of thwarting the cavalry forces of neighbouring tribes when they made plundering raids on them. They had succeeded in making hedges that were almost like walls, by cutting into saplings, bending them over, and intertwining thorns and brambles among the dense side-branches that grew out. These hedges provided such protection that it was impossible to see through them, let alone penetrate them. Since the march of our column would be hindered by such obstacles, the Nervii thought that the proposed plan should be tried.

18   We had chosen a site for our camp at a place where a hill sloped down evenly from its summit to the river Sambre, which I have already mentioned. Opposite this, on the other side of the river, there was another hill with the same sort of slope, open for about 200 paces on its lowest slopes, but so thickly wooded higher up that it was not easy to see into it. Inside this wood the main enemy force stayed hidden, while on the open ground by the river, a few cavalry pickets could be seen. The river was about three feet deep.

19   I had sent the cavalry on in advance and was following with the rest of my troops. However, the marching order of my column was quite different from that which the Belgae had described to the Nervii: because we were approaching the enemy, I followed my usual practice of leading my forces with six legions in light marching order; behind these I had placed the baggage train of the entire army, with the two recently recruited legions bringing up the rear to guard them.

Our cavalry, with the slingers and archers, crossed the river and engaged the enemy's cavalry in battle. However, they kept on withdrawing to their main force in the wood and then coming out again to charge our men, who did not attempt to pursue them beyond the edge of the open ground. Meanwhile the six legions who had arrived first marked out the ground and began to construct the camp.

The main army of the Nervii, concealed in the wood, had formed up in battle order there, full of confidence. They had agreed that the appearance of our baggage train should signal the moment for their attack. So as soon as they caught sight of it, they suddenly dashed out in full force and charged our cavalry, easily driving them back and throwing them into confusion. They then ran down to the river with such incredible speed that it seemed to us as if they were at the edge of the wood, in the river, and on top of us almost all in the same moment. Then with the same speed they swarmed up the opposite hill towards our camp and attacked the men who were busy fortifying it.

I had to do everything at once — hoist the flag that was the signal for   20
running to arms, sound the trumpet, recall the men from their work on the fortifications, bring back the men who had gone further afield in search of material for the rampart, get the troops into battle formation, address the men, then give the signal for attack.

There was not time to do most of these things because the enemy was almost on us, but in this very difficult situation two things helped us. First, the knowledge and experience of the soldiers; their training in earlier battles meant that they could decide for themselves what had to be done without waiting to be told. Second, the order I had given to all the legionary commanders that they must stay with their legions and not leave the work until the fortification of our camp was completed. Because the enemy was so close and advancing at such speed, the commanders of the legions did not wait for further orders from me, but did what seemed best on their own initiative.

I issued only essential orders, then ran down to speak to the troops where   21
I could first find them; it was the Tenth legion that I came across first. I ·
addressed them keeping my words to a minimum. I said they should remember their traditional valour and not lose their nerve, but meet the enemy's attack bravely. Then as the Nervii were a mere javelin's throw away, I gave the signal for battle.

Next I set off for the other wing to address the men there as well, but found them already fighting. There had been so little time, and the enemy had been so keen to fight it out, that our men had had no chance to put on their helmets or take the covers from their shields, let alone put on badges and decorations. To avoid wasting valuable time looking for his own unit, each soldier took up position by the first standards he happened to see wherever he met them, as he came from the work of fortifying the camp.

The formation of my troops was dictated more by the features of the site,   22
the slope of the hill, and the demands of the immediate occasion than by the theories of any military rule book. The legions were isolated and had to fight the enemy in different directions; their view was hampered by the very thick hedges described above; it was impossible to find fixed points at which to position our reserves, or to see ahead what was needed in each part of the

Battles between Gauls and Romans were bloody affairs, the fierce energy of which is brilliantly captured by this Roman sarcophagus. Details of Gaulish manners and armour are carefully portrayed if somewhat idealized. The Gauls sometimes went naked into battle magically protected by their neck torcs and armed only with their swords and shields. Classical writers frequently refer to their long hair and drooping moustaches.

field, or indeed for any one man to give all the commands that were necessary. And so, since conditions were so unpredictable, fortunes too inevitably fluctuated.

23   The soldiers of the Ninth and the Tenth were on the left of our line, with the Atrebates facing them. They hurled their javelins and wounded many of the enemy, who were already breathless and exhausted with running, and rapidly drove them downhill into the river. My men pursued them as they tried to get across, and with their swords killed great numbers of them as they struggled in the water. The legionaries did not hesitate to cross the river themselves, and once across, they moved forward up the difficult ground. They met with resistance, the battle was renewed and they put the enemy to flight.

    Similarly in another part of the field, the Eleventh and Eighth legions, facing in a slightly different direction, had engaged the Viromandui, driven them downhill and were fighting right on the river bank. However, our camp was now almost entirely exposed on the left and in front.

The Twelfth and the Seventh legions were drawn up quite close together on the right, and it was on this position that the entire army of the Nervii, led by their commander-in-chief Boduognatus, moved in a solid mass. Some of them began to surround the legions on their right flank; others made for the top of the hill, where the camp was.

At the same time, our cavalry and the light-armed infantry who had been   **24**
with them and had been routed, as I have described above, by the enemy's first attack, were retreating into the camp when they were confronted by the enemy face to face. They took to flight once more, this time in a different direction. The army servants, watching from the rear gate on the crest of the hill, had seen our victorious troops crossing the river, and so had gone out to plunder. However, on looking back they saw the enemy in our camp, so they too took to their heels in flight. At the same time, there was an uproar as those coming up with the baggage began to rush off in different directions yelling in panic.

Among our cavalry were some sent to assist us by the Treveri. They have a unique reputation for courage among the Gauls, but they were thoroughly alarmed by all that was happening. They saw our camp filled with vast numbers of the enemy, our legions hard pressed and almost surrounded, servants, cavalry, slingers, and Numidians scattered and fleeing in every direction, and so they concluded that our position was hopeless and made off home. There they reported to their tribe that the Romans were utterly defeated and their camp and baggage train fallen into enemy hands.

After addressing the Tenth, I made my way to the right wing, where I   **25**
found our troops under severe pressure. All the standards of the Twelfth had had been collected into one cramped space so its men were packed close together and getting in each other's way as they fought. All the centurions of the fourth cohort had been killed; so had the standard bearer, and the standard was lost.

In the other cohorts nearly all the centurions had been either killed or wounded, including the very brave senior centurion, Publius Sextius Baculus, who had so many terrible wounds that he could no longer stand. The rest of the men were slowing down, and some in the rear ranks had given up fighting and were intent on getting out of range of the enemy. And all the while, the enemy in front kept pouring up the hill and were pressing us on both flanks.

I recognized that this was a crisis; there were no reserves available. I had no shield with me but I snatched one from a soldier in the rear ranks and went forward to the front line. Once there, I called out to all the centurions by name and shouted encouragement to the rest of the men. I ordered them to advance and to open out their ranks so that they could use their swords more effectively. My arrival gave the troops fresh hope; their determination was restored because, with the commander-in-chief looking on, each man was eager to do his best whatever the risk to himself. As a result the enemy's attack was slowed down a little.

26   I then saw that the Seventh legion, which stood close to the Twelfth, was also under pressure from the enemy. I told the military tribunes to join the legions together gradually and adopt a square formation so that they could attack the enemy in any direction. This they did, with the result that our men began to offer tougher resistance and to fight more bravely; they could now support one another and were no longer afraid of the enemy moving to their rear and surrounding them.

Meanwhile, the soldiers of the two legions that had been acting as a guard to the baggage train at the rear of the column had quickened their pace on receiving reports of the battle and were now visible on the top of the hill, in full view of the enemy.

Titus Labienus had captured the enemy camp and from the high ground on which it stood, could see what was happening in our camp. He now sent the Tenth legion to our assistance. Just by observing the flight of our cavalry and the army servants, the soldiers of the Tenth could tell how things stood and how great was the danger threatening the camp, the legions and their commander-in-chief. They therefore moved up to join us with the utmost speed.

27   Their arrival changed things entirely. Even those of our men who had fallen to the ground wounded, began to fight again, propping themselves up on their shields. The servants, seeing the enemy's panic, ran to face them, even though the enemy were armed and they were not. The cavalry too, anxious to wipe out the disgrace of their flight by showing bravery now, were fighting anywhere and everywhere, trying to outdo the legionary soldiers.

But the enemy showed enormous courage even though their hopes of survival were almost gone; when their front lines had fallen, those behind stepped forward onto the bodies and fought from there. They too were brought down and the corpses piled up, but the survivors moved up and, as if from the top of a mound, kept on hurling their spears, intercepting our javelins and flinging them back at us. It is quite right to say that they were men of outstanding courage, having dared to cross a very wide river, clamber up its steep banks, and move on over very difficult ground. Surely only great fighting spirit could have made light of such difficulties.

28   So ended this battle by which the tribe of the Nervii, and even their name, were virtually wiped out. Their old men had, as I have already said, been sent away with the women and children into the tidal creeks and marshes, and when news of the battle reached them they realized that nothing could stop the victorious Romans or save the defeated Nervii. With the consent of all the survivors they sent envoys to me and surrendered. In describing the disaster their tribe had suffered, they said that from their council of 600, only three men had survived, and barely 500 from their fighting force of 60,000. Wishing it to be seen that I treated unfortunate suppliants mercifully, I took the greatest care to keep them safe. I told them to keep their lands and *oppida*, and I gave orders to the neighbouring tribes to refrain from doing them any damage or injury and to see that their people did the same.

3 The Aduatuci

I have already mentioned that the Aduatuci were on their way with all their 29
troops to help the Nervii. When news of the battle reached them, they
turned and marched back home. They abandoned all their other *oppida* and
strongholds and collected all their possessions into one *oppidum*, which had
remarkable natural defences. It was ringed around by very high, sheer rocks
except at one point, where there was a gently sloping approach no more
than 200 feet wide. They had fortified this place with a very high double
wall on which they were now setting heavy stones and great wooden beams
sharpened to a point.

These Aduatuci were descendants of the Cimbri and Teutoni, who, on
their march to our province and Italy, had left on the west bank of the
Rhine cattle and baggage they could not drive or carry with them, together
with 6,000 of their own people to guard it. After the destruction of the main
body of the Cimbri and Teutoni, these 6,000 struggled for many years with
the neighbouring tribes, sometimes invading their territory, at others defending their own. Eventually, with the agreement of all these tribes, peace
had been made and this was the place they chose for their home.

When our army first arrived in their territory, the Aduatuci made 30
numerous sorties from their *oppidum* and engaged in minor skirmishes with
our troops. But later, when we had shut them in with an earthwork 12 feet
high, with a circuit of five miles and redoubts at frequent intervals, they
stayed inside. We brought up our protective sheds and constructed a
siege-terrace.

When the enemy saw us building a siege-tower some distance away, they
shouted down insults at us from their wall, jeering at us for building such a
huge piece of apparatus so far away. Mostly the Gauls are very scathing
about our small stature, contrasting it with their own great size, and now
they mockingly asked us if we, little men that we were, imagined that our
feeble hands and strength could set a great tower like that on a wall.

But it was a different matter when they saw the tower moving and coming 31
near to their walls. This strange and unfamiliar sight alarmed them, and they
sent envoys to me to ask for peace.

The gist of their speech was this. They now believed that we Romans
must have divine help in fighting wars, if we could move up a piece of apparatus of such a height as quickly as that. They placed themselves and all their
property at our disposal, making only one plea; if I showed that mercy and
forbearance that others had told them of, and decided they were to be spared,
they begged me not to strip them of their weapons. Almost all the neighbouring tribes were hostile to them and resented their fighting spirit; if I
made them hand over their weapons, they could not defend themselves
against them. And if they were reduced to that, they would rather suffer any
fate at the hands of the Romans than be tortured to death by people they were
used to dominating.

To this appeal I replied that I would not destroy their tribe, more because 32
it was my habit to be merciful than because they deserved to be spared; but
only on condition that they surrendered before the battering ram touched

their wall. I made it clear, however, that there would be no question of my accepting their surrender unless they handed over their weapons. I would do for them what I had done for the Nervii and forbid the neighbouring tribes to do them any harm once they had surrendered to Rome.

The envoys reported this back to their people, then returned and said they were ready to comply with my instructions. They threw a great number of weapons down from the wall into the ditch in front of their *oppidum*; there were so many that the piles of weapons reached nearly to the top of the wall and of our siege-terrace. However, as became clear afterwards, they kept back about a third of their weapons, hidden in the *oppidum*. Then the gates were opened and for that day they enjoyed peace.

33   In the evening I ordered my troops to leave the *oppidum* and had the gates closed so that the inhabitants should not suffer any ill-treatment from our soldiers during the night. The enemy, however, as we discovered later, had a plan already made. They believed that once they had surrendered to us, we would withdraw our pickets or at any rate keep watch with less vigilance. Some of them were armed with the weapons they had kept hidden, others with shields made of bark or wickerwork, which they had hastily covered with skins, for they had no time to spare.

Soon after midnight they suddenly burst out of the *oppidum* in full force at a point where they thought it would be easiest to scale our fortifications. The alarm was quickly given by fire signals; I had already given orders to that effect. Our troops came running up from the nearest redoubts. The enemy fought fiercely, as you would expect of them: they were brave men with very little hope of survival, fighting on difficult ground against an enemy who could hurl down weapons at them from a rampart and towers, and their only hope lay in their own valour.

About 4,000 of them were killed and the rest driven back into their *oppidum*. Next day we smashed the gates open. There was no longer anyone defending and I sent in my troops. I sold all I found inside by auction, in one lot. It was reported to me by the purchasers that the number of people sold in that auction was 53,000.

34   I had sent Publius Crassus with one legion to deal with the tribes on the Atlantic seaboard — the Veneti, Venelli, Osismi, Curiosolites, Esubii, Aulerci, and Redones. At about this same time I received information from Crassus that all these tribes had been brought into submission to Rome.

35   With these operations, peace had been brought to the whole of Gaul. Reports of this war had made such a great impression on the natives that the tribes living beyond the Rhine sent envoys to me promising to give hostages and do what I ordered. I was in a hurry to leave for Italy and Illyricum, so I told them to come back at the beginning of the following summer. I sent the legions into winter quarters in the territory of the Carnutes, the Andes, the Turones, and the tribes who lived near to where we had just been engaged in war. When my dispatches were read in Rome, a public thanksgiving was decreed lasting 15 days; no one had been granted this honour before.

BOOK III · 56 BC

1 Galba in the Alps

When I was starting for Italy, I sent Servius Galba with the Twelfth legion 1
and a section of our cavalry to the territories of the Nantuates, the Veragri,
and the Seduni, which stretch from the borders of the Allobroges, Lake
Geneva, and the Rhône to the high Alps. My reason for sending them was
that I wanted to open up the route through the Alps. Merchants had regularly used this route, but only at great risk and on payment of heavy tolls.
I gave Galba permission to quarter his legion in this area for the winter, if he
thought it necessary.

Galba fought several successful engagements and took a number of the
enemy's strongholds by storm; envoys were sent to him from all the districts.
He took hostages from the tribes and made peace. He decided to station two
cohorts in the country of the Nantuates and to spend the winter himself with
the remaining cohorts of the legion in Octodurus, a village of the Veragri,
which is situated in a valley with little level ground around it, and is hemmed
in on all sides by very high mountains. A river divided the village into two
parts; one part he allowed the Gauls to keep, the other he made them evacu-
ate. He assigned this part to his cohorts and fortified it with a rampart and
a ditch.

Several days had gone by in this encampment and Galba had given 2
orders for grain to be brought in, when suddenly he was informed by his
patrols that during the night all the Gauls had left the part of the village he
had allotted to them, and that the surrounding mountains were occupied
by an enormous number of Seduni and Veragri.

There were several reasons why the Gauls had taken this sudden decision
to renew hostilities and try to crush our legion. First, the legion was under
strength since the two cohorts had left, several individuals had been sent
out in search of supplies, and so the Gauls despised it because of its reduced
numbers. Second, the site of their quarters meant that Galba's men were at
a disadvantage; the Gauls would be charging down from the mountains
hurling their spears into the valley, and they believed that we would not be
able to withstand even their first attack. In addition, they resented having
their children taken away from them in the name of hostages, and they
were convinced that we were trying to get possession of the Alpine heights
not just to open up the routes, but to control them for all time and to annex
the region to the neighbouring Province.

At this point, the work of fortifying the camp was not yet absolutely 3
finished, nor had adequate provision been made for grain and other supplies, because when Galba had received hostages from the Gauls after their

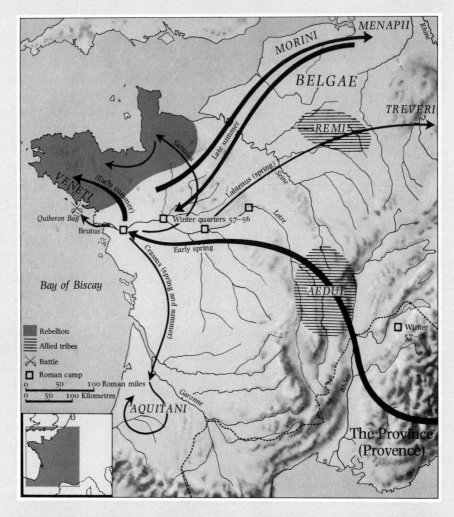

The campaign of 56 BC was dominated by the rebellion of the tribes of Normandy and Brittany. Whatever the immediate cause the real reason probably lay in the fact that the submissions obtained in the previous year by Crassus were nominal. When the tribes realized what the presence of Rome really meant (and they would have had ample opportunity to observe this during the winter with the legions garrisoned nearby) revolt was inevitable.

Caesar dealt brilliantly with the potentially very dangerous situation. First he sent orders that warships were to be built and then he deployed his forces. Labienus was sent to the territory of the Belgae. Crassus moved south into Aquitania while Sabinus was given the task of dealing with the recalcitrants of Normandy and northern Brittany. Thus each potential danger area was placed under surveillance and the tribes were prevented from uniting. When these preparations were complete Caesar moved against the rebels. The savage nature of his reprisals demonstrated to a shocked Celtic world the high price to be paid for rebellion against Rome.

Caesar's firsthand contact with the maritime tribes would have impressed upon him the significance of cross-channel trade with Britain and would in all probability have confirmed his desire to visit the island for himself. Experience of the Atlantic, gained during the great sea battle in Quiberon Bay against the Veneti, was an invaluable prelude to his Channel crossing in 55.

surrender, he had assumed that there was no need to fear any further out-
break of hostilities. So when he received this information, he lost no time in
calling a council of war and asking for opinions.

The danger was sudden and unexpected; it was also serious. Already
almost all the heights were clearly filled with hordes of armed men. The
roads were cut, so it was impossible for relief to get through or supplies to
be brought up. Some of the members of the council thought the situation
was already almost beyond hope and they proposed abandoning the baggage, breaking their way out and trying to reach safety by the same route
as they had used when they came. But the majority decided that such a
plan should be kept as a last resort, and that in the meantime they should
defend the camp and wait to see how things developed.

There was a short interval, scarcely enough to post the troops and making   4
the other arrangements agreed on. Then the enemy gave their signal, ran
down from all sides, and began to hurl stones and spears at the rampart.

At first, while they were fresh, our men fought back bravely and every
weapon that they hurled down from their position on the rampart hit its
mark. If any part of the camp was stripped of defenders and seemed to be
under pressure, they ran there and gave support. What got the better of
them was that when the enemy withdrew from the battle exhausted by prolonged fighting, fresh troops filled their places. But it was impossible for us to
do anything like that because the legion was under strength; not only was
there no chance for exhausted men to withdraw from the action, but even
the wounded could not abandon their posts in order to recover their strength.

The fighting went on without a break for more than six hours. Our men   5
were running out of weapons as well as stamina, while the enemy were pressing harder, and, as our men became weaker, had started to break down
the rampart and fill in the ditches. Our position was now desperate.

The senior centurion Publius Sextius Baculus, whom I mentioned as
having been very badly wounded in the battle against the Nervii, and the
military tribune Gaius Volusenus, a man of sound judgment and great
courage, ran up to Galba and told him that they must now resort to the
emergency plan: their only hope of getting away safely was to break through
the enemy's lines.

The centurions were called together and the men were quickly told
what to do. They were to leave off fighting for a time and merely fend off
the weapons hurled at them by the enemy; in this way they would be able
to recover from their exertions. Then when the signal was given, they were
to break out from the camp. Their hopes of getting away safely would depend
entirely on their courage.

Our men did as they were told. They suddenly burst out through all the   6
gates of the camp, giving the enemy no chance to realize what was happening or to close ranks. So fortune now turned the other way. The Gauls, who
thought they had come close to capturing our camp, were surrounded and
cut off on all sides. Of more than 30,000 native troops known to have come
to attack our camp, more than a third were killed. The rest of their panic-
stricken forces we put to flight, not allowing them to stop even on the higher

ground. When the entire enemy force had been routed and stripped of its weapons, our men withdrew behind the fortifications of the camp.

After this battle Galba did not want to take any more risks. He was aware that the situation he had been confronted with was quite different from what he had intended when he came there for the winter. He was very worried too about the shortage of grain and other supplies. Next day, therefore, he burned every building in the village and then set out to return to the Province. No enemy tried to stop him or delay his march. He led his legion safely into the territory of the Nantuates and from there into that of the Allobroges, where he spent the winter.

2 The Venetic campaign

7   After these operations I had every reason to think that Gaul had been pacified – the Belgae had been overcome, the Germans driven out, and the Seduni defeated in the Alps – and so at the beginning of the winter, I set out for Illyricum. I wanted to visit the tribes there and get to know that area as well. But at that point war suddenly broke out again in Gaul.

The cause of the war was this. Young Publius Crassus had been in winter quarters with the Seventh legion near the Atlantic, in the territory of the Andes tribe. Because there was a grain shortage in this region, he sent prefects and military tribunes into several of the neighbouring tribes to get food supplies. Titus Terrasidius went to the Esubii, Marcus Trebius Gallus to the Curiosolites, and Quintus Velanius and Titus Silius to the Veneti.

8   Now of all the peoples of the coastal part of that area, the Veneti are by far the strongest. They have a great many ships and regularly sail to and from Britain. When it comes to knowledge and experience of navigation, they leave all the other tribes standing. The sea on that coast is extremely violent and open, and the harbours few and far between. Since the Veneti control these, they are able to exact tolls from almost all who regularly use those waters.

It was these Veneti who started the trouble by detaining Silius and Velanius. They thought that by doing this they would get back the hostages they had given to Crassus. Their neighbours followed their lead – it is characteristic of Gauls to take sudden impulsive decisions – and detained Trebius and Terrasidius for the same reason.

After a swift exchange of envoys, they pledged themselves through their leaders to take no action except by joint decision, and to face together whatever was coming. They urged the other tribes to hold fast to the freedom they had inherited from their ancestors rather than endure slavery at the hands of the Romans. All the tribes of the seaboard area were quickly won over. A joint embassy was sent to Publius Crassus telling him that if he wanted to get his officers back he should return their hostages.

9   Because I was some distance away, in Illyricum, I learned of these developments from Crassus. I gave orders that in the time before I could get there, warships should be built on the river Loire, which flows into the Atlantic, and that oarsmen should be recruited from the Province and crews and pilots procured. This was quickly seen to, and I made my way to the army as soon as the season allowed.

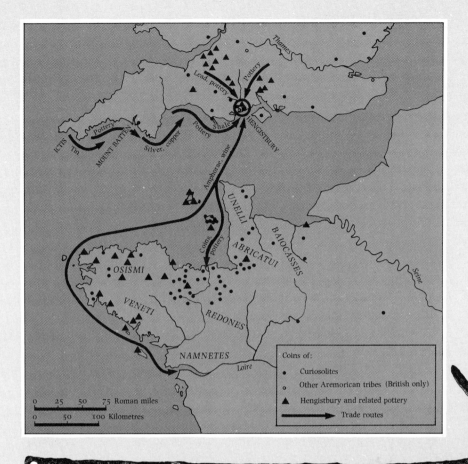

The tribes of Aremorica were in direct trading contact with their neighbours in southern Britain: Caesar says as much, and archaeological evidence confirms his statement. The principal axis was N–S between the harbours dominated now by St. Malo in Brittany and Hengistbury Head in Dorset. Hengistbury served as a port-of-trade where British goods were exchanged for luxury imports, one of which was Italian wine shipped to the island in large ceramic amphorae. British exports would have included metals from the west country, in particular tin from Cornwall, together with corn, slaves, and hunting dogs (all mentioned by the classical geographer Strabo).

The archaeological evidence for this trade is impressive. At Hengistbury excavations have brought to light large quantities of imported Aremorican pottery as well as fragments of Italian amphorae. Aremorican coins, particularly those of the Coriosolites, occur in some number both at Hengistbury and on neighbouring sites.

These vigorous trading links seem to have come to an end in the middle of the first century BC quite possibly as the direct result of Caesar's campaigns. It may be that he forbade trade between these regions and rerouted it through the pro-Roman tribes of eastern England of whom he specifically mentions the Trinobantes.

A fascinating scrap of evidence for cross-channel trade was found at the Dorset hillfort of Bulbury. It was an iron anchor complete with a long iron chain similar to those that Caesar describes in use among the Veneti.

The Veneti, and the other tribes too, learned of my arrival and at the same time began to realize the extent of the crime they had committed in detaining envoys and putting them in chains. (That category of men has always been sacred and inviolable to all peoples.) So they decided to prepare for war on a scale that matched the danger they were in, paying particular attention to the provision of equipment for their ships.

Their hopes were all the greater because they had such confidence in the terrain itself. They knew that the land routes were intersected by tidal inlets, and that our sailing would be hampered by our ignorance of the terrain and by the lack of harbours; they were confident too that our troops could not stay long in their country because of lack of provisions. And besides, if everything turned out quite differently, they still had great naval power; we Romans, however, had no ships available and no knowledge of the shoals, harbours, and islands in the area where we were going to be fighting. They realized that sailing on the vast open Atlantic was not at all the same as what we were used to on the Mediterranean, which is a land-locked sea.

So, having agreed on this policy, they fortified their *oppida*, stocked them with grain from the surrounding fields, and assembled as many ships as possible in Venetia, where it was generally assumed I should begin my operations. As allies for the campaign they secured the Osismi, the Lexovii, the Namnetes, the Ambiliati, the Morini, the Diablintes, and the Menapii. And they summoned extra forces from Britain, which lies opposite that part of Gaul.

10 As I have already indicated, there were difficulties in conducting this campaign, but even so there were many reasons why I wanted to undertake it.

First, there was the crime involved in detaining Romans of equestrian rank; then there was the fact that fighting had again broken out after surrender, and that a revolt had occurred when hostages had been given. Moreover, a great many tribes were involved in the hostile alliance, and above all there was the danger that if this part of Gaul were not dealt with, other tribes would think they were free to do the same. I was aware that almost all the Gauls were eager for political change, and were quickly and easily roused to war, and I knew that all people naturally want freedom and hate to be enslaved. And so I decided I must split up my army and disperse it over a larger area before more tribes could join in the revolt.

11 I therefore sent my legate Titus Labienus with a force of cavalry to the country of the Treveri, which is close to the Rhine. This officer's instructions were to approach the Remi and the rest of the Belgae and keep them loyal. It was said that the Belgae had sent for German troops to help them; if these Germans tried to force their way across the Rhine in their ships, Labienus's orders were to stop them.

I ordered Publius Crassus to set out for Aquitania with twelve cohorts of legionaries and a large number of cavalry, to stop reinforcements being sent from those tribes to Gaul, and to prevent such powerful peoples joining forces.

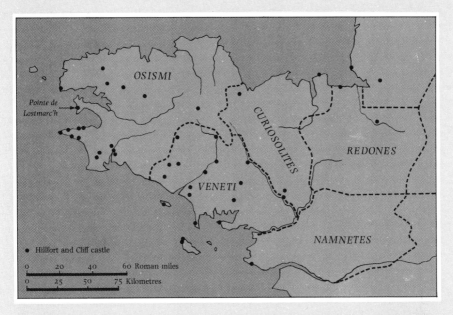

Caesar makes specific reference to the promontory fortifications of the Aremorican tribes. Many of these are known, particularly along the southern shore of the peninsula. They were mapped and studied in detail by Sir Mortimer Wheeler before World War II. Typically promontory forts, or cliff castles as they are often called, were sited on fingers of land projecting into the sea, defended only by ramparts and ditches thrown across the narrowest point. The natural defences of these locations together with the shelving beaches far below where the ships could be hauled to safety made them virtually impregnable. Caesar realized this, which was one reason why he chose to meet his enemies in a pitched battle at sea.

The cliff castle pictured below is that on the Pointe de Lostmarc'h near the entrance to the Bay of Douarnez.

I sent the legate Quintus Titurius Sabinus with three legions to the country of the Venelli, the Curiosolites, and Lexovii, to make sure that that group was kept separate from the rest.

I put young Decimus Brutus in charge of the fleet and of the Gallic ships that I had ordered the Pictones, the Santoni, and the other pacified districts to supply. His instructions were to set out for the territory of the Veneti as soon as he could. I myself marched there with the land forces.

12   The *oppida* of the Veneti were mostly on the far ends of spits, or headlands. They were sited in such a way that they could not be approached on foot when the tide rushed in from the open sea, as happens regularly every twelve hours; they were not accessible by sea either, because ships would be damaged on the shoals when the tide went down. So in both respects there were problems in attacking such *oppida*.

Sometimes, however, we had the Veneti beaten by the sheer scale of our siegeworks; we managed to keep the sea out with great dams, which we built as high as the walls of their *oppida*. But whenever this happened and the Veneti began to realize the hopelessness of their position, they would bring up numbers of ships, of which they had an unlimited supply, load them with their possessions and retreat to other *oppida* nearby, where they would once more defend themselves by the same advantages of terrain.

These tactics they pursued for a great part of the summer, all the more easily because of the bad weather, which kept our ships in port, and the extreme difficulties we experienced sailing on the vast, open sea, where the tides were high and the harbours, if any, were few and far between.

13   The Gauls' own ships were built and rigged in a different way from ours. Their keels were somewhat flatter, so they could cope more easily with the shoals and shallow water when the tide was ebbing; their prows were unusually high, and so were their sterns, designed to stand up to great waves and violent storms. The hulls were made entirely of oak to endure any violent shock or impact; the cross-beams, of timbers a foot thick, were fastened with iron bolts as thick as a man's thumb; and the anchors were held firm with iron chains instead of ropes. They used sails made of hides or soft leather, either because flax was scarce and they did not know how to use it, or, more probably, because they thought that with cloth sails they would not be able to withstand the force of the violent Atlantic gales, or steer such heavy ships.

When we encountered these vessels, our only advantage lay in the speed and power of our oars; in other respects the enemy's ships were better adapted for the violent storms and other conditions along that coast. They were so solidly built that our ships could not damage them with rams, and their height made it hard to use missiles against them or seize them with grappling irons. Not only that; when a gale blew up and they ran before it, they could weather the storm more easily and heave to more safely in shallow water, and if left aground by the tide, they had nothing to fear from rocks and reefs. To our ships, on the other hand, all these situations were a source of terror.

14   After capturing several of their *oppida*, I realized that all this effort was

being wasted: even when we had done so, it was impossible to stop the enemy getting away, or to do them any real damage. So I decided I must wait for our fleet to arrive.

As soon as it came into view, about 220 enemy ships, absolutely ready for action and perfectly equipped with every kind of weapon, sailed out of harbour and took up position opposite ours. It was far from clear to Brutus, the fleet commander, or to the military tribunes and centurions entrusted with individual ships, what to do or what tactics to adopt. They knew it was impossible to inflict damage with the rams; on the other hand, if we built turrets on our ships, the sterns of the enemy vessels still towered above them. This meant that it was difficult for our men to hurl their missiles properly, whereas those thrown by the Gauls fell with greater effect.

But our men had one piece of equipment, prepared beforehand, which proved very effective – sharp-pointed hooks inserted into long poles, rather like the grappling hooks employed in sieges. These were used to grab and pull tight the ropes fastening the yardarms to the masts of the enemy ships. The ropes were then snapped by a sudden spurt of rowing, and the yardarms inevitably collapsed. As the Gallic ships relied entirely on their sails and rigging, when they lost these they were at once robbed of all power of manoeuvre.

The rest of the conflict was a matter of valour, in which our soldiers were easily superior. This was all the more true because they were fighting under my own eyes and those of the whole army. Our troops occupied all the hills and high ground from which there was a good view down to the sea, so any deed of above average bravery could not fail to be noticed.

With the enemy's yardarms wrenched off in the way I have described, **15** two or three of our ships would position themselves around individual vessels, and our soldiers would make the most determined efforts to board them. The enemy realized what was happening, and after several of their ships had been taken in this way, they determined to save themselves by flight, since they could find no means of thwarting our tactics.

They had already turned their ships before the wind when suddenly there was such a dead calm they were unable to move. This certainly happened at just the right moment for us to make our victory complete: our ships pursued theirs one by one and captured them, with the result that when night fell only a very few vessels from the entire enemy fleet managed to reach land. The engagement had lasted from about ten in the morning until sunset.

This battle marked the end of the war with the Veneti and the peoples **16** of the whole Atlantic coast. Not only had they assembled all the men of military age there, and all the older men too who had any authority or distinction, but they had concentrated their entire force of ships in that one place. So when these were lost, the rest had nowhere to retreat and no means of defending their *oppida*.

They therefore surrendered themselves and all their property to me. I decided that they must be punished with particular severity, so that in future the Gauls would have a greater respect for the rights of envoys. I put all their elders to death and sold the rest into slavery.

3 Sabinus in Normandy

17   While these operations were taking place in the country of the Veneti,
Quintus Titurius Sabinus arrived in the territory of the Venelli with the
troops I had assigned to him. The chief of these Venelli, Viridovix, was
commander-in-chief of all the rebel tribes of that area and had formed a
considerable army out of them. In the last few days the Aulerci, the Eburovices, and the Lexovii had killed all their councillors because they refused
to sanction going to war, then closed their gates against us and joined Viridovix. In addition a large number of bandits and desperadoes had come together from all over Gaul; the prospect of plunder and the attractions of
fighting had more appeal than daily work on the land.

Sabinus stayed within his camp, which occupied an ideal position; but
Viridovix, who had encamped opposite him two miles away, led out his
troops every day and gave him an opportunity of fighting a pitched battle.
The result was that the Gauls began to despise Sabinus and even some of
our own men voiced their criticisms of him. He gave such an impression
of being frightened that the enemy eventually dared to come right up to the
rampart of our camp.

The reason for Sabinus's behaving like this was his belief that a subordi-
nate commander ought not to fight an engagement with such a vast enemy
force, especially in the absence of his commander-in-chief, unless he enjoyed
the advantage of position or some particularly favourable opportunity presented itself.

18   Having established this reputation for timidity, Sabinus selected from his
auxiliary troops a clever Gaul who seemed ideal for his plan. By promising
this man large rewards he persuaded him to go over to the enemy; he explained to him what he wanted done. The man went to the enemy,
pretending to be a deserter. He told them all about the Romans' fear, explaining that I myself was being hard pressed by the Veneti and that the very
next night Sabinus would lead his army secretly out of camp and set out to
go to my aid.

When they heard this, they all shouted out that such a chance of success
was not to be lost; they must march against our camp. In deciding on this
plan the Gauls were influenced by many things – the hesitation of Sabinus
in the last few days, the assurances of the deserter, the shortage of food that
had resulted from their own inadequate attention to supplies, their expectations about the outcome of the Venetic campaign, and of course the general
willingness of people to believe what they want to believe.

Spurred on by such considerations, they would not let Viridovix and the
other chiefs leave the council until they had agreed that they should arm
and march on our camp. When this consent was given, they were exultant;
it was almost as if the victory was already theirs. They set out towards the
camp, with bundles of brushwood and faggots for filling up our ditches.

19   The site of our camp was high ground at the top of a gentle slope about a
mile long. The enemy ran up to it at great speed so as to give us as little time
as possible to get ourselves organized and armed. When they reached us,
they were out of breath. Sabinus addressed his men and gave them the

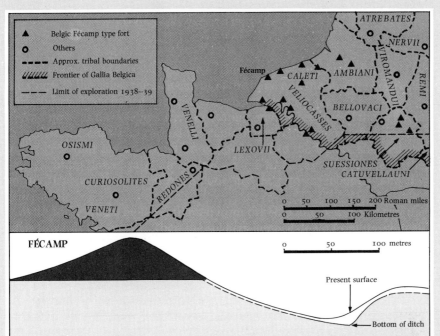

FÉCAMP

0   50   100 metres

Present surface

Bottom of ditch

Sir Mortimer Wheeler's detailed survey of the hillforts of northern France identified a very specific type of defence that occurred mainly in the territory of the Belgic tribes. He named this type after the fort of Fécamp sited on the coast of Normandy overlooking the English Channel. The Fécamp type of fortification is characterized by a huge rampart of heaped rubble and soil fronted by a wide flat-bottomed ditch. This kind of ditch may well be a local response to the tactics of Roman siege warfare. Battering rams would have been difficult to use while the ditch, easy to jump into but difficult to escape from, would have been a death-trap if properly defended.

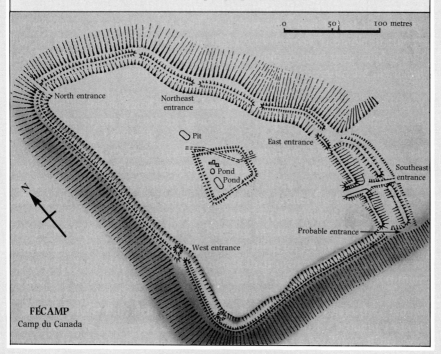

0   50   100 metres

North entrance

Northeast
entrance

Pit

East entrance

O Pond
Pond

Southeast
entrance

N

Probable entrance

West entrance

FÉCAMP
Camp du Canada

67

signal they were eager to hear. He ordered them to make a sudden sortie from two of the gates while the Gauls were still at a disadvantage because of the bundles they were carrying.

We had the advantage of position, and our men were brave and had all the experience of their earlier battles. The enemy, on the other hand, were so exhausted and so lacking in military skills that they could not stand up to even a single attack from our men, but immediately turned and fled.

They were hampered by what they were carrying and our troops, being fresh, pursued and killed a large number of them. Our cavalry ran down the rest and caught all but a few who had managed to get away. So it happened that Sabinus heard of my naval battle and I heard of his victory at one and the same time.

All the tribes there immediately surrendered to him, for while the Gauls are quick and eager to start wars, they lack the determination and strength of character needed to carry on when things go against them.

4 Crassus in Aquitania

20 About the same time Publius Crassus reached Aquitania, which, as I have already said, must be considered to constitute a third of the country of Gaul as a whole because of its population and the area it covers.

Crassus was well aware that he had to fight in country where a few years earlier the legate Lucius Valerius Praeconinus had been defeated and killed, and from which the proconsul Lucius Manlius had fled with the loss of all his heavy equipment. He realized therefore that he must be extremely careful. And so he made arrangements about grain supplies, raised a force of auxiliary troops and cavalry, and called up individually many good fighting men from Toulouse, Carcasonne, and Narbonne, towns in the Province near Aquitania.

He then led his army into the territory of the Sontiates. This tribe, hearing of Crassus's approach, assembled a large army and force of cavalry, in which they were particularly strong, and attacked our column on the march. The first engagement was between cavalry, then, when their horsemen had been driven back and were being pursued by ours, they suddenly brought out into the open the infantry troops they had been keeping hidden in a valley. These troops renewed the battle, attacking our men while they were scattered.

21 The battle was long and fierce. The Sontiates, confident because of their earlier victories, thought that the survival of the whole of Aquitania depended on their valour; our men were keen to show what they could do under a young leader, without their commander-in-chief and the rest of the legions. In the end, exhausted by their wounds, the enemy turned and fled. Large numbers of them were killed by Crassus, who then marched straight for their *oppidum* and began to attack it.

Meeting with stiff resistance, he brought up protective sheds and siege towers. The Sontiates first tried to break out, then they dug tunnels up to our rampart and sheds. (The Aquitani are extremely skilful at this because there are copper mines and quarries in many parts of their country.) But when they realized that even by doing this they could achieve nothing, because of the vigilance of our men, they sent envoys to Crassus asking him to accept their surrender. He agreed, and they handed over their weapons as he ordered.

While all our troops were fully occupied with these events, the enemy   22
commander-in-chief, Adiatunnus, attempted to break out from another part of the *oppidum* with 600 companions all bound by a vow of loyalty.

The Sontiates call such people *soldurii*, and they observe the following rule of life: they share all the good things of life with those to whom they have pledged themselves in friendship, and if any such friend meets a violent death, they all either share his fate or kill themselves. And as yet, in the memory of man, no one has been known to refuse to die after the death of a comrade to whom he had pledged friendship.

When a shout went up from the part of our fortifications where Adiatunnus was making his attempt, our men ran to arms and there was a fierce battle there. Adiatunnus was driven back into his *oppidum*, but in spite of all that, he succeeded in his request that Crassus should accept his surrender on the same terms as the others.

Crassus received the weapons and hostages and then set out for the   23
country of the Vocates and the Tarusates.

By now the natives were thoroughly alarmed: they had heard that an *oppidum* that had excellent natural defences and strong fortifications had been captured within a few days of Crassus's arrival. So they began to send envoys to all the neighbouring tribes, take oaths of allegiance, exchange hostages, and mobilize their forces. They even sent envoys to those peoples of northern Spain who are on the borders of Aquitania, asking them for men and leaders.

When these reinforcements arrived, the enemy were able to take the field with an army strengthened not only in numbers but also in prestige. The men chosen to lead their forces were those who had been with Quintus Sertorius in all his campaigns and so were considered to be military experts. They followed Roman practice and began to choose their sites, build and fortify camps, and cut off our supplies.

Seeing all this, Crassus realized that his own troops were too few to be easily divided, whereas the enemy were ranging over the country and blocking roads, but were still able to leave their camp adequately garrisoned; this meant that it was less easy for us to get grain and other supplies through, and all the while the enemy's numbers were increasing. His conclusion was that he must fight a pitched battle without delay. He referred the matter to a council of war, and finding that everyone there shared his view, decided to fight the next day.

At dawn he led out all his troops and drew them up in two lines, with the   24
auxiliaries in the centre. He then waited to see what plan of action the enemy would take.

The Gauls were confident that they would not be at risk in the engagement, because of their own numbers and long established military record, and because of our numerical weakness. But even so, they thought it would be safer to block the roads, cut off our supplies and so win a victory without bloodshed; if, starved of supplies, our men began to retreat, they planned to attack them on the march, when they were at a disadvantage, dispirited and hampered by the packs they were carrying. Their leaders approved of this plan and so, when our troops were led out, the Gauls kept themselves inside their camp.

Crassus observed all this. The enemy by delaying had created the impression that they were afraid. This made our men even keener to fight, and they could be heard saying that they ought to attack the enemy camp immediately. Crassus addressed his men and then, with all his troops eager for action, marched on the enemy camp.

25 Once there, some of our troops began to fill in the ditches, while others kept up a constant hail of missiles and drove the defenders from the rampart and fortifications. The auxiliaries, in whose fighting qualities Crassus had little confidence, kept the others supplied with stones and javelins, and carried up turf for building an earth bank, and in this way they gave all the appearance of being fighting men. The enemy too fought with courage and determination, hurling their weapons down on us from above with great effect.

Then some of our cavalry rode round the enemy's camp and reported to Crassus that the back was not so carefully fortified and offered easy access.

26 Crassus addressed his cavalry officers, telling them to rouse the spirits of their men by promising generous rewards, and then explained what he wanted done.

They carried out his instructions, and led out the cohorts who had been left to guard or camp and were therefore still fresh. To avoid being seen from the enemy camp they took these troops round by a long detour while everyone's attention was concentrated on the fighting, and quickly reached the section of their fortifications mentioned above. They tore this down and had established themselves in the enemy camp before the enemy themselves could see them clearly or understand what was happening.

Hearing the shouts that came from this sector, our men began to attack all the more keenly; they now expected to win, and as usually happens in such cases, this gave them fresh strength. The enemy were completely surrounded, all their hopes gone; they threw themselves down from their fortifications and fled for their lives.

Our cavalry pursued them over perfectly open plains, and of the 50,000 men known to have assembled from the Aquitani and Cantabri, hardly one quarter survived. It was late at night when our cavalry returned to camp.

27 When news of this battle spread, most of the tribes of Aquitania surrendered to Crassus, sending hostages of their own accord. These tribes included the Tarbelli, the Bigerriones, the Ptianii, the Vocates, the Tarusates, the Elusates, the Gates, the Ausci, the Garumni, the Sibuzates, and the Cocosates. A few of the most remote tribes, relying on the approach of winter to save them, did not submit.

28 At about the same time, even though the summer was now almost over, I led my army against the Morini and the Menapii. All the rest of Gaul had

been subdued, but these tribes remained in arms and had never sent envoys to me to discuss peace terms.

I thought that my campaign against them could be completed quickly, but they began to use tactics quite different from those employed by the rest of the Gauls. Realizing that even the strongest tribes had been defeated and routed when they fought pitched battles, they withdrew with all their possessions into an area of their land consisting of a continuous belt of forests and marshland.

When I reached the edge of these forests, I began to build a camp. There had so far been no sign of the enemy and our men were in scattered groups, working on constructing the camp, when suddenly the Gauls rushed out from all parts of the forest and charged at us. My men quickly armed them-themselves and drove their attackers back into the forests, killing quite a number of them. However, they kept up their pursuit too far over the rather difficult country and so a few of our own troops were killed too.

In the days that followed this incident I ordered that the forests should be cut down. To prevent any attack being made on my troops from the flank when they were unarmed and not ready to fight, I had all the timber that had been felled put as a barrier against the enemy, piled up to act as a rampart on each side. **29**

The men worked extraordinarily quickly and in a few days a large area was cleared. We had already caught up with the enemy's cattle and the end of their baggage train, though they were going farther and farther into the forests, when such bad weather came on that we had to leave off the operation, and as the rain continued, it was impossible to keep the men in tents any longer.

So after ravaging all the enemy's fields, and burning their villages and farm buildings, I led my army back and quartered it for the winter in the country of the Aulerci and the Lexovii and the other tribes who had recently fought against us.

One of the characteristics of Aremorican culture was the high technical and artistic quality of its pottery. Pottery was wheel turned, evenly fired and often elaborately decorated, sometimes with complex curvilinear motifs copied from contemporary fine metal-work. This outstanding example is from Saint-Pol-de-Léon on the north coast of Brittany.

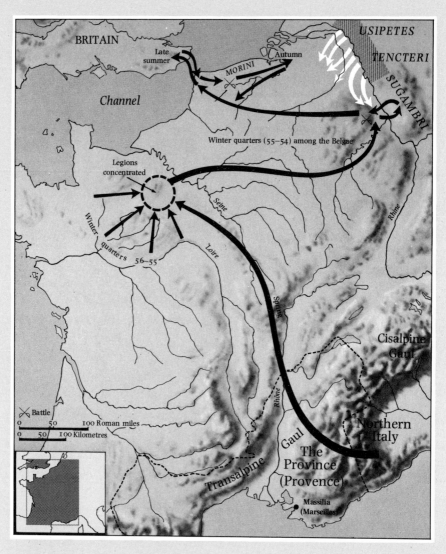

The year 55 BC saw Caesar's exploits at their most spectacular. In a single year he accomplished two feats of daring either of which would have shaken his Italian audience with excitement – the crossing of the Rhine and the landing in Britain. He was venturing into the unknown to lands which, in the minds of many, were peopled with mythical beings and with monsters. Tactically neither adventure was necessary. Caesar could offer some self-justification in terms of the help that his enemies in Gaul were receiving from abroad and of the potential build-up of hostile troops north of the Rhine, but this kind of special pleading was hardly convincing. Caesar was an adventurer and a showman who could not resist the lure of the exciting.

The German campaign began with some provocation but the actual Rhine crossing and the devastation wrought in the territory of the Sugambri was little short of terrorism, indeed Caesar virtually admits as much.

While the Rhine crossing was a relatively safe operation the landing in southeastern Britain verged on the foolhardy. Inexperience of Channel tides, bad luck, and errors of judgment combined to make it a near disaster but Caesar rescued the situation and returned to Gaul intent on trying again in the next year.

BOOK IV · 55 BC

1 The German campaign

In the following winter, in which Gnaeus Pompeius and Marcus Crassus   1
began their consulship, the German tribes of the Usipetes and the Tencteri
crossed the Rhine in large numbers not far from where that river meets the
sea. Their reason for crossing was that for several years they had been
harassed by attacks from the Suebi and prevented from cultivating their
own land.

The Suebi are by far the largest and most warlike of all the German tribes.
It is said that they have 100 cantons and from each of these they draw 1,000
armed men every year to fight in wars outside their own territory. The rest,
who stay at home, support both themselves and the fighting force, but in
the following year they in their turn become the warriors, while the others
stay at home.

In this way both agriculture and military instruction and practice go on
without interruption. However, no private ownership of land exists in their
communities, and no one is allowed to settle down and cultivate any one
plot for more than a year. They do not eat much cereal food but mostly live
on milk and meat, spending much time in hunting.

From childhood they are not restrained by any discipline or sense of duty
to others, and they never do anything at all against their own inclinations.
Such freedom from restraint, together with their diet and daily exercise,
produces in them enormous bodily stature and strength. They live in an
extremely cold climate and yet they have made a practice of bathing in the
rivers and of wearing only animal skins, so scanty that they leave a large
part of the body naked.

Traders are admitted into their country so that they will have purchasers   2
for their booty rather than because they want to import anything. And
whereas the Gauls are particularly fond of horses and pay huge prices for
them, the Germans do not import them at all. They use only their homebred
animals, which, though small and ugly, are made remarkably strong and
efficient through daily training.

In cavalry engagements they often jump down from their horses and
fight on foot, and because their horses have been trained to stand perfectly
still, the warriors can quickly get back to them when the need arises. They
believe nothing is more disgraceful or effeminate than to use a saddle. And
so however few they may be, they are bold enough to attack any body of
saddled cavalry, however large.

The import of wine into their country is absolutely forbidden; they think
that it makes men soft and effeminate and incapable of enduring hardship.

73

3   They consider that the greatest glory a nation can have is to keep the widest possible area of uninhabited land next to its borders, because that shows the number of other tribes unable to withstand their fighting strength. So, for example, it is said that on one side of the Suebic territory there is uninhabited land stretching for 600 miles.

On the other side the Ubii are their nearest neighbours, once a large and prosperous nation by German standards. Although they are Germans too, they are slightly more civilized than the rest; they live on the Rhine and are often visited by traders, and because they are so close to Gaul, they have adopted Gallic customs. The Suebi have frequently attempted to drive them out of their country by force of arms, but have been thwarted by their strength and numbers. However, they have succeeded in making the Ubii pay tribute, greatly reducing their pride and power.

4   The Usipetes and the Tencteri, mentioned above, were in just the same position. Having withstood attacks from the Suebi for many years, they were in the end driven from their land, and after wandering about for three years in various parts of Germany, they reached the Rhine.

The area they had come to was inhabited by the Menapii, who had lands, buildings, and villages on both banks of the river. The arrival of such a horde so terrified these people that they abandoned their buildings on the right bank and posted guards on the left bank to stop the Germans crossing.

The Germans tried every means of getting across, but without success; they could not force their way over because they had no boats, and the Menapian guards foiled any attempts at crossing by stealth. So they pretended to go back to their own country and home, and for three days marched in that direction. Then they turned back; their cavalry covered the whole distance back in one night, and caught the Menapii when they were off their guard. They did not expect to be attacked, because their patrols had told them that the Germans had withdrawn, and so they had gone back with no fears to their settlements across the Rhine.

The Germans killed them and seizing their boats, crossed the river before news of all this could reach the Menapii on the left bank. Once across, they seized all the buildings that the Menapii had there, and lived on their supplies of food for the rest of the winter.

5   When I was informed about these events, I felt uneasy because of the temperament of the Gauls: they are always ready to change one plan for another and in general are always eager for political change, and I thought I ought not to rely on them.

It is a custom of theirs to force travellers to stop, even if they don't wish to, and question them about what they have heard or found out on this subject or that; in the *oppida* a crowd gathers around traders and forces them to say what country they have come from and what information they have gathered there. Influenced by these reports, even when they are hearsay, the Gauls frequently adopt plans about important matters, which they are bound to regret almost immediately, since they are slaves to unsubstantiated rumours and most of the people they question make up answers they think will please them.

Being aware of this habit of theirs and not wishing to have to face a more   6
serious campaign, I set out to join the army rather earlier in the season than
I usually did.

When I reached them, I discovered that what I had suspected would
happen had happened. Some tribes had sent embassies to the Germans
inviting them to withdraw from the Rhine, and undertaking to supply them
with all they had asked for. This encouraged the Germans to range over a
wider area, until they had reached the country of the Eburones, and the
Condrusi, dependents, of the Treveri.

I called a meeting of the leading men of Gaul, but thought I ought not
to reveal to them what I had found out. Instead, after calming their fears
and giving them encouragement, I told them to provide cavalry for the
campaign I intended to conduct against the Germans.

After making arrangements about grain supplies and selecting my   7
cavalry troops, I began the march to the area where the Germans were
said to be. When I was only a few days' march away from them, they sent
envoys to me with the following message.

'We Germans are not initiating hostilities against the Roman people, but
neither shall we be slow to fight if we are provoked. It is a custom handed
down from our forefathers to resist any aggressor and to ask no mercy.
One thing, however, we wish to say: we came to Gaul not from choice, but
because we were driven out of our homes. If you Romans wish to be on
friendly terms with us, we can be of use to you. Either assign to us land to
live in or allow us to keep that which we have fought over and won. The
Suebi are the only tribe we acknowledge as our superiors, for not even the
immortal gods can match them; there is no other tribe on earth that we
cannot overcome.'

I gave what I considered an appropriate reply, and ended by saying that   8
if they remained in Gaul there could be no question of friendship between us:
it was unreasonable for people who were unable to protect their own territory to seize other people's, and besides there was no land available in Gaul
that could be given to them without causing resentment, especially considering their great numbers. I told them they could, if they wished, settle
in the country of the Ubii, whose envoys were then in our camp, complaining about the wrongs done them by the Suebi and asking me for help; I
would give instructions to the Ubii about this.

The German envoys said they would report back to their people and then   9
return to me in three days when they had discussed the matter. They asked
me in the meantime not to move my camp any nearer to them. I told them
that it was impossible for me to grant that request either.

I had found out that they had some days earlier sent a large detachment
of cavalry across the river Meuse to the territory of the Ambivariti for plunder
and grain supplies. I thought that they were trying to delay matters with me
because they were waiting for these cavalry troops to get back.

The Meuse rises in the Vosges mountains, in the country of the Lingones.   10
It is joined by a tributary from the Rhine, called the Waal, and forms the
island of the Batavi. The Meuse itself flows into the Rhine about 80 miles

from the sea. The Rhine rises in the country of the Lepontii, who live in the Alps. Its course is long and swift, passing through the territory of the Nantuates, the Helvetii, the Sequani, the Mediomatrices, the Triboci, and the Treveri. As it nears the sea it divides into several streams, thus making many large islands. A great number of these are inhabited by fierce, savage tribes, some of whom are believed to live on fish and birds' eggs. The river flows into the sea at many mouths.

11   When I was no more than twelve miles from the enemy, their envoys returned to me, as had been agreed. They met me on the march and earnestly begged me not to advance any farther. I did not agree to this request, so they asked me to send word to the cavalry who had gone on ahead of our column, telling them not to engage in battle. They also asked me to give them the chance of sending envoys to the Ubii, saying that if the chiefs and the council of that tribe would pledge themselves by oath, they would accept the terms I suggested. They asked me to allow them three days for completing these arrangements.

I thought all this was being proposed with the same motive as before, that is, to obtain a three-day delay in which their absent cavalry could get back again. However, I said that on that day I would advance no more than the four miles necessary to get water. I asked them to meet at that point on the next day with as many of their tribesmen as possible so that I could hear their requests.

Meantime I sent orders to the officers who had gone on in front with all the cavalry telling them not to attack the enemy, and if attacked themselves, to hold out until I approached with the main body of the army.

12   Our cavalry force was 5,000 strong, whereas the enemy's numbered no more than 800 because those who had crossed the Meuse in search of provisions had not yet returned. However, the Germans charged our force as soon as it came into view.

Our men, who were not expecting trouble from the enemy, because their envoys had only just left me and had asked for a truce for that day, were quickly thrown into confusion. But when they fought back once more, the enemy, following their usual practice, jumped down and unseated a number of our men by stabbing their horses in the belly. The rest they put to flight, driving them on in such panic that they did not stop until they came into sight of our marching column.

Seventy-four of our cavalry were killed in this engagement, among them a very gallant Aquitanian called Piso. He came from a most distinguished family, his grandfather having been king of his tribe and granted the title 'Friend' by our senate. In this engagement he went to the help of his brother, who was cut off by the enemy, and succeeded in rescuing him; his own horse was wounded and he was thrown. He fought back most courageously as long as he could, but in the end he was surrounded by Germans and fell covered in wounds. His brother had by this time got away from the fighting, but seeing Piso fall, he spurred on his horse, rode straight at the enemy and was himself killed.

13   After this battle it was clear that I was dealing with an enemy who with-

out provocation had launched a treacherous attack when they had asked for peace. I therefore decided that I should not listen to any more of their deputations or accept any proposals they might make.

However, I considered it to be the height of folly to wait until the enemy's forces could be increased by the return of their cavalry, and knowing the unstable character of the Gauls, I realized what a deep impression the Germans had already made on them with just one battle; so I decided that they must be given no time to make plans. Having reached this decision, I told my legates and quaestor of my intention not to let a single day go by before bringing the enemy to battle.

The next morning we had a great stroke of luck. A large number of Germans, including all their chiefs and elders, came to visit me in my camp. They were resorting once more to the same treachery and deceit because, though they claimed to have come in order to excuse themselves for having the previous day attacked us, thus breaking the agreement they themselves had asked for, they intended to deceive me if they could into granting their requests about a truce.

I was delighted that they were in my power and I ordered that they should be detained. I led the whole of my army out of the camp, telling the cavalry to bring up the rear, because I thought that its morale had been undermined by its recent defeat.

My troops were formed in three parallel columns and quickly marched **14** the distance of eight miles, reaching the enemy camp before the Germans could realize what was happening. Everything threw them into sudden panic – the speed of our advance and the absence of their own leaders. They were given no time to make plans or arm themselves, and they were in too much confusion to decide whether it was best to lead their troops out against us, or to defend their camp, or to try to save themselves by running away. We could tell they were in a panic by the way they were shouting and running about, and our men, spurred on by the treachery of the previous day, burst into their camp.

There, those Germans able to arm themselves fast enough resisted our men for a short time, fighting among their carts and baggage wagons. But because the Germans had brought everything they had with them when they left their homes and crossed the Rhine, there was also a great crowd of women and children and these now began to flee in all directions. I sent the cavalry to hunt them down.

When the Germans heard cries behind them and saw that their own **15** people were being killed, they threw away their weapons, abandoned their standards, and rushed out of the camp. When they reached the confluence of the Moselle and the Rhine, they saw they had no hope of escaping farther. A large number of them were killed and the rest flung themselves into the river, where they perished overcome by panic, exhaustion, and the force of the current.

Our men returned to camp without a single fatal casualty and with only a very few injured, after fearing that they would be involved in a very difficult campaign since the enemy had numbered 430,000. I gave the Germans detained in our camp permission to leave. But they were afraid of being killed or tortured by the Gauls whose lands they had ravaged, and they said they wanted to stay with me. I allowed them to retain their liberty.

16　　With the German war concluded, I decided that I must cross the Rhine. Several reasons prompted me. The strongest was that I could see the Germans were all too ready to cross into Gaul, and I wanted them to have reasons of their own for anxiety when they realized that an army of the Roman people could and would cross the Rhine. There was also the fact that the section of cavalry of the Usipetes and the Tencteri, which, as I have already mentioned, had crossed the Meuse in search of plunder and grain and so had not taken part in the battle, had crossed the Rhine after the rout of their countrymen, entered the territory of the Sugambri and joined forces with them.

When I sent messengers to the Sugambri to demand the surrender of those who had made war on me and on Gaul, they replied that the Rhine was the limit of Roman power: if I thought the Germans had no right to cross into Gaul against my will, why should I claim any power or authority on the German side of the Rhine?

Then too there was the fact that the Ubii – the only tribe across the Rhine who had sent envoys to me, established ties of friendship, and given hostages – were urgently begging me to go to their help because they were being severely harassed by the Suebi. If it was impossible for me to do that because of political preoccupations, they asked me merely to take my army across the Rhine; that would be enough to give them help and provide them with confidence for the future.

They said that with the defeat of Ariovistus and this latest victory of ours, the name and reputation of my army was so great even among the most distant tribes of Germany that they would be protected merely by the fact that others knew of their friendship with Rome. They promised to provide a large number of boats to get the army across the river.

17　　These were the reasons that had made me decide to cross the Rhine. However, I thought that to cross in boats would be too risky, and would not be fitting for my own prestige and that of Rome. And so, even though building a bridge involved enormous difficulties, because of the breadth and depth of the river and its strong current, that is what I thought I must attempt, or else give up any thoughts of taking the army across.

This is the method I used in building the bridge. Two piles a foot and a half thick, slightly pointed at their lower ends and of lengths dictated by the varying depth of the river, were fastened together two feet apart. We used tackle to lower these into the river, where they were fixed in the bed and driven home with piledrivers, not vertically, as piles usually are, but obliquely, leaning in the direction of the current.

Opposite these, 40 feet lower down the river, two more piles were fixed, joined together in the same way, though this time against the force of the current. These two pairs were then joined by a beam two feet wide, whose ends fitted exactly into the spaces between the two piles of each pair. The pairs were kept apart from each other by means of braces that secured each pile to the end of the beam. So the piles were kept apart, and held fast in the

The bridging of the Rhine was a brilliant feat of
construction, but since the Roman army had within
it many of the most able engineers, and every
soldier had some building skills, Caesar could
approach his task with a degree of assurance. His
evident fascination with the scheme, witnessed by
the detail in which he describes it, suggests that he took a
personal interest in the proceedings. It would have demonstrated to
the Germans, perhaps more than anything else, the invincibility of Rome.

opposite direction, the structure being so strong and the laws of physics such that the greater the force of the current, the more tightly were the timbers held in place.

A series of these piles and beams was put in position and connected by lengths of timber set across them, with poles and bundles of sticks laid on top. The structure was strong, but additional piles were driven in obliquely on the downstream side of the bridge; these were joined with the main structure and acted as buttresses to take the force of the current. Other piles too were fixed a little way upstream from the bridge so that if the natives sent down tree trunks or boats to demolish it, these barriers would lessen their impact and prevent the bridge being damaged.

18 Ten days after the collection of the timber was begun, the work was completed and the army led across. I left a strong guard at each end of the bridge and then marched into the territory of the Sugambri.

Meanwhile deputations came to me from several tribes asking for peace and friendship. I replied courteously and told them to have hostages brought to me. From the moment we had started building the bridge, the Sugambri had been preparing for flight. They were urged to do so by those of the Tencteri and the Usipetes who were with them, and so they left their own country and disappeared into uninhabited forests, taking all their belong-
19 ings with them. I stayed a few days in their territory, burning all their villages and buildings and cutting down their crops. Then I returned to the country of the Ubii.

I promised this people help if they were harassed by the Suebi, and they gave me the following information. When the Suebi had learned from their scouts that a bridge was being built, they followed their usual custom and called a council. They sent messengers to every part of their country telling their people to leave their *oppida*; they were to take their women, their children, and all their property into the forests and then all men capable of fighting were to assemble in one place, that chosen being about the middle of their territory. There, the Ubii informed me, the Suebi were waiting for us to arrive and that was the place where they had decided to fight it out.

On receiving this information, I crossed back into Gaul, breaking the bridge behind me. I had accomplished all the objectives that had made me decide to take my army across the Rhine – to intimidate the Germans, to punish the Sugambri, to relieve the Ubii from Suebic harassment. We had spent 18 days in all across the Rhine and I considered I had done all that honour or interest required.

2 Reconnaissance to Britain

20 Not much of the summer was left, and winter sets in early in these regions because the whole of this part of Gaul faces north. Nevertheless I went ahead with plans for an expedition to Britain, because I knew that in almost all of our campaigns in Gaul our enemies had received reinforcements from the Britons.

Even if we should not have enough time for conducting a campaign that season, I thought it would be very useful merely to have visited the island, to have seen what sort of people lived there, and to get some idea of the terrain and the harbours and landing places. The Gauls knew practically nothing about all this. In the ordinary way no one goes to Britain except traders, and even they are acquainted only with the sea coast and the areas that are opposite Gaul. And so, although I summoned traders from all parts, I could not find out about the size of the island, the names and populations of the tribes who lived there, their methods of fighting or the customs they had, or which harbours there could accommodate a large number of big ships.

In order to get this information before venturing on an expedition to 21 Britain, I sent Gaius Volusenus there first with a warship. I thought he was a suitable man for the task, and gave him instructions to make enquiries about all these points and come back to me as quickly as he could.

I myself took all the army and set off for the territory of the Morini, because from there the crossing to Britain was shortest. I gave orders that ships should assemble there from the neighbouring districts, together with the fleet built the previous summer for the campaign against the Veneti.

Meanwhile my plan became known and traders reported it to the Britons. Several of their tribes sent envoys to me to promise that they would give hostages and submit to the authority of Rome. I heard what they had to say and gave them generous promises, urging them to keep their word.

I sent them back home and with them Commius, whom I had made king of the Atrebates after I had subdued that tribe. I had a high opinion of his courage and judgment and I believed him to be loyal to me; his authority was greatly respected in those regions. I told him to visit as many tribes as he could, to encourage them to seek the protection of Rome, and to tell them I should soon be arriving in Britain.

Volusenus reconnoitred all the coastal areas he could, without venturing to disembark and so put himself in the power of the natives. Four days later he returned to me and reported his findings.

While I was in this part of the country, waiting for our ships to be made 22 ready, envoys came to me from a large section of the Morini to apologize for their previous policy, explaining that it was only because they were foreigners and not used to our ways that they had made war on the Roman people, and to promise in future to do what I told them. This seemed to me to have happened just at the right time. I did not want to leave an enemy at my rear, but I had no chance of conducting a campaign, because it was too late in the season and I thought the expedition to Britain more important than settling these trivial problems. So I ordered the Morini to produce a large number of hostages, and when these had been brought, I accepted the submission of their tribe.

About 80 transport ships had been obtained and assembled, enough in my opinion to take two legions across to Britain. There were also some warships that I assigned to the quaestor, the legates, and the officers commanding auxiliary troops. In addition to these, there were 18 transports at a point eight miles away, prevented by the wind from reaching the same harbour as the rest. These I assigned to the cavalry.

I left the rest of the army with the legates Quintus Titurius Sabinus and Lucius Aurunculeius Cotta, to be led against the Menapii and those clans of the Morini who had not sent envoys to me. I ordered another legate, Publius Sulpicius Rufus, to guard the harbour with what I considered was a strong enough force.

23 These arrangements were completed, and, finding the weather suitable for sailing, we put to sea about midnight. I had told the cavalry to proceed to the farther port, embark there, and follow me.

Although they acted rather too slowly in carrying out their instructions, I myself reached Britain with the leading ships about nine o'clock in the morning, and saw the enemy's forces, armed, in position on all the hills there.

At that point steep cliffs came down close to the sea in such a way that it was possible to hurl weapons from them right down on to the shore. It seemed to me that this place was altogether unsuitable for landing and so I waited at anchor until about three o'clock for the rest of the ships to arrive.

Meanwhile I summoned my legates and the military tribunes and explained to them what Volusenus had reported and what I wanted done. I warned them that military tactics, particularly those involved in warfare at sea, where things happen quickly and unpredictably, demanded that every order should be carried out instantly and without question; then I dismissed them.

Both the wind and the tide were now in our favour, so I gave the signal for the anchors to be weighed. We moved on about seven miles and ran the ships ashore on a flat and open beach.

24 But the natives had discovered our intention. They had sent on ahead their cavalry and the chariots, which they regularly use in battle. The rest of their troops came on behind and were stopping our men landing.

We were now faced with grave difficulties, for the following reasons. Because of their size, our ships could not be run ashore except where the water was deep; the soldiers were unfamiliar with the terrain, their hands were full and they were weighed down by the heavy weapons they carried; they had to jump down from their ships, get a footing in the waves and fight the enemy all at the same time.

The enemy, on the other hand, were standing on dry land or moving out just a little way into the water; all their limbs were unencumbered and they knew the ground very well, so they boldly hurled their javelins and spurred on their horses, which were trained for this kind of thing. Our men were terrified at this. They were completely unfamiliar with this kind of fighting and did not show the same spirit and keenness as they usually did in battles on land.

25 I noticed this and acted. Our warships were swifter and easier to handle than the transports, and also their shape was something the enemy had never seen before. So I ordered them to be moved a short distance from the transports, and then to be rowed hard and run ashore on the enemy's exposed flank. From there they were to drive the Britons back with slings, arrows, and artillery, and dislodge them from their position.

This manoeuvre was very effective. The natives were greatly disturbed by the shape of the ships, the movement of the oars, and the strange devices of our artillery. They halted and then moved back a short way.

And now, as our soldiers were hesitating, mostly because of the depth of the water, the man who carried the eagle of the Tenth legion, after praying to the gods that his act would bring good luck to the legion, shouted out loudly, 'Jump down, men, unless you want to betray your eagle to the enemy. I at any rate shall have done my duty to my country and my general'.

With these words he flung himself from the ship and began to carry the eagle towards the enemy. Then the soldiers jumped down from the ship all together, urging each other not to allow a disgrace like that to happen. When the men from the next ships saw what these soldiers did, they followed them and advanced towards the enemy.

The fighting was fierce on both sides. Our men, however, could not keep 26 ranks or get a firm footing or follow their proper standards, and men from different ships grouped themselves under the first standards they came across. There was great disorder as a result.

But the enemy knew all the shallows. When from the beach they saw any of our men disembarking one by one, they spurred on their horses, attacking while we were at a disadvantage in the water, and swarmed around, outnumbering our men. Others attacked entire groups, hurling spears at their exposed flank.

When I realized what was happening, I ordered the boats from the warships and also the scouting vessels to be filled with troops, and then sent these to help where I had seen my men in difficulties. As soon as our men had a footing on dry land and all their comrades had joined them, they charged the enemy and put them to flight. But they were unable to pursue very far because our cavalry had not been able to hold their course and reach Britain. This was the one thing that prevented me enjoying my usual good luck.

As soon as the defeated Britons had regrouped after the rout, they sent 27 envoys to me at once to ask for peace. They promised to give hostages and in future to do as I ordered.

With these envoys came Commius the Atrebatian, whom, as mentioned above, I had sent on in advance to Britain. When he had disembarked and was delivering my instructions to the Britons in the role of an envoy, they had seized him and thrown him into chains; now, after the battle, they sent him back to me. In asking for peace they put the blame for Commius's treatment on the common people, begging me to pardon what had been done through their ignorance. I reproached them for having started hostilities without provocation when they had of their own accord sent envoys to me on the continent asking for peace. But I said I would forgive their ignorance and told them to send me their hostages.

Some of these they delivered at once, but others they said they would hand over in a few days' time, because they had to be brought from a distance. Meanwhile they ordered their men to go back to their fields, and

28 the chiefs began to come from all parts of the island to put themselves and their communities under my protection. With this peace was established.

On the fourth day after our arrival in Britain, the 18 ships already mentioned above, which had taken on the cavalry, set sail from the northern port on a gentle breeze. When they were getting close to Britain and could be seen from our camp, suddenly such a violent storm blew up that none of them could hold course. Some were carried back to where they had started from; others were swept down to the southwest part of the island, at great peril to themselves, but even so they dropped anchor. However, when they began to ship water, they were forced to put out to sea into the darkness of the night and make for the continent.

29 That night there happened to be a full moon. This time of the month, though we did not realize it, regularly brings the highest tides in the Atlantic. So the warships I had used for transporting my army, and which had been hauled up on the beach, were engulfed by the tide, and at the same time the transports that were riding at anchor were battered by the storm. And our men had no chance of doing anything to save them. Several of the ships were smashed; the rest were unusable, having lost their cables, their anchors, and the rest of their gear.

Naturally this threw the whole army into great confusion. We had no other ships in which they could be taken back, and none of the materials needed for making repairs. No arrangements had been made about grain supplies for spending the winter in Britain because it had been generally assumed that we should winter in Gaul.

30 Realizing the difficulties we were in, the British chieftains who had assembled at my headquarters after the battle discussed the situation together. They knew that we had no cavalry, ships, or corn, and they realized that the small size of our camp reflected the numerical weakness of our forces. (The camp was all the smaller because I had brought the legions across without most of their heavy equipment.) They therefore concluded that the best thing to do was to renew hostilities, stop us getting grain and other supplies, and prolong the campaign into the winter.

They were confident that if we were defeated or prevented from returning, no one in future would cross to invade Britain. And so once again they renewed their oaths of mutual loyalty and began gradually to leave the camp and to call up in secret the men who had gone back to their fields.

31 Although I had not yet discovered what the enemy's plans were, the disaster that had struck our ships and the fact that they had stopped sending hostages made me suspect what did in fact happen. So I prepared to meet any eventuality.

Grain was brought into the camp every day from the surrounding fields; timber and bronze were salvaged from the most seriously damaged ships and used to repair the rest; I ordered the other equipment needed for the job to be sent from the continent. The soldiers worked very hard, so although 12 ships were lost, we were able to make the rest tolerably seaworthy.

32 While this work was going on, as usual one legion, in this case the Seventh, had been sent out to get grain. As yet there had been nothing to

make us suspect that the Britons would renew hostilities, since some of them were still working in the fields and others even came quite frequently to the camp. But the guards on duty at the gates reported to me that an unusually large cloud of dust could be seen in the direction in which the legion had gone.

I guessed what it was – the natives had embarked on a new plan – and ordered the cohorts on guard duty to set out with me in that direction, two of the other cohorts to relieve them, and the rest to arm and follow us at once. We advanced a little way from the camp and then saw that the legion was being hard pressed by the enemy; they were having difficulty holding their ground, packed close together as they were, with weapons hurled at them from every side.

The reason for their predicament was this. Because all the grain had been cut everywhere but in this one place, the enemy had guessed that our men would go there and had hidden in the woods by night. When our men were busy reaping, scattered and with their weapons laid aside, the Britons had suddenly attacked them; they had swarmed around with cavalry and chariots, killing a few of our men and throwing the rest into confusion before they could form up.

These are the tactics of chariot warfare. First they drive in all directions hurling spears. Generally they succeed in throwing the ranks of their opponents into confusion just with the terror caused by their galloping horses and the din of the wheels. They make their way through the squadrons of their own cavalry, then jump down from their chariots and fight on foot. Meanwhile the chariot-drivers withdraw a little way from the fighting and position the chariots in such a way that if their masters are hard pressed by the enemy's numbers, they have an easy means of retreat to their own lines. 33

Thus when they fight they have the mobility of cavalry and the staying power of infantry; and with daily training and practice they have become so efficient that even on steep slopes they can control their horses at full gallop, check and turn them in a moment, run along the pole, stand on the yoke and get back into the chariot with incredible speed.

I came to the rescue just in time, for our men were unnerved by these tactics, which were strange to them. As I approached, the enemy halted and the soldiers of the Seventh recovered from their fear. But after that, thinking that this was not the time for attacking or fighting a general engagement, I stayed where I was, and then, quite soon afterwards, led the legions back into camp. While all our men were occupied with this, the rest of the natives who had been working in the fields made off. 34

There followed several days of continuous bad weather, which kept our men in camp and prevented the enemy attacking us. In the meantime the natives sent messengers all over the country, telling the people about the small number of our troops and pointing out what a splendid opportunity this gave them of getting booty and of freeing themselves for all time, once they had driven us out of our camp. In this way they quickly collected a large force of infantry and cavalry and marched towards our camp.

35   I could see that what had happened before would happen again; even if we defeated the Britons, they would get safely away because of their speed. However, I had about 30 cavalrymen whom Commius, the Atrebatian mentioned above, had brought over with him, so I drew up my legions in battle formation in front of the camp.

When battle was joined, the enemy were not able to withstand our attack for long; they turned and fled. We pursued them as far as our speed and strength would allow, and killed a number of them. Then we set fire to all the buildings over a wide area before returning to camp.

36   The same day the enemy sent envoys to me to ask for peace. From these I demanded twice as many hostages as before and ordered them to be sent to the continent, because it would soon be the equinox and I did not think it wise to risk sailing with damaged ships in wintry weather. Soon after midnight I set sail, taking advantage of a favourable wind, and my entire fleet reached the continent safely.

However, two of the transports were not able to make the same harbours
37   as the rest and were carried a little way farther south. When about 300 soldiers had disembarked from these two ships and began to march towards our camp, the Morini, who had been in a state of peace when I set out for Britain, thought that here was a chance of plunder. They surrounded them, at first with only a small group of men, and told them to put down their weapons if they didn't want to be killed. Our men formed a ring and defended themselves, but at the sound of the shouting about 6,000 natives quickly collected there.

When this was reported to me, I sent all the cavalry in the camp out to relieve them. Meanwhile our soldiers held out, and for more than four hours fought with the utmost bravery, killing some of the enemy but suffering only a few wounds themselves. As soon as our cavalry came in sight, the enemy threw away their weapons and fled. We killed a great number of them.

38   Next day I sent the legate Titus Labienus, with the legions I had brought back from Britain, against the Morini, who had thus started hostilities again. Because the marshes where they had taken refuge the previous year had now dried up, the Morini had nowhere to retreat, and so almost all of them submitted to Labienus.

But the legates Quintus Titurius and Lucius Cotta, who had led their legions into the territory of the Menapii, discovered that these people had all gone into hiding in the very dense forests. So they laid waste all their land, cut down their corn, and set fire to their buildings before returning to me.

I arranged winter quarters for all the legions in the country of the Belgae. Only two of the British tribes obeyed my orders and sent their hostages there; the rest failed to send any.

At the end of this campaign, when my dispatches reached Rome, the Senate decreed a public thanksgiving of 20 days.

BOOK V · 54 BC

1 Indutiomarus and Dumnorix

In the consulship of Lucius Domitius and Appius Claudius, when I was   1
leaving winter quarters to go into Italy, as I did every year, I ordered the
legates in charge of the legions to have as many new ships as possible built
and to see to the repair of the old ones during the winter.

I explained exactly how I wanted the new ships to be constructed. So that
they could be loaded quickly and beached easily, I had them made slightly
lower than the vessels we usually use in the Mediterranean, especially as I
had discovered that in the Channel the waves are comparatively small
because of the frequent ebb and flow of the tides. But for the heavy cargo
they would carry, and the large numbers of animals to be shipped across,
I had them made slightly wider than those we use in other waters. I ordered
that all these vessels should be suitable for both rowing and sailing, an
arrangement made all the easier because of their low freeboard. I gave
instructions that the materials needed for equipping the ships should be
brought from Spain.

After the assizes in northern Italy were completed I set out for Illyricum,
because I had been told that the Pirustae were making raids and doing
damage in that part of the province that bordered on their land.

When I got there, I ordered the tribes to raise troops and to assemble at
the place I specified. The Pirustae, hearing about this, sent spokesmen to me
to explain that what had happened had nothing to do with their government's policy. They said they were ready to make every kind of reparation
for the damage.

I accepted what they said and told them to provide hostages, to be
delivered by a specified date. If these were not produced, I said, I should
make war on their tribe. The hostages were delivered on time, as I had
ordered, and I appointed arbitrators to assess the damage each community
had suffered and decide on the reparation due to them.

After this had been dealt with and the assizes in Illyricum were com-   2
pleted, I returned to northern Italy, and from there set out to rejoin the
army. On arrival, I made a tour of all the winter quarters. I found that, in
spite of a very great shortage of materials, the men had worked with such
outstanding keenness that about 600 ships of the type described above and
28 warships had been built; these would all be ready for launching within
a few days.

I congratulated the soldiers and the officers who had been in charge of
the operation. I explained to them what I wanted done next, telling them
all to assemble at Portus Itius. I had discovered that from there one could
cross to Britain most easily, a distance of about 30 miles from the continent.

I left a sufficient force of men for this task and taking with me four

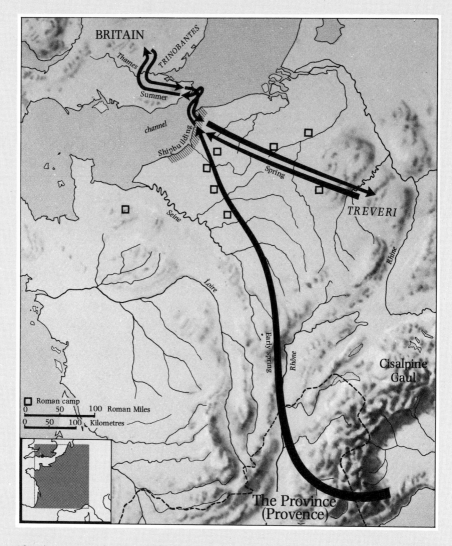

The year 54 BC was a busy time for Caesar. Once more Britain claimed his attention. This time, with the experience of the previous year and with a much larger force, he achieved an adequate military and diplomatic success. The Britons were backward compared to the Gaulish tribes: they still used old-fashioned war chariots obsolete in Gaul for at least half a century (IV 24, 32) and apart from the tribes of the southeast, much of the country seems to have still retained the primitive social system of chiefdoms. In the southeast, however, larger tribal groupings existed and it is probable that a market economy was beginning to develop. One of the tribes, the Trinobantes of Essex, benefited considerably from Caesar's patronage and it seems that in the aftermath of the expeditions much of the cross-channel trade was conveyed through their territory. It may be that they were granted a monopoly by Caesar in return for their pro-Roman attitude. In any event in the next 90 years their leaders grew rich and were able to acquire quantities of Roman luxury goods such as wine, fine pottery, and silver ware.

With the approach of autumn the campaign was still dragging on but Caesar decided to quit the island to get back to Gaul for the winter. In the event he reached French soil just in time to avert a crisis (V 26).

legions, unencumbered by heavy baggage, and 800 cavalry, I set off for the country of the Treveri. This was because the Treveri had not come to the annual councils of chieftains; they had not submitted to my authority, and were said to be making overtures to the Germans across the Rhine.

The Treveri have much the most powerful cavalry in the whole of Gaul, and also a large infantry force. Their territory, as I have already said, borders on the Rhine. Two men, Indutiomarus and Cingetorix, were struggling at the time for supreme power in the tribe. As soon as Cingetorix heard that I was approaching with my legions, he came and assured me that he and all his supporters would remain loyal and abide by their alliance with the Roman people. He also explained what was going on among the Treveri.

Indutiomarus, however, began to prepare for war. He assembled cavalry and infantry, and hid any of his people who were too old or too young to fight in the huge forest of the Ardennes, which stretches from the Rhine right across the country of the Treveri to their borders with the Remi. But some of the leading men of the tribe who were friends of Cingetorix and were alarmed by the approach of our army, came to me. They began to ask for my support for their personal position, because, they said, it was impossible for them to act in the public interest of their tribe.

Indutiomarus was now afraid of being deserted by everyone, and so sent envoys to me to say that the reason he had been unwilling to leave his people and come to me was that it would be easier for him to keep the tribe loyal if he stayed among them; if all the nobles of the tribe left, the common people would, through ignorance, go astray. As a result he had the tribe under control and, if I gave permission, he would come to my camp and put himself and his tribe under my protection.

I knew perfectly well the motive behind these words and what it was that deterred Indutiomarus from continuing with his original plan. However, all my preparations for the campaign in Britain had been made and I did not want to be forced to spend the summer among the Treveri, so I ordered Indutiomarus to come to me himself and bring 200 hostages with him.

The hostages were delivered, and included his son and all his relatives, who had been specified by name. I reassured Indutiomarus about their safety and encouraged him to stay loyal. But even so I sent for the other leading men of the tribe and reconciled them one by one to Cingetorix, for I was aware that he deserved this help from me, and I thought it was very important that as he had displayed such outstanding loyalty to me, his authority among his people should be kept as great as possible. Indutiomarus bitterly resented this curtailment of his influence; he had been hostile to us before, but now his hostility became much more intense.

When this business with the Treveri had been settled, I marched to Portus Itius with my legions. There I learned that 60 ships that had been built in the country of the Meldi had been driven off course by a storm and had returned to their starting point; but the rest I found completely equipped and ready to sail.

Four thousand cavalry from all parts of Gaul and leading men from all the tribes assembled there too. I had decided to leave behind just a few of these men, whose loyalty to me had been proved, and to take the rest with me as hostages, because I was afraid there might be a rising in Gaul while I was away in Britain.

6   Among these chieftains was Dumnorix the Aeduan, who has already appeared in my narrative. I had decided to keep him in particular with me because I knew that he was eager for revolution; he was ambitious and daring, and had great influence among the Gauls. In addition, during the council of the Aedui Dumnorix had said that I was offering to make him king of his tribe, a statement the Aedui greatly resented even though they did not dare to send spokesmen to me to protest or ask me to give up the idea. I heard about this from some Gauls with whom I stayed.

To begin with, Dumnorix proceeded to use every kind of reason to support his request to be left behind in Gaul. He said he was not used to sailing and was afraid of the sea, and also that religious considerations prevented him. Then, when he saw that I was determined not to yield to such pleas, and that he had no hope at all of getting what he wanted, he began to make overtures to the other Gallic chieftains, taking them aside one by one and urging them to stay behind on the continent.

He started to play on their fears by claiming that it was no accident that Gaul was being stripped of all its leading men. My intention, he alleged, was to take across all those whom I dared not kill in the sight of their fellow Gauls and put them to death in Britain. He extracted a pledge of loyalty from the rest, demanding that they swear an oath to work together for what they knew to be the good of Gaul.

7   I received reports of his activities from several people, and when I realized how things stood, decided that in view of the high regard I had for the Aedui, I must do all in my power to control Dumnorix and thwart his plans; I could see his recklessness increasing and therefore I thought I should take steps to prevent him doing any harm to me personally or to Rome.

We were held up for about 25 days at Portus Itius because the northwest wind, which is the prevailing wind at all seasons in these parts, prevented us sailing. I took steps to keep Dumnorix loyal, but at the same time to find out what he intended to do. Eventually the weather changed in our favour and I ordered the infantry and cavalry to embark. But while this operation was engaging everyone's attention, Dumnorix took some Aeduan calvary-men and, unknown to me, started for home.

When I heard of this, I postponed the sailing, and letting everything else wait, sent a large cavalry detachment to pursue him and bring him back. I told them that if Dumnorix resisted and refused to obey, he was to be killed, because I did not think that a man who had flouted my authority to my face would behave rationally when I was not there.

When he was ordered to return, Dumnorix began to resist, fighting to defend himself and begging his followers to help him, all the while shouting again and again that he was a free man and the citizen of a free state. In accordance with my instructions, he was surrounded and killed. All the Aeduan cavalrymen who had been with him returned to our camp.

2 The British campaign

After this I set sail, leaving Labienus on the continent with three legions and   8
2,000 cavalry to guard the ports. Their orders were to make arrangements
for grain supplies, get to know what was happening in Gaul and take such
measures as the time or circumstances might require. I took with me five
legions and a force of cavalry equal in numbers to that which I had left
with Labienus.

We set sail about sunset, carried along by a gentle southwest breeze, but
about midnight the wind dropped and we could not maintain course. The
tide carried us on too far and when dawn came we saw Britain far behind us
on our left. Once again we followed the turn of the tide and used our oars
to reach the part of the island that last summer's experience had shown to
have the best landing places. The efforts of the soldiers in this were magnificent, for by pulling on the oars without stopping, they managed to make the
heavily laden transports keep up with the warships.

All our vessels reached Britain about midday. Not one of the Britons was
to be seen. I discovered later from prisoners that large numbers of them had
assembled there, but they had left the shore in terror and hidden themselves
on the higher ground when they saw so many ships; more than 800 vessels
were visible simultaneously, including those that had survived from the
previous year and also the privately owned ones built by individuals for
their own use.

The army disembarked and a suitable place was chosen for our camp.   9
When I discovered from prisoners where the British troops had taken up
position, I left ten cohorts and 300 cavalry on the shore to guard the ships
and then marched towards the enemy soon after midnight. I did not feel
anxious about the ships because I had left them anchored on an open shore
of soft sand, with Quintus Atrius responsible for their safety.

We marched by night for about 12 miles before coming in sight of the
enemy forces. They had moved with their cavalry and chariots down from

STRUCTURE OF ROMAN LEGION

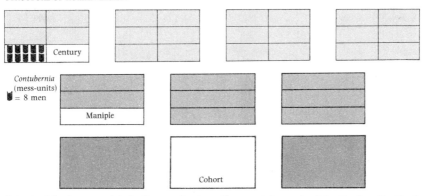

A typical legion consisted of 10 cohorts – the most important tactical units. Each
cohort was composed of 6 centuries (of about 80 men) arranged in 3 maniples. A
century was divided into 10 *contubernia*, or mess-units, of 8 men – shown here by black
shields. (See also Translators' Notes.)

the higher ground to a river and were trying to stop our progress and engage us in battle. When our cavalry drove them back, they hid in the woods, where they enjoyed a position with extremely good natural and manmade defences. It was clear that they had prepared it previously for some war among themselves, because many trees had been cut down and used to block all the entrances to it.

The Britons came out of the woods in small groups to fight, and tried to stop our men penetrating their fortifications. But the soldiers of the Seventh legion, holding up their shields to form a protective shell, piled up earth against the fortifications and captured the place, driving the Britons out of the woods at the cost of only a few wounded. But I forbade them to pursue far, because I was unfamiliar with the terrain and also because most of the day had already gone and I wanted to leave time for fortifying our camp.

10 Next morning I divided the infantry and cavalry into three sections and sent them to pursue the fleeing enemy. They had advanced some way and only the rearguards of the columns were in sight, when cavalrymen from Quintus Atrius came and reported to me that on the previous night there had been a great storm that had damaged almost all our ships and cast them up on the shore; the anchors and cables had not held firm, and the sailors and pilots could not cope with the force of the gale; as a result a great deal of damage had been caused by the ships colliding with each other.

11 When I heard this I ordered the legions and the cavalry to be recalled, telling them to defend themselves if they were attacked on the march. I returned to the ships and saw for myself that things were almost exactly as the messengers and their dispatches had described.

About 40 ships were totally lost; but it seemed that the rest could be repaired, though with a great deal of effort. I therefore picked out the skilled craftsmen from the legions and ordered others to be sent for from the continent. I wrote asking Labienus to have the men with him set about building as many ships as they could.

I decided that the best thing for me to do, even though it involved an enormous amount of work, was to beach all the ships and enclose them within the fortifications of the camp. All this took us about ten days; the men worked non-stop day and night.

With the ships beached and the camp strongly fortified, I left the same troops as before to guard them and set off for the place from which I had returned. When I got there, I found that larger British forces had now assembled from all parts of the country. By general agreement the supreme command and direction of the campaign had been given to Cassivellaunus.

His territory lies about 80 miles from the sea and is separated from the maritime tribes by a river called the Thames. Previously Cassivellaunus had been in a continual state of war with the other tribes, but our arrival had frightened the Britons into appointing him commander-in-chief for the campaign.

12 The interior of Britain is inhabited by people who claim, on the strength of their own tradition, to be indigenous. The coastal areas are inhabited by

Caesar was evidently fascinated by the chariots that were still used by the Britons in warfare (IV 24, 32). From his description, the discovery of the metal fittings belonging to chariots, and representations like the above on the reverse of a Roman denarius minted in *c.* 48 BC, it is possible to build up an accurate idea of the Celtic chariot in action. It was a light and highly manoeuvrable two-wheeled platform, with side panels probably of wicker work, joined by a long pole to a yoke by which the ponies were harnessed. A skilled driver guided the vehicle about the battle leaving the war-lord free to fight as he pleased.

invaders who crossed from Belgium for the sake of plunder and then, when the fighting was over, settled there and began to work the land; these people have almost all kept the names of the tribes from which they originated. The population is extremely large, there are very many farm buildings, closely resembling those in Gaul, and the cattle are very numerous.

For money they use bronze or gold coins, or iron ingots of fixed standard weights. Tin is found there in the midland area, and iron near the coast, but not in large quantities. The bronze they use is imported. There is timber of every kind, as in Gaul, but no beech or fir. They think it wrong to eat hares, chickens, or geese, keeping these creatures only for pleasure and amusement. The climate is more temperate than in Gaul, the cold season being less severe.

The island is triangular in shape, with one side facing Gaul. One corner of 13 this side points east and is on the coast of Kent, the landing point for almost all ships from Gaul; the lower corner points south. The length of this side is some 500 miles. The second side of the island faces westward, towards Spain. In this direction lies Ireland, which is thought to be half the size of Britain and is the same distance from Britain as Gaul is. Midway between Ireland and Britain is the Isle of Man, and it is believed that there are several smaller islands too, where, some writers say, there is continual darkness for 30 days in midwinter. We made numerous inquiries about this, but found out nothing. However, from accurate measurements with a water clock, we could tell that the nights were shorter than on the continent. This western side of Britain is, in the opinion of the natives, 700 miles long. The third side of the island faces north; there is no land opposite this side, but the eastern corner of it points roughly towards Germany. The length of this side is reckoned to be 800 miles, which means that the whole island is some 2,000 miles in circumference.

14   By far the most civilized of the Britons are those who live in Kent, which is an entirely maritime area; their way of life is very like that of the Gauls. Most of the tribes living in the interior do not grow grain; they live on milk and meat and wear skins. All the Britons dye their bodies with woad, which produces a blue colour and gives them a wild appearance in battle. They wear their hair long; every other part of the body, except for the upper lip, they shave. Wives are shared between groups of ten or twelve men, especially between brothers and between fathers and sons; but the children of such unions are counted as belonging to the man with whom the woman first cohabited.

15   There was a fierce engagement as the British cavalry and charioteers clashed with our men on the march. However, our men were superior everywhere and drove the enemy off into the woods and hills, killing a number of them, though suffering some casualties themselves through pressing the pursuit too far. Then after a short interval, when our men were off their guard and busy fortifying the camp, the Britons suddenly rushed out of the woods, charged down on those on picket guard duty in front of the camp, and started a fierce battle there.

I sent two cohorts to help, the first of their respective legions, and they took up position very close to each other. But the enemy, showing very great daring, broke through between them and got away safely because our men were unnerved by these unfamiliar tactics. Quintus Laberius Durus, a military tribune, was killed that day. I sent up more cohorts and the enemy were eventually driven back.

16   Throughout the whole of this peculiar combat, fought in front of the camp in full view of everyone, it was clear that because of the weight of their armour our men were at a disadvantage in dealing with such an enemy. They could not pursue the Britons when they retreated and they did not dare to abandon their regular formation. The cavalry, too, were at grave risk when they engaged in battle, because the enemy would generally retreat on purpose, and after drawing our cavalry some way from the support of the legions, would jump down from their chariots and fight on foot, which meant they had the advantage. Cavalry tactics brought exactly the same element of risk to those retreating and those in pursuit. There was also the fact that they never fought in close order but in scattered groups widely spaced, and they had reserves posted at intervals so that the various groups could cover each other's retreat and strong, fresh troops could take over from those who were tired.

17   Next day the enemy took up position on hills some distance from our camp. They showed themselves only in small groups and began to harass our cavalry, though less vigorously than on the previous day. But at midday, when I had sent out three legions and all my cavalry under the command of the legate Gaius Trebonius on a foraging expedition, the enemy suddenly

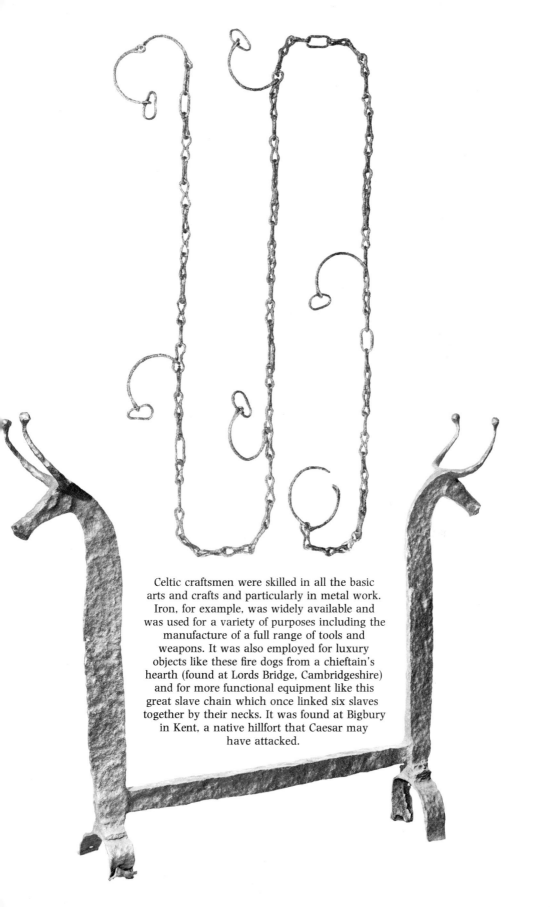

Celtic craftsmen were skilled in all the basic arts and crafts and particularly in metal work. Iron, for example, was widely available and was used for a variety of purposes including the manufacture of a full range of tools and weapons. It was also employed for luxury objects like these fire dogs from a chieftain's hearth (found at Lords Bridge, Cambridgeshire) and for more functional equipment like this great slave chain which once linked six slaves together by their necks. It was found at Bigbury in Kent, a native hillfort that Caesar may have attacked.

swooped down on them from all sides, pressing their attack right up to the legions' standards.

Our men made a fierce counter-attack, drove them back and kept up their pursuit until the cavalry, gaining confidence from the fact that they could see the legions supporting them from behind, drove the Britons headlong in flight. A great many of the natives were killed and the rest were given no chance of closing ranks and making a stand, or jumping down from their chariots.

After this rout the additional forces that had assembled from all over the country immediately dispersed, and after that the enemy never fought against us in a general action.

18   When I discovered what the enemy's plans were, I led the army to the river Thames and the territory of Cassivellaunus. There is only one place where the river can be forded, and even there with difficulty. When we reached it, I noticed large enemy forces drawn up on the opposite bank. The bank had also been fortified with sharp stakes fixed along it, and, as I discovered from prisoners and deserters, similar stakes had been driven into the river bed and were concealed beneath the water.

I immediately gave orders for the cavalry to go ahead and the legions to follow them. As the infantry crossed, only their heads were above the water, but they pressed on with such speed and determination that both infantry and cavalry were able to attack together. The enemy, unable to stand up to this combined force, abandoned the river bank and took to flight.

19   As I have already indicated, Cassivellaunus had now given up all hope of fighting a pitched battle. He disbanded most of his forces, keeping only some 4,000 charioteers, with whom he kept a close watch on our line of march. He kept a short way from our route, concealing himself in the woods and thickets, and when he had discovered the areas through which we should be marching, he drove the inhabitants and their cattle out of the fields there and into the woods. Then, whenever our cavalry had ventured any distance into the fields to get plunder or devastate the country, he sent his charioteers out of the woods by every road and track to attack them.

Our men were in great danger from such clashes, and fear of them prevented us from ranging far afield. The result was that I could not allow the cavalry to go any distance from the column of infantry; thus the damage our cavalry could inflict on the Britons by burning and ravaging their land was limited by the capacity of our infantry, when they were tired from strenuous marching, to give them protection.

20   In the meantime the Trinobantes sent a deputation to me. They are perhaps the strongest tribe in the southeast of Britain and it was from them that young Mandubracius had come to me in Gaul to put himself under my protection, having had to flee for his life after his father, the king of the tribe, was killed by Cassivellaunus.

The envoys promised that the tribe would surrender and carry out my orders; they begged me to protect Mandubracius from Cassivellaunus and send him back to them to rule as king. I told them to send me 40 hostages and grain for my army, and then I sent Mandubracius back to them. They quickly carried out my instructions, sending me grain and the required number of hostages.

Now that the Trinobantes were under our protection and so in no danger 21 of harm at the hands of our troops, other tribes sent embassies to me and surrendered. These included the Cenimagni, the Segontiaci, the Ancalites, the Bibroci, and the Cassi.

From these tribes I discovered that we were quite close to Cassivellaunus's *oppidum*. It was protected by forests and marshes, and a great number of men and cattle had been collected in it. I should mention that the Britons give the name 'oppidum' to *any* densely wooded place they have fortified with a rampart and trench and use as a refuge from the attacks of invaders.

I set off there with my legions and found that the site had excellent natural defences and was very well fortified. Nevertheless we proceeded to attack it on two sides. After putting up brief resistance, the enemy were unable to hold out against our men's onslaught, and they rushed out of their *oppidum* on the other side. Many of these fugitives were captured and killed. Inside the fortress we found a great quantity of cattle.

While these operations were going on there, Cassivellaunus sent mes- 22 sengers to Kent, an area by the sea as I have said above. There were four kings in that region, Cingetorix, Carvilius, Taximagulus, and Segovax, and Cassivellaunus ordered them to collect all their troops and make a surprise attack on our naval camp. When these forces reached the camp, our men made a sudden sortie, killing many of them and capturing one of their leaders, a nobleman called Lugotorix, before retiring again without loss.

When reports of this battle reached him, Cassivellaunus, alarmed by the many reverses he had suffered, the devastation of his country, and especially the defection of the other tribes, sent envoys to me to ask for terms of surren-der, using Commius the Atrebatian as an intermediary.

I had decided to winter on the continent because of the danger that sudden risings might break out in Gaul. There was not much of the summer left and I realized that the Britons could easily hold out for that short time, so I accepted their surrender, ordering hostages to be given and fixing the tribute to be paid annually by Britain to Rome. I gave strict orders to Cassi-vellaunus not to molest Mandubracius or the Trinobantes.

When the hostages were delivered, I led the army back to the coast, 23 where I found the ships had been repaired. We launched them, and because we had a great many prisoners and had lost some of our ships in the storm, I decided to make the return journey in two trips.

It happened that out of such a fleet of ships, making so many voyages both in that and the previous year, not a single one with troops on board was lost. But of those sent back to me empty from the continent (that is, those on their way back from Gaul after disembarking our first contingent, and the 60 that Labienus had had built after the start of the expedition), very few reached their destination, almost all the rest being driven back. I waited some time for these ships, but in vain. Then, because I was afraid that the approaching equinox would prevent us sailing, I was obliged to pack the men on board more tightly than usual on those ships that we had.

The sea then became very calm, so we set sail late in the evening and reached land at dawn. I had brought all the ships across in safety and we beached them.

3 The winter camps: Cotta and Sabinus

24 After this, a council of the Gallic leaders was held at Amiens. The grain harvest that year in Gaul had been poor because of drought, so I was compelled to change my usual methods of arranging winter quarters for my legions, and distribute them among a larger number of tribes.

I sent one legion into the country of the Morini under the command of the legate Gaius Fabius, another under Quintus Cicero to the Nervii, and a third under Lucius Roscius to the Esubii. I ordered a fourth legion, under the command of Titus Labienus, to winter in the territory of the Remi on the borders of the Treveri, and three more were quartered among the Belgae under the quaestor Marcus Crassus and the legates Lucius Munatius Plancus and Gaius Trebonius. I sent one legion, recently raised in the country north of the river Po, together with five cohorts under the legates Quintus Titurius Sabinus and Lucius Aurunculeius Cotta into the territory of the Eburones. Most of this tribe's land lies between the Meuse and the Rhine and their chiefs at that time were Ambiorix and Catuvolcus.

I thought that by distributing the legions in this way I could best cope with the shortage of grain. But, in fact, the winter quarters of all these legions, with the exception of the one under Lucius Roscius, which had been sent to a perfectly quiet and peaceful area, were within 100 miles of each other. Meanwhile I decided to stay in Gaul myself until I knew that all the legions had reached their destinations and fortified their winter camps there.

25 Among the Carnutes was a man of noble birth called Tasgetius, whose ancestors had been kings of their tribe. In all the campaigns he had been remarkably useful to me, and so in return for his merit and his loyalty to me I had restored him to the position his ancestors once held. He had been ruling for more than two years when his enemies assassinated him, with the open approval of many members of the tribe.

This crime was reported to me. Many individuals were involved in it, and I was afraid that they would persuade the whole tribe to revolt. So I ordered Lucius Plancus to leave Belgium with his legion and set off at once for the territory of the Carnutes. I told him to spend the winter there, and to arrest those he found responsible for the death of Tasgetius and send them to me. Meanwhile all the legates and quaestors in command of legions sent reports to me that they had reached their quarters and fortified the camps there.

26 About a fortnight later there was sudden trouble. A revolt broke out, and the instigators of it were Ambiorix and Catuvolcus. After coming to meet Sabinus and Cotta on the frontiers of their country and bringing supplies of grain to our winter camp, they had been induced by messages from Indutiomarus the Treveran to summon all their people to arms.

They made a sudden attack on a group of our men who were getting wood, and then came with a large force to attack the Roman camp. Our

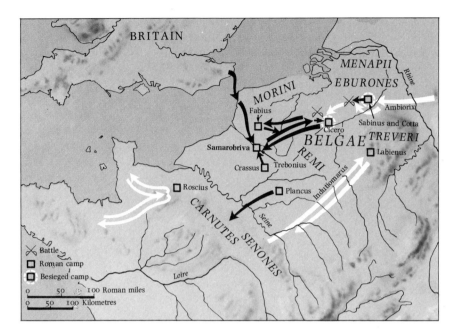

On returning to Gaul from Britain in the autumn of 54 BC Caesar was faced with a crisis – lack of grain forced him to site the winter quarters of his legions more widely throughout Belgic territories than he would otherwise have chosen. The political situation was tense and rebellion flared up led by Ambiorix. In the confusion of marching and countermarching that ensued, a substantial Roman force and its two commanders Sabinus and Cotta, were surrounded and annihilated. Although the situation was retrieved, not least by Caesar's own decisive action, the events of that autumn were a firm reminder that Gaul was by no means conquered. Further rebellions, even more serious, were to follow.

troops quickly armed and mounted the rampart, and some Spanish horsemen, sent out on one side, were victorious in the cavalry engagement that ensued. The enemy gave up all hope of success and withdrew from the attack. Then, following their usual practice, they shouted out for someone from our side to go out and parley, claiming that they themselves had something to say that concerned both sides and could lead to a settlement of the conflict.

Gaius Arpineius, a Roman of equestrian rank and a friend of Sabinus, was sent to parley with them, and with him went a Spaniard called Quintus Junius, who had already been employed by me on numerous missions to Ambiorix. When they arrived, Ambiorix addressed them as follows:

'I acknowledge that I am greatly indebted to Caesar for his acts of kindness to me. For it was by his doing that I was relieved of the tribute I used to pay to my neighbours, the Aduatuci, and it was Caesar who restored to me my son and my nephew, who had been sent to them as hostages and then enslaved and kept in chains.

When I attacked the Roman camp I was not acting in accordance with my own will and judgement but because of pressure from my fellow tribes-

27

men; my position as ruler is such that my people have as much control over my actions as I have over theirs. My tribe's reason for making war was that it could not stand out against the sudden joint action to which all the Gauls had pledged themselves. I can easily prove the truth of this by pointing to my own lack of importance, for I am not so naive as to imagine that my troops can defeat the Romans.

The whole of Gaul agreed on a common plan; we had to attack all the Roman winter camps today – that is, the attacks had to be simultaneous to make it impossible for any one legion to go to help another. It would not have been easy for us to refuse our fellow Gauls, especially as it was clear that the plan was designed to regain our national liberty. But I have done my duty as far as the claims of patriotism are concerned and now I am in mind of the duty I owe to Caesar in return for his kindness to me.

I urge and implore Sabinus, as one with whom I have ties of hospitality, to think of his own safety and that of his soldiers. A large force of German mercenaries has crossed the Rhine and will be here in two days. It is for the Roman generals themselves to decide whether to withdraw their troops from the camp before the neighbouring tribes can realize what is happening, and take them to Cicero's camp, about 50 miles away, or to that of Labienus, which is slightly farther.

I promise on my solemn oath that I will give them safe conduct through my territory. In doing so, of course, I am acting in the interests of my tribe by relieving them of the burden of having a Roman winter camp in their territory, and at the same time repaying Caesar for his kindness to me.' When he had made this speech, Ambiorix withdrew.

28   Arpineius and Junius reported what they had been told to the legates, who were surprised and alarmed by what they heard. Even though the information had come from an enemy, they still thought it should be taken seriously. What alarmed them most was the scarcely credible fact that a tribe as obscure and insignificant as the Eburones had dared to make war on Rome on its own initiative. And so they called a council of war to discuss the matter.

The views expressed there differed widely. Lucius Aurunculeius and several of the military tribunes and senior centurions believed that they should do nothing in a hurry nor leave the camp without specific instructions from me. They argued that however many German troops came, they could be kept out of such a well-fortified camp; experience proved this, because they had held out very bravely against the enemy's first attack and had inflicted many casualties as well. They went on to point out that there was no shortage of grain and before long help would be coming not only from the nearest camps but also from me. Finally, they argued, what could be more irresponsible or disgraceful than to follow the advice of an enemy when making a decision of vital importance?

29   Sabinus disagreed with their arguments, insisting that they would be leaving it too late to act when enemy forces, reinforced by the Germans, had assembled in larger numbers or when some disaster struck in the neighbouring Roman camps. They had only a short time to decide what to do.

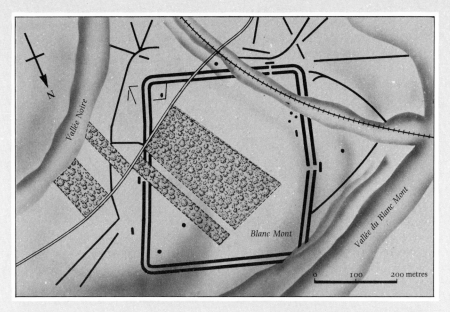

The discovery of Roman campaign camps is a very difficult task not least because they were built of relatively insubstantial earthworks fronted by slight ditches. In the heavily farmed landscape of northern France all surface trace has long since been obliterated. The ditches do, however, survive buried beneath the fields and can, under certain conditions when the crop is ripening, be seen from the air. Recently Roger Agache has carried out a detailed aerial photographic survey of large areas of northern France and has discovered several Roman camps. At Folleville in the Somme valley he has discovered a large camp 36 acres in extent, large enough to support an entire legion. Its double ditches were broken at three points where the entrances lay, each entrance gap being protected in front by a short length of bank and ditch known as a *tutulus*. Inside the enclosure the soldiers would have pitched their tents. Precise dating is impossible on present evidence but the camp could have belonged to the Caesarian campaigns.

'It is my belief,' he said, 'that Caesar has already set out for Italy, for otherwise the Carnutes would not have decided on killing Tasgetius, nor, if Caesar had been in Gaul, would the Eburones have shown such contempt for us as to attack our camp.

My argument depends not on Ambiorix's advice but on the facts. The Rhine is nearby; the Germans bitterly resent the death of Ariovistus and our victories in past campaigns; the Gauls are burning with indignation at all the insults they have suffered since they were brought under the control of Rome and lost their former military glory. Finally, who can imagine that Ambiorix has decided to act in this way without being absolutely confident of the outcome of his action?

My own proposal is safe either way: if there is no real danger, we shall reach the nearest legion with no risk at all; if the whole of Gaul is in league with the Germans, our only chance of escape is to act quickly. As to the plan proposed by Cotta and the others who disagree with me, what would that lead to? It may not involve us in any danger at the moment, but it certainly involves a long siege and the risk of death by starvation.'

30   The two opposing views were discussed, with Cotta and the senior centurions still vigorously objecting to Sabinus's proposal. Then, in a voice loud enough for most of the ordinary soldiers to hear, Sabinus shouted out, 'Have it your own way then, if that's what you want. I am no more frightened of death than the rest of you are. These men will know what has happened and if things go wrong, it is you, Cotta, they will hold responsible. If you would give your consent, by the day after tomorrow they would be with their comrades in the nearest camp sharing the fortunes of war with them, instead of being abandoned and isolated from the rest, to perish either by starvation or by the sword.'

31   The members of the council sprang up, laid hold of the two generals, and begged them not to cause a crisis by persisting in their disagreement. If only everyone would agree on one course of action there was no real problem, whether they stayed in the camp or set out from it, but if the disagreement continued, there was no chance of escape. The discussion went on until midnight. Eventually Cotta, in great distress, gave in. Sabinus's proposal prevailed and it was announced that they would leave the camp at dawn.

No one slept during the rest of the night, each soldier going through his kit to see what he could take with him and how much of his winter equipment he was forced to leave behind. They went through every possible argument to convince themselves that danger was inevitable if they remained, and that it would be increased as they became exhausted by constant night watches.

At dawn they set out from the camp in a long straggling column with a very great deal of heavy baggage; they seemed to be convinced that Ambiorix, who had suggested the plan, was not an enemy but the best of friends.

32   The enemy, hearing the noise and aware of activity in the night, realized that our men were going to leave the camp. So they placed two ambushes in a good spot in the woods about two miles away and waited there, hidden from view, for the Romans to arrive.

The massacre of the Roman troops led by Cotta
and Sabinus was a blow to Caesar's prestige:
it showed the Gauls for the first time that Rome was
not invincible. Although, by the winter of 54 the
army had re-established its supremacy, the troops
posted in their winter camps among the Belgae
must have felt distinctly uneasy.

When the greater part of our column had descended into a deep defile the Gauls suddenly appeared at each end of it and began to harass the rear-guard and stop the head of the column climbing the hill to get out. They forced our men to engage in battle on ground that was very unfavourable to them.

33   Sabinus had entirely failed to anticipate the possibility of such an attack, so now he became panic-stricken and ran about arranging the cohorts. But he did even this nervously, in a way that made it clear he no longer had control of the situation – as usually happens when someone is forced to take decisions after the action has already started.

Cotta, on the other hand, had thought that such an attack was possible during the march, and for that very reason had been against leaving the camp. However, he did everything possible to save the army, calling on the men and encouraging them as a commander-in-chief would, and fighting in the line like an ordinary soldier.

The length of the marching column made it difficult for the two legates to attend to everything personally and to see what should be done at every point, so they had word passed along the line that the men should abandon the baggage and form into a circle. In such circumstances that is a sensible plan, but on this occasion it had unfortunate results; it lowered the morale of our men, and made the enemy keener to fight, because they thought we would not have adopted that formation unless we were in a panic and had given up hope. What is more, as was inevitable, soldiers were everywhere leaving their units and rushing to look for and rescue their most cherished possessions from the baggage. Their shouting and weeping could be heard on all sides.

34   The enemy, on the other hand, knew exactly what to do. Their leaders ordered the word to be passed around their whole force that no one was to leave his position; the plunder would be theirs and whatever the Romans left would be kept for them, so they must realize that everything depended on their winning.

The Gauls were equal to our men in courage and keenness for the fight. But although our troops were let down by their commander and deserted by their luck, they still put all their hope of survival in their own fighting abilities, and whenever one of our cohorts charged, a large number of the enemy fell.

Ambiorix saw this and ordered his troops to hurl their weapons at long range without getting too close; wherever the Romans charged they were to give ground (they could do this without suffering any harm themselves, because they were lightly armed and trained by daily practice), but they were to pursue when our men retreated to their lines.

35   These instructions were carried out most carefully. Whenever a cohort left the circle and charged, the Gauls retreated very rapidly. Meanwhile, of course, that cohort was unprotected and exposed to missiles on its right flank. And when it began to return to its original place in the circle, it was surrounded both by the Gauls who had given ground and by the nearest of those who had stayed in position. But if the Romans tried simply to hold their ground, they had no chance to use their fighting ability, and because

they were packed close together, no opportunity to avoid the weapons hurled at them by that great throng.

Nevertheless, in spite of all the disadvantages that beset them and the many injuries they suffered, our men held out. Although the fighting lasted for much of the day, from dawn until about two o'clock, they did nothing in that time to disgrace themselves. Titus Balventius, a gallant and highly respected soldier who had been chief centurion of his legion the previous year, had both thighs pierced with a spear in this battle; and Quintus Lucanius, another centurion of the same rank, was killed fighting most courageously in an attempt to rescue his son, who had been surrounded. The legate Lucius Cotta was wounded by a sling stone, which hit him full in the face as he was going around encouraging all the cohorts and companies of men.

All this thoroughly alarmed Sabinus. When he caught sight of Ambiorix 36 in the distance encouraging his men, he sent his interpreter Gnaeus Pompeius to him to ask quarter for himself and his men. In reply to this appeal Ambiorix said that Sabinus was free to come and speak with him, if he wished. He hoped that his men could be persuaded to spare the lives of the Roman troops; and he personally would guarantee that Sabinus himself would certainly come to no harm.

Sabinus proposed to the wounded Cotta that if he agreed, they should both withdraw from the battle and go together to parley with Ambiorix. He said he hoped that Ambiorix could be persuaded to spare them and their troops. But Cotta said he would not go to an enemy who was still in arms, and he refused to change his mind.

Sabinus ordered the military tribunes and senior centurions who were 37 with him at the moment to follow him. When he was quite close to Ambiorix, he was told to lay down his weapons. He obeyed and told those with him to do the same. Then he began to discuss terms with Ambiorix. The Gaul deliberately prolonged the conversation and Sabinus was gradually surrounded, and then killed.

At this the Gauls, as is their custom, raised a shout of victory, and with loud yells charged at our men and broke through our ranks. Cotta was killed fighting there and so were most of the soldiers with him. The others retreated to the camp from which they had come. One of these survivors, Lucius Petrosidius the standard bearer of the legion, was beset by great numbers of the enemy; he threw the eagle inside the rampart and died fighting valiantly in front of the camp. The rest, with difficulty, managed to keep the enemy off until nightfall; in the night, because they had no hope left, every single one of them committed suicide. The few who had slipped away during the battle made their way by ill-defined tracks through the forests to Labienus's camp, and told him what had happened.

4 The winter camps: Cicero

Ambiorix was elated by this victory. Ordering his infantry to follow, he 38 immediately set out with his cavalry, riding day and night without a halt, for the country of the Aduatuci, who lived next to his kingdom. He told the Aduatuci what had happened and persuaded them to take up arms.

The next day he went on to the country of the Nervii and urged them not to let slip the chance of freeing themselves for all time and punishing the Romans for the wrongs they had inflicted upon them. He explained that two Roman legates had been killed and a large part of the Roman army wiped out; they would have no difficulty in suddenly overwhelming Cicero's winter camp and destroying that legion too. And he promised that he would help them to do this.

39 The Nervii were easily convinced by his words. And so messengers were sent at once to the Ceutrones, the Grudii, the Levaci, the Pleumoxii, and the Geidumni; all these tribes were under the rule of the Nervii. They assembled the largest force they could and with these they suddenly swooped down on Cicero's camp.

News of Sabinus's death had not yet reached Cicero, and so it inevitably happened with him too that some of his men who had gone into the forests to get wood for the fortifications were cut off by the unexpected arrival of the enemy cavalry and surrounded. Then a large force of Eburones, Nervii, and Aduatuci, together with their allies and dependants, launched their attack on the legion in the camp.

Our men quickly ran to arms and mounted the rampart. They managed to hold out that day but only with difficulty, for the enemy placed all their hopes in the speed of their attack and were convinced that if they won this battle they would be victorious ever after.

40 Cicero wrote to me at once and offered large rewards to anyone who could get the letters through to me. But all the roads were blocked and those carrying the letters were intercepted.

During the night, using the timber that had been collected for the fortifications and working with incredible speed, Cicero's men built about 120 towers and made good any parts of the defences that seemed inadequate. Next day, with much larger forces than before, the enemy attacked the camp and filled in the ditch. Our men put up the same resistance as on the previous day. Similar attacks were made and resisted day after day.

There was no let up in the work during the nights, and not even the sick or wounded had a chance of sleeping. Whatever was needed to meet the next day's attack was got ready during the night; quantities of stakes, with their points hardened in the fire, and large numbers of siege-spears were made; the towers were fitted with extra storeys, and battlements and wicker breastworks were attached to them. Although Cicero's health was very poor, he did not allow himself any time for rest even during the night, until the men actually went and told him that he must look after himself.

41 Then leaders and chieftains of the Nervii who had been on friendly terms with Cicero, and so had some reason to go and talk to him, said they wanted to parley. Their request was granted. They told the same story Ambiorix had used with Sabinus, that is, that the whole of Gaul was in arms, the Germans had crossed the Rhine, and my winter camp and those of the other commanders were being attacked.

They then told him about Sabinus's death as well, and produced Ambiorix to prove that their story was true. 'You are making a mistake,' they said, 'if you are hoping for any help from troops who have no confidence about their own safety. But we have nothing against you or the Roman people, except that we object to having Roman winter camps in our country and do not want them to become a regular habit. As far as we are concerned, you may leave your camp in safety and go wherever you like without fear.'

To this Cicero made only one reply. 'It is not the practice of the Roman people to accept any terms from an enemy who is still armed. If you agree to lay down your weapons, you can count on my support when you send your envoys to Caesar. As he is a just man, I expect Caesar will grant your requests.'

With their hopes of success in this direction dashed, the Nervii surrounded our camp with a rampart nine feet high and a ditch 15 feet wide. They had learned how to do this by watching our methods in previous years, and prisoners taken from our army without our knowing also gave them some instruction. But they were without the proper tools for the work and could be seen cutting the sods with their swords and removing the earth with their hands and in their cloaks.   **42**

From this it was possible to get some idea of their numbers, for in less than three hours they completed a fortification three miles in circumference. In the days that followed, with the Roman prisoners instructing them again, they began to build towers high enough to dominate our rampart, and to make grappling hooks and protective sheds.

When the siege was in its seventh day, a very strong wind blew up and the enemy started slinging red-hot missiles made of moulded clay and hurling incendiary darts at the huts in the camp. These huts were thatched with straw in the Gallic fashion and so caught fire quickly, and the strong wind spread the flames all over the camp. With a great cheer, as if they had already gained the victory completely, the enemy set about bringing up their towers and sheds and scaling the rampart with their ladders.   **43**

But our men displayed enormous courage and presence of mind. Even though they were being scorched by the fire that burned all around them and attacked by a hail of missiles, and knew perfectly well that their baggage and all their possessions were going up in flames, not a man left his place on the rampart. Scarcely anyone even looked back at the blaze. At that moment of crisis every soldier fought with the utmost determination and valour.

This was by far the hardest day's fighting for our men, but even so, it turned out that they killed and wounded more of the enemy that day than any other, for the Gauls had crowded in a mass right at the foot of our rampart and those at the back prevented those in front from retreating.

When the flames had subsided a little, an enemy tower was brought right up at one point until it touched the rampart. The centurions of the third cohort withdrew from the point where they were stationed, moved all their men back, and then began to make signs and shout to the enemy to come inside if they wanted. But none of them dared to move forward. Then our men hurled stones from all sides to dislodge them and the tower was set on fire.

44   In that legion there were two outstandingly brave individuals, Titus
Pullo and Lucius Vorenus, both centurions who were getting close to the
senior grade. They were always arguing about which of them was the
better soldier, and every year they vied with one another over the question
of promotion.

When the fighting near the fortifications was at its fiercest, Pullo called
out, 'Why are you hesitating, Vorenus? What sort of opportunity are you
looking for to win glory through your courage? Today will decide between
our rival claims.' With these words he advanced beyond the fortifications
and charged the enemy where their ranks seemed to be thickest. Of course
Vorenus did not stay behind within the protection of the ramparts, but went
after Pullo, because he was afraid of what everyone would think if he did not.

When Pullo was just a short distance from the enemy, he hurled his
javelin at them and ran one of the Gauls through as he was running forward
from their lines. The wounded man fainted and his comrades covered him
with their shields. Then they all hurled their weapons at Pullo, leaving him
no chance to retreat. A javelin pierced his shield and stuck in his swordbelt.
This forced his scabbard out of place, making it impossible for him to draw
his sword quickly with his right hand, and as he was struggling in his
attempts to do so, the enemy surrounded him.

His rival Vorenus ran up and rescued him in this extremity. The Gauls
immediately left Pullo, thinking he had been killed by the javelin, and all
turned on Vorenus, who drew his sword and engaged them at close quarters,
killing one and driving the rest off a little. But he pressed on too eagerly and
stumbled and fell into a hollow in the ground.

He was now surrounded in his turn, and it was Pullo's turn to come to his
aid. Both men escaped unharmed, and after killing several of the Gauls,
they returned to the protection of our fortifications having earned for themselves the highest possible praise. In this way fortune played with the rivals
in their struggles; they had been enemies to each other and yet each other's
saviours too, and it was impossible to decide between the two of them in
gallantry.

45   The siege was becoming more difficult and more dangerous every day,
especially because with so many men out of action wounded, only a few were
left to carry on defending the camp. As the situation became more critical,
Cicero sent more and more messengers to me with dispatches.

Some of these were captured and put to death by torture in full view of
our soldiers. But there was in the camp a Nervian, a man of good family
called Vertico. He had deserted to Cicero at the start of the siege and had
been loyal to him. By promising freedom and large rewards, Vertico persuaded one of his slaves to carry a dispatch to me. The slave tied this round
a javelin and so got it out; as he was himself a Gaul, he passed through the
enemy lines without exciting any suspicion, and so reached me. It was
from him I learned of the dangers threatening Cicero and his legion.

46   It was early evening when I received the dispatch. I at once sent a messenger to the quaestor Marcus Crassus, whose winter camp was 25 miles
away in the territory of the Bellovaci, ordering him to set off with his legion

at midnight and join me with all speed. As soon as my message reached him, Crassus set out.

I sent another messenger to the legate Gaius Fabius, telling him to take his legion into the country of the Atrebates, through which I knew I should have to march on my way to Cicero's camp.

I wrote to Labienus asking him to bring his legion to the frontier of the Nervian territory if he could do so without risk. I did not think it wise to wait for the rest of the legions, who were rather too far away, but I collected about 400 cavalry from the nearest camps.

At about nine o'clock next morning I was informed by his advance guards **47** that Crassus was approaching, so I set out and covered 20 miles that day. I left Crassus with his legion in charge of Amiens, where I had left the army's heavy baggage, the hostages sent by various tribes, the official papers, and all the grain that had been collected to see us through the winter.

Fabius carried out his instructions, making good speed, and joined me with his legion on the march.

Labienus had heard of Sabinus's death and the destruction of the cohorts. As all the forces of the Treveri had moved against him, he was afraid that if he set out from his camp and gave the impression he was running away, the Gauls would attack and he would not be able to hold out against them, especially as he knew they were elated by their recent victory. So he wrote back to me explaining the danger he would be risking if he led his legion out of the camp. He also wrote a detailed account of what happened in the the country of the Eburones, and told me that all the forces of the Treveri, cavalry and infantry, had taken up position three miles away from his camp. Although it meant that I had only two legions instead of the three I **48** had expected, I approved of Labienus's decision.

I thought the only way of saving the situation left to me now was to act quickly. By forced marches we reached the territory of the Nervii, where I discovered from prisoners what was happening in Cicero's camp, and how dangerous the situation was.

I then managed to persuade one of my Gallic cavalrymen, by promising him a large reward, to take a letter to Cicero. I wrote the letter in Greek characters, so that if it were intercepted the Gauls should not discover what our plans were. I told the man that if he could not get into the camp, he must fasten the letter to the thong of his spear and then throw this inside the rampart.

In the letter, I wrote that I had set out with the legions and would soon be there, and I urged Cicero to keep up his former confidence and courage.

The Gaul was afraid to risk going close up to the camp, so he threw the spear as he had been told. It happened to stick in one of the towers and for two days remained there unnoticed. But on the third day one of the soldiers spotted it, pulled it out, and took it to Cicero. Cicero read it through, then had his men drawn up on parade and read the letter aloud to them. They were all overjoyed. Soon the smoke of burning buildings could be seen in the distance, and this dispelled all doubt about the approach of the legions.

When the Gauls heard news of our approach from their patrols, they **49** raised the siege and marched against me with all their forces, numbering about 60,000. Cicero made use of this chance and again asked the same Vertico, mentioned earlier, for a Gaul to carry a dispatch to me.

In his letter he warned me to proceed very warily and carefully, and described how the enemy had left the camp and had now directed their entire army against me. This dispatch reached me about midnight. I told my troops what it contained and encouraged them to face the coming battle with confidence.

At dawn the next day we struck camp and advanced about four miles, until we could see the great throng of the enemy on the far side of a valley, which had a stream running through it. Since my force was so small, it would have been very risky to fight on unfavourable ground; and as I knew that Cicero was no longer besieged, I thought I need not be so concerned about speed. So I halted and made a fortified camp in the most advantageous position I could find.

Since I had barely 7,000 men and no heavy baggage, the camp would have inevitably been small, but by limiting the width of the roads inside it, I had made it even smaller, so that the enemy would think it utterly contemptible. Meanwhile I sent scouts out in all directions to discover the best way for crossing the valley.

50   That day there were some cavalry skirmishes near the stream, but the two armies stayed in their positions. The Gauls were waiting for larger forces, which had not yet joined them. I was hoping that if we made a pretence of being afraid, we could entice the Gauls onto our own ground and so engage them in battle on our side of the valley in front of our camp. If that didn't work, I hoped to be able to cross the valley and the stream with less risk once the routes had been explored.

At dawn the enemy cavalry came up to the camp and engaged our cavalry. I told my cavalry to fall back deliberately and withdraw to the camp. At the same time I gave instructions for the height of the rampart to be increased all round, and the gates to be blocked up; while carrying out these tasks, the men were told to run about as much as possible and give the impression that they were afraid.

51   All this induced the Gauls to bring their troops across the valley and form them up on unfavourable ground. I then withdrew my men even from the rampart, which made the enemy come nearer still. They hurled missiles from all sides into our fortifications and sent heralds round with orders to announce that any Gaul or Roman who wanted to go over to their side, could do so safely before nine o'clock; after that there would be no chance to. And they so despised our troops that, thinking they could not break through the gates of our camp because these were blocked (though there was only a single row of sods that looked like a barricade) they began to break down the rampart with their hands and fill the ditches with earth.

At that point, our troops burst out from all the gates and the cavalry were sent out too. They quickly put the Gauls to flight, so completely that not a single one of them stood his ground to fight. We killed great numbers of them, stripping them all of their weapons.

I was afraid to pursue too far, because there were woods and marshes 52
in the way and because I could see that there was no opportunity of doing
the enemy even the slightest harm. So I marched on and reached Cicero's
camp the same day, with all my men safe.

I was amazed to see the towers and shelters and earthworks the enemy
had built there. When Cicero's legion was led out on parade, I discovered
that not one in ten of them remained unwounded. From all this I could tell
the extent of the danger they had been in and the great courage they had
shown in the face of it. I praised Cicero very highly, as he deserved, and
congratulated the legion too. I spoke individually to the centurions and military tribunes whose outstanding valour had been mentioned to me by
Cicero.

I received from prisoners a fuller account of the deaths of Sabinus and
Cotta, and next day held an assembly of the soldiers at which I explained
what had happened, and then reassured them. I told them the disaster we
had suffered had been caused by the legate's rashness, and that they should
not take it too much to heart; with the help of the gods and their own valour
they had avenged the defeat. The enemy's triumph had been short-lived,
and there was no need for them to let it rankle any longer.

Meanwhile news of my victory was brought with incredible speed to 53
Labienus by the Remi. He was about 60 miles away from Cicero's camp and
I did not reach it until about two o'clock in the afternoon; but before midnight there was the sound of shouting at the gates of the camp and Labienus
realized it was the Remi announcing a victory and offering their congratulations. The news spread to the Treveri, and Indutiomarus, who had decided
to attack Labienus's camp the next day, fled in the night and took all his
forces back into their own country.

I sent Fabius and his legion back to their winter quarters and decided to
spend the winter myself in quarters near Amiens with my three legions in
three separate camps there.

5 The winter camps: Labienus

Because such serious disturbances had broken out in Gaul, I decided to
remain with the army for the entire winter. For as news spread of the disaster
in which Sabinus had been killed, almost all the tribes in Gaul had been
discussing the possibility of going to war; they were sending messengers and
envoys all over the country, finding out what the other tribes were intending
to do and who would make the first moves in such a war, and holding meetings at night in deserted places. Throughout the whole winter there was
scarcely a time when I was not anxious, and not receiving some report
or other about plans for a rising among the Gauls.

For instance, the legate Lucius Roscius, whom I had put in command
of the Thirteenth legion, sent me a report that large Gallic forces from the
tribes called Aremorican had assembled to attack him and had been as close
as eight miles to his winter camp; but when they heard of my victory they had
gone away, and with such speed that their departure had resembled flight.

I summoned the leading men of each tribe, and partly by frightening 54 them, declaring that I knew what was going on, and partly by persuading them, I managed to keep a large part of the country loyal.

But on the instructions of their council, the Senones, a tribe particularly strong and influential among the Gauls, attempted to kill Cavarinus, whom I had established as their king; his brother, Moritasgus, had been king at the time of my arrival in Gaul, and his ancestors before that. Cavarinus had found out about their intention and escaped. They had pursued him as far as the frontier, deprived him of his throne, and banished him; then they sent envoys to me to justify their action. I ordered that their entire council should appear before me, but they did not obey.

So great an impact had been made on the barbarian Gauls by the appearance of a people ready to take the initiative in making war on us, and such a profound change had this brought about in the attitude of them all, that there was scarcely a tribe we did not suspect of plotting against us. The only exceptions were, of course, the Aedui and the Remi, whom I had always regarded with particular respect, the Aedui because of their longstanding and unbroken record of loyalty to Rome, the Remi because of the help they had recently given us in the Gallic campaigns.

I suppose this state of affairs was not especially surprising; although there were many reasons, there was, above all, the very deep resentment felt by those who used to be considered the best warriors in the world but had now so completely lost that reputation as to be subject to the sovereignty of Rome.

55   Throughout the winter Indutiomarus and the Treveri never stopped their efforts against us – sending envoys across the Rhine, stirring up the German tribes, promising them money, and telling them that most of our army had been destroyed and only a small fraction remained. But he did not succeed in persuading any German tribe to cross the Rhine. They said they had tried it twice already, in the campaign under Ariovistus and when the Tencteri had made their crossing, and were not going to tempt fortune again.

Although disappointed in his hopes in that direction, Indutiomarus continued gathering and training troops, procuring horses from the neighbouring tribes, and enticing exiles and criminals to join him from all over Gaul by offering them large rewards. In this way, he had now gained such prestige for himself in Gaul that deputations came to him from all parts of the country seeking his favour and friendship for their governments and for individuals.

56   Indutiomarus was aware that people were coming to him of their own accord and he knew that in one direction the Senones and the Carnutes were ready to revolt because they were conscious of their own guilt, while in another the Nervii and the Aduatuci were preparing to attack the Romans. Thinking therefore that he would have no lack of volunteers if he began to advance beyond the boundaries of his own land, he gave notice of an armed muster.

This is the Gauls' customary way of starting a war. A law, common to all the Gallic tribes, requires all adult males to come to the muster armed; the last man to arrive is most cruelly tortured and put to death, watched by the assembled throng.

At that meeting, Indutiomarus declared his son-in-law Cingetorix a public enemy and confiscated his property. Cingetorix was leader of the rival party and, as already mentioned, had put himself under my protection; he had remained loyal to me. When that business had been dealt with, Indutiomarus announced to the assembly that he had been sent for by the Senones, the Carnutes, and several other Gallic tribes. He said he intended to march to them through the country of the Remi, which he would lay waste as he went, but that before doing this he would attack Labienus's camp. He issued instructions for what he wanted done.

Labienus was inside a camp that occupied a strong position and had   57
been very well fortified. Consequently he felt no anxiety for himself or his legion; but he was concerned not to lose any chance of winning a victory. So when he learned from Cingetorix and his relatives what Indutiomarus had said at the muster, he sent messengers to the neighbouring tribes on every side calling on them to provide cavalry by a certain date.

Meanwhile almost every day Indutiomarus with all his cavalry would roam about near the camp, sometimes to reconnoitre its position, sometimes to parley or intimidate our men. Usually all the cavalry would hurl missiles inside our rampart. Labienus kept his men inside the fortifications and did all he could to make the enemy more convinced that he was afraid of them.

Each day Indutiomarus showed greater contempt for us as he came   58
up close to the camp. But in a single night Labienus brought into the camp all the cavalry which he had summoned from the neighbouring tribes. He took such care that the guards should keep all his men inside the camp that there was no chance of the news getting out or reaching the Treveri.

Meanwhile Indutiomarus followed his usual practice and came up to the camp, and spent most of the day there. His cavalry hurled missiles and, yelling insults, challenged our men to go out and fight. When they got no reply from us, towards evening, when they felt like it, they broke up into scattered groups and went away.

Suddenly, Labienus opened two of the gates and sent out all his cavalry. He had given them strict instructions that after the enemy had panicked and been put to flight (as he knew would happen, and it did), everyone was to go for Indutiomarus and no one else; they were not to strike a blow at any other Gaul until they had seen Indutiomarus killed. Labienus did not want his men to spend time pursuing the rest and so give Indutiomarus the chance to escape, and he had offered large rewards to those who succeeded in killing him. He sent some infantry cohorts to support the cavalry.

Fortune favoured the plan that the legate had devised. Since all our troops were after him, and him alone, Indutiomarus was caught and killed just as he was fording a river, and his head was brought back to the camp. While the cavalry were returning they chased and killed as many as they could.

The forces of Eburones and Nervii who had already assembled dispersed when the news reached them. After this success my province of Gaul was somewhat more peaceful.

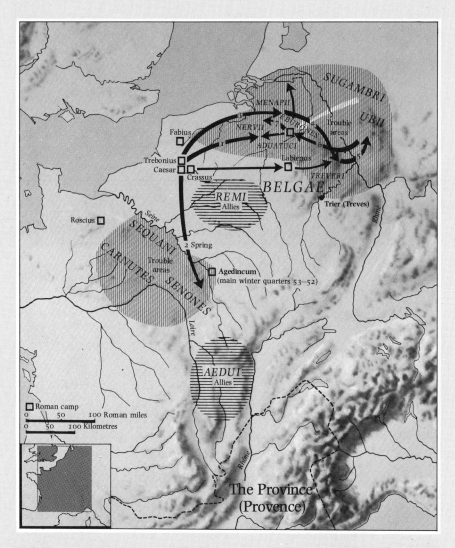

The sixth campaigning season in 53 BC was decisive for the future of northern Gaul. The uneasy winter was over and the recalcitrant Belgae had to be taught a lesson once and for all. In a rapid thrust Caesar was among the Nervii, forcing them to surrender. Then followed campaigns against the Menapii, in the marshlands of the Rhine mouth, and the powerful Treveri, who occupied the district around modern Trier, culminating with a second crossing of the Rhine. Further campaigning ensued in the north until by sheer weight of numbers Caesar had destroyed the Belgic resistance. It had been a relentless war of attrition. In the long term Roman discipline and Caesar's ability to regroup and to bring up reserves could not fail against an ill-disciplined native foe distracted by jarring factions and weakened by the devastation of their crops and herds.

One interesting aspect of the year's campaigning was Caesar's need to bring the Senones and Carnutes to heel. Both tribes occupied land south of the Seine and had hitherto been left largely unmolested. The reason for the action may have been that the Carnutes were providing a haven for religious dissidents. Caesar himself tells us that the Druids met annually in their territory. The Druids could unite the Gauls — indeed they were the only power who could; perhaps it was this that Caesar feared.

114

BOOK VI · 53 BC

1 The Treveran campaign

I had many reasons for expecting a more serious disturbance in Gaul before 1
long, and so I instructed the legates Marcus Silanus, Gaius Antistius Reginus,
and Titus Sextius to levy fresh troops. At the same time I sent a request to
Gnaeus Pompeius, who was now proconsul. For reasons of state, he was
staying near Rome though still keeping his military command. I asked him
to mobilize the recruits from northern Italy whom he had sworn in when
he was consul, and give them orders to march to join me.

I wanted to impress public opinion in Gaul not only for the present but for
the future as well. It was important to show that our resources in Italy were
so great that we could quickly make good any setback we suffered in the
war, and even increase the number of our forces.

Pompeius showed himself to be a patriot and a friend by doing what I
asked, and my legates also quickly raised the new troops. Before the winter
was over, three legions had been formed and brought to Gaul, thus providing
twice as many cohorts as those Sabinus had lost. The size of the reinforcements, and the speed with which they had been assembled, showed what
Roman organization and resources could achieve.

After Indutiomarus had been killed, as I have described, the Treveri 2
handed over his command to members of his family, who continued to
make overtures to the nearest German tribes, promising them money in
return for their support. Making no headway with the tribes closest to them,
they tried to win the support of those more remote, and were successful with
a number of these. Oaths were exchanged to confirm the alliance, and
hostages were given to guarantee the payment of the promised money.
They admitted Ambiorix as an ally in their league.

These developments were reported to me. I could see that preparations
for war were being made on every side. The Nervii, the Aduatuci, and the
Menapii were in arms and had been joined by all the German tribes on the
west bank of the Rhine; the Senones refused to come at my command and
were intriguing with the Carnutes and other neighbouring tribes; the
Treveri were continually sending deputations to woo the German tribes. I
concluded, therefore, that I must make plans for a campaign earlier in the
season than usual.

So, with the winter not yet over, I concentrated the four nearest legions 3
and marched into the territory of the Nervii, taking them by surprise. Before
they could either assemble or escape, we took a great many cattle and prisoners, which were given to the soldiers as booty. We laid waste the fields
and forced the Nervii to surrender and give hostages. That business was
quickly dealt with, and I took the legions back again into winter quarters.

At the beginning of spring I summoned the Gallic council as usual. All the tribes turned up except the Senones, the Carnutes, and the Treveri. I interpreted their failure to attend as the first step towards a war of rebellion, and to make it clear that everything else was of secondary importance, I transferred the council to Paris. The Parisii shared a frontier with the Senones and in the previous generation had united with them to make one state; but no one thought they were involved in the present policy of their neighbours.

I announced this decision from the platform in my camp, and then that same day set out with the legions against the Senones. After a series of forced marches we reached their territory.

4   When Acco, who had been the leader of the conspiracy, heard of my approach, he ordered the whole population to gather inside their *oppida*. This they tried to do, but before they could complete the operation, news came that the Romans had arrived. The Senones had no alternative but to abandon their plan and send envoys to me to ask my forgiveness.

They made this approach through the Aedui, under whose protection their tribe had been from ancient times. At the request of the Aedui I gladly pardoned them and accepted their excuses. I did this because I thought that summer was the time for fighting the war on hand and not for holding an inquest. I told the Senones to provide 100 hostages, and these I gave to the Aedui to look after.

The Carnutes also sent envoys and hostages while I was in the same area. They used the Remi, whose dependants they were, to plead their cause. My reply to them was the same. I then completed the business of the Gallic council and ordered various tribes to supply contingents of cavalry.

5   Now that this part of Gaul had been pacified, I turned all my thoughts and energies towards war against the Treveri and Ambiorix. I told Cavarinus to accompany me with the cavalry of the Senones to prevent any trouble being caused in the tribe by his hasty temper or the hatred he had incurred. Having made these arrangements, I looked around to see what other plans Ambiorix might have, since I was convinced he was not going to fight a pitched battle.

Close to the territory of the Eburones, and protected by a continuous line of marshes and forests, were the Menapii, the only Gallic tribe who had never sent envoys to me to ask for peace. I knew that ties of friendship existed between them and Ambiorix, and I had discovered that, with the aid of the Treveri, he had formed an alliance with the Germans. I thought I ought to deprive him of these allies before attacking him directly in war, to prevent him, in desperation, hiding among the Menapii or being forced to join the Germans beyond the Rhine.

Having decided on this plan, I sent the baggage of the entire army to Labienus in the territory of the Treveri, and ordered two legions to move there as well. I myself set out for the territory of the Menapii with five legions in light marching order. The Menapii did not collect any troops together; they relied instead on the protection given by the terrain, and fled into the forests and marshes, taking their belongings with them.

I divided our forces into three, entrusting detachments to the legate   6
Gaius Fabius and the quaestor Marcus Crassus. Bridges were quickly constructed and the three columns advanced, burning isolated buildings and
villages, and carrying off large numbers of cattle and prisoners.

This forced the Menapii to send envoys to me to beg for peace. I accepted
their hostages, but made it clear that I should regard them as enemies if
they allowed Ambiorix or his agents into their territory. When this had been
settled, I left Commius the Atrebatian with a detachment of cavalry to keep
watch on the Menapii. I myself set out for the territory of the Treveri.

While I was thus occupied, the Treveri had assembled large forces of   7
infantry and cavalry, and were preparing to attack Labienus and the one
legion that had been wintering in their territory. They were already no
more than two days' march from his camp when they heard of the arrival of
the two legions I had sent. They pitched camp about 15 miles away and
decided to await reinforcements coming from the Germans.

Labienus discovered what they were intending to do, and hoped that
their recklessness would provide him with a chance of fighting. So he left
five cohorts to guard the baggage, and set out against the enemy with the
other 25 cohorts and a large force of cavalry. When he was about a mile
away from the enemy, he entrenched a camp.

Between Labienus and the enemy there was a river with steep banks,
very difficult to cross. He had no intention of crossing it himself and did not
think the enemy would either.

Each day the Gauls' hope of being joined by reinforcements increased.
So Labienus deliberately said, quite openly, that since the Germans were
reported to be approaching, he was not going to put his own safety or that
of his army at risk, but would strike camp at dawn the next day. His words
were quickly reported to the enemy; it was only natural that among the
large number of Gallic cavalry in his camp there should be some who supported the Gallic cause.

During the night Labienus summoned the military tribunes and senior
centurions and explained his plan. So that it would be easier to make the
enemy believe the Romans were afraid, Labienus gave orders that when
camp was struck, there should be more noise and disturbance than is usual
in a Roman army. By doing this he made their departure look like flight.

Because the two camps were so close together, all this was reported to
the enemy by their patrols before dawn. The Gauls urged one another not   8
to let the plunder they had hoped for slip from their grasp: the Romans
were panic-stricken; to wait for reinforcements from the Germans would
take too long; they would be disgracing themselves if, with such a large
army, they hadn't the spirit to attack a mere handful of men, especially
men who were running away and hampered by baggage.

So when our rearguard had hardly got clear of the fortifications of the
camp, the Gauls boldly crossed the river, intending to join battle with us
even though the ground was unfavourable to them. Labienus had expected
this, and in order to entice them all to come across the river, he moved quietly
on, keeping up the pretence that he was marching away.

At this point he sent the baggage a little way ahead to a position on some higher ground. Then he said to his men, 'Here is the chance you've been looking for. You've got the enemy in your grasp, and they are in a bad position and on unfavourable ground. Show the same courage now, under my command, as you have often shown under the commander-in-chief. Imagine he is here, watching all this in person.'

With these words he ordered his troops to turn to face the enemy and form up for battle. He sent a few squadrons of cavalry to guard the baggage and stationed the rest on the flanks.

Our men quickly raised a shout and launched their javelins at the enemy. The Gauls had thought our men were running away, but now against all their expectations they saw them advancing to attack. They could not even stand up to the charge, but were routed as soon as the lines met, and made for the nearest woods. Labienus hunted them down with his cavalry, killing a large number and taking many prisoners.

A few days later he received the submission of the tribe. For when the Germans who were coming to help them realized the Treveri had been routed, they went back home. The relatives of Indutiomarus, who had been the instigators of the revolt, left their country and returned with the Germans. Cingetorix, as I have already said, had remained loyal from the start, and he was now given the supreme civil and military power over his tribe.

9   After marching from the territory of the Menapii into that of the Treveri, I decided to cross the Rhine. I had two reasons for doing this: the Germans had sent reinforcements to the Treveri to use against us, and I wanted to prevent Ambiorix taking refuge among the German tribes.

Having made this decision, I set about building a bridge a little way above the place where the army had crossed before. The method of construction was now perfectly familiar, and by working with great determination the soldiers completed the task in a few days. Leaving a strong guard on the bridge in Treveran territory in case there should be any sudden rising in that tribe, I took the rest of my forces, including the cavalry, across.

The Ubii, who had previously given hostages and submitted, sent envoys to me to clear themselves and to explain that they had not broken faith with me; their tribe had not sent any troops to help the Treveri. They earnestly begged me to spare them and not allow innocent people to be punished for the guilty, through an indiscriminate hatred of all Germans. They promised to provide more hostages if I wanted them. I made inquiries, and discovered that it was the Suebi who had sent the reinforcements. So I accepted the explanation given by the Ubii and began to investigate possible routes leading to the country where the Suebi lived.

10   Meanwhile I was informed a few days later by the Ubii that the Suebi were collecting all their forces into one place and sending messages to their subject tribes telling them to provide contingents of infantry and cavalry.

On hearing this, I made arrangements for the supply of grain and chose a suitable position for a camp. I told the Ubii to take in their cattle and transfer all their possessions from the fields into their *oppida*. I hoped that shortage of food might induce the Suebi, being ignorant and uncivilized, to fight on unequal terms.

I gave instructions that they were to send frequent patrols into the territory of the Suebi to find out what was going on there. The Ubii carried out my instructions and after a few days made the following report. On getting reliable information about the Roman army, the Suebi had taken all their own forces and those collected from their allies, and withdrawn deep into the most remote part of their country, where there was an enormous forest called Bacenis. This stretched far into the interior and formed a natural barrier between the Suebi and the Cherusci, preventing either tribe from making damaging raids into the territory of the other. It was at the edge of this forest, they reported, that the Suebi had decided to wait for the Romans to arrive.

2 Customs of the Gauls and Germans

It seems appropriate, at this point, to describe the customs of the Gauls and   11 the Germans, and the differences between these two nations.

In Gaul, not only every tribe, every canton, and every subdivision of a canton, but almost every individual household is divided into rival factions. The leaders of these factions are men thought by their followers to have the greatest prestige, and it is to their judgment and assessment that they turn in any question or discussion of policy. The reason for this long-established custom seems to have been to ensure that every man among the common people should have protection against those more powerful than himself; for no leader allows his supporters to be oppressed or cheated, and if he fails to protect them, he loses all his authority over them.

The same principle applies to the country of Gaul as a whole; all the tribes are grouped in two factions. When I first came to Gaul, the Aedui were   12 leaders of one of these groups, and the Sequani of the other. The Sequani were the weaker of the two when considered as a power by themselves, because the Aedui had from ancient times enjoyed very great prestige and had many dependent tribes.

The Sequani had therefore made an alliance with Ariovistus and his Germans, and by making considerable concessions and promises to them, had brought them in on their side. They fought several successful battles against the Aedui, wiping out all the nobles of that tribe, with the result that they became so much more powerful that they were able to take over a great many of the dependent tribes of their rivals. They took as hostages the sons of the leading men of the Aedui, and compelled the tribe to swear an oath never to plot against the Sequani. They kept occupied a section of Aeduan land bordering on their own territory, which they had seized by force, and, in fact, established their dominance over the whole of Gaul.

This state of affairs had led Diviciacus to go to Rome to ask help from the Senate, but he had returned without achieving anything. With my arrival in Gaul the situation changed. The Aedui had their hostages returned to them, their former dependent tribes were restored and with my help new ones were acquired, because those who had been their allies before realized

CELTIC SOCIETY
THE TRIBE

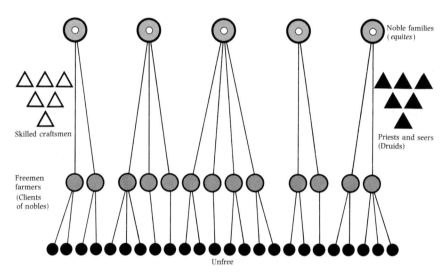

Chieftan and family

Noble families
(*equites*)

Skilled craftsmen

Priests and seers
(Druids)

Freemen
farmers
(Clients
of nobles)

Unfree

The Gauls with whom Caesar came into contact were not a nation, they were a complex of tribal groups in different stages of social development. Since the situation was varied the description of Celtic social structure, which Caesar offers, is at best a generalization. It is probably true, however, that in many tribes the noble families (the *equites*) were removed from the day-to-day routine of food production: so too were the men of skill (*druides*), who were patronized by the rich. What Caesar fails to mention are the freemen farmers, responsible, with their slaves, for working the land. Such men would have owed allegiance to a particular noble who in return provided protection. In some Celtic groups the noble owned large herds of cattle, which were hired out to their farmer-clients in return for food and services.

that they were better treated and more justly governed than in the past. In other respects too, the influence and prestige of the Aedui were increased.

The Sequani lost their supremacy and the Remi took their place. It was known that my favour towards this tribe was as great as to the Aedui. So tribes that could not be induced to join the Aedui – because of long-standing feuds – began to place themselves under the protection of the Remi, who took good care of them and so held on to the new authority they had suddenly acquired. At that time, the position was that the Aedui were acknowledged to be easily the most powerful tribe in Gaul, with the Remi next in importance.

13   Throughout Gaul there are only two classes of men who are of any account or importance. For the common people are regarded almost as slaves; they never venture to do anything on their own initiative and are never consulted

on any subject. Most of them, crushed by debt or heavy taxes or the oppression of more powerful men, pledge themselves to serve the nobles, who exercise over them the same rights as masters have over slaves.

The two privileged classes are the Druids and the knights. The Druids are in charge of religion. They have control over public and private sacrifices, and give rulings on all religious questions. Large numbers of young men go to them for instruction, and they are greatly honoured by the people.

In almost all disputes, between communities or between individuals, the Druids act as judges. If a crime is committed, if there is a murder, or if there is a dispute about an inheritance or a boundary, they are the ones who give a verdict and decide on the punishment or compensation appropriate in each case. Any individual or community not abiding by their verdict is banned from the sacrifices, and this is regarded among the Gauls as the most severe punishment. Those who are banned in this way are reckoned as sacrilegious criminals. Everyone shuns them; no one will go near or speak to them for fear of being contaminated in some way by contact with them. If they make any petitions there is no justice for them, and they are excluded from any position of importance.

There is one Druid who is above all the rest, with supreme authority over them. When he dies, he is succeeded by whichever of the others is most distinguished. If there are several of equal distinction, the Druids decide by vote, though sometimes they even fight to decide who will be their leader.

On a fixed date each year they assemble in a consecrated place in the territory of the Carnutes; that area is supposed to be the centre of the whole country of Gaul. People who have disputes to settle assemble there from all over the country and accept the rulings and judgments of the Druids.

It is thought that the doctrine of the Druids was invented in Britain and was brought from there into Gaul; even today those who want to study the doctrine in greater detail usually go to Britain to learn there.

The Druids are exempt from military service and do not pay taxes like the **14** rest. Such significant privileges attract many students, some of whom come of their own accord to be taught, while others are sent by parents and relatives.

It is said that during their training they learn by heart a great many verses, so many that some people spend 20 years studying the doctrine. They do not think it right to commit their teachings to writing, although for almost all other purposes, for example, for public and private accounts, they use the Greek alphabet. I suppose this practice began originally for two reasons: they did not want their doctrines to be accessible to the ordinary people, and they did not want their pupils to rely on the written word and so neglect to train their memories. For it does usually happen that if people have the help of written documents, they do not pay as much attention to learning by heart, and so let their memories become less efficient.

The Druids attach particular importance to the belief that the soul does not perish but passes after death from one body to another; they think that this belief is the most effective way to encourage bravery because it removes the fear of death. They hold long discussions about the heavenly bodies and

The Celtic deities were varied. In trying to
explain them in terms that his Roman
audience would understand Caesar fails to
grasp the essential point – that the many
hundreds of local gods can be divided quite
simply into two groups, the earth mother
deities, frequently associated with springs
and the underworld and with fertility, and
the local tribal gods, the idealized war
leader – male gods who were good at
everything. Each tribal group would
worship their own manifestations of these
two primitive ideals.

Top left: bronze head, probably a god, from
Garancières-en-Beauce and *right*: Celtic
Boar-god from Euffigneix, Haute Marne.

their movements, about the size of the universe and the earth, about the nature of the physical world, and about the power and properties of the immortal gods, subjects in which they also give instruction to their pupils.

The second class is that of the knights. Whenever a war breaks out and 15 their services are required – and before my arrival in Gaul, almost every year saw them involved either in an offensive or a defensive war – they are all involved in the campaign, each one attended by as many retainers and dependants as his birth and wealth make possible. The size of a knight's following is the only criterion of influence and power they recognize.

The Gallic people as a whole are extremely superstitious. Consequently, 16 people suffering from serious illnesses, and people involved in the dangers of battle, make, or promise to make, human sacrifice; the Druids officiate at such sacrifices.

The Gauls believe the power of the immortal gods can be appeased only if one human life is exchanged for another, and they have sacrifices of this kind regularly established by the community. Some of them have enormous images made of wickerwork, the limbs of which they fill with living men; these are set on fire and the men perish, enveloped in the flames. They believe that the gods prefer it if the people executed have been caught in the act of theft or armed robbery or some other crime, but when the supply of such victims runs out, they even go to the extent of sacrificing innocent men.

The god they worship most is Mercury, and they have very many images 17 of him. They regard him as the inventor of all the arts, the guide of all their roads and journeys, and the god who has greatest power for trading and moneymaking. After Mercury they worship Apollo, Mars, Jupiter, and Minerva, having almost the same ideas about these gods as other peoples do: Apollo averts diseases, Minerva teaches the first principles of industry and crafts, Jupiter has supremacy among the gods, and Mars controls warfare.

When they have decided to fight a battle, it is to Mars that they usually dedicate the spoils they hope to win; and if they are successful, they sacrifice the captured animals and collect all the rest of spoils in one place. Among many of the tribes it is possible to see piles of these objects on consecrated ground. It is most unusual for anyone to dare to go against the religious law and hide his booty at home, or remove any of the objects that have been placed on such piles. The punishment laid down for that crime is death by the most terrible torture.

The Gauls claim that they are all descended from Father Dis; they say this 18 is the tradition handed down to them by the Druids. For this reason they reckon periods of time not in days but in nights; in celebrating birthdays, the first of the month, and the beginning of a year, they go on the principle that night comes first and is followed by day.

As for the other customs of daily life, one difference between the Gauls and other peoples is their attitude to their children. They do not allow their sons to approach them in public until they are youths old enough for military service, and they regard it as disgraceful for a son who is still a boy to stand where his father can see him in a public place.

19   When a man marries, he contributes from his own property an amount calculated to match whatever he has received from his wife as her dowry. A joint account is kept of all this property and the profits from it are set aside. Whichever of the two outlives the other gets both shares, together with the profits that have accumulated with the years. Husbands have power of life and death over their wives as well as over their children. When the head of a distinguished family dies, his relatives meet and if there have been any suspicious circumstances connected with his death, they examine his wives under torture, as we examine slaves; if they are found guilty, they are burnt to death, suffering the most terrible torment.

    Although Gaul is not a rich country, funerals there are splendid and costly. Everything the dead man is thought to have been fond of is put on the pyre, including even animals. Not long ago slaves and dependants known to have been their masters' favourites were burned with them at the end of the funeral.

20   The tribes that are considered most efficient in running their affairs have it laid down by law that if anyone hears from a neighbouring tribe any rumour or news, he must report it to a magistrate and not tell anyone else. This is because such tribes have discovered that impulsive and ignorant people are often frightened by false rumours, and driven to commit criminal acts and interfere with important affairs of state. The magistrates suppress whatever they think fit, publishing only what they consider good for the people to know. It is forbidden to discuss politics except in assembly.

21   The customs of the Germans are very different from those of the Gauls. They have no Druids to supervise religious matters and they do not show much interest in sacrifices. They count as gods only things that they can see and from which they obviously derive benefit, for instance Sun, Fire, and Moon. Of the other gods they have never even heard.

    Their whole life is centred round hunting and military pursuits; from childhood they devote themselves to toil and hardship. Those who preserve their chastity longest win the highest approval from their friends; some think that this increases their stature, others that it develops their strength and muscles. They consider it the utmost disgrace to have had intercourse with a woman before the age of twenty. But there is no secrecy about the facts of sex; men and women bathe together in the rivers, and they wear only hides or short garments of hairy skin, leaving most of the body bare.

22   The Germans are not interested in agriculture; their diet consists mainly of milk, cheese, and meat. No one possesses a definite portion of land to call his own property; each year the magistrates and chiefs of the tribe allot a piece of land to clans and groups of kinsmen and others living together, deciding on the size and position of such allotments at their own discretion, and in the following year they compel them to move to another piece of land.

    They give many reasons for this practice. They say it is to prevent people becoming so accustomed to living in one place that they lose their keenness for war and take up agriculture instead; to prevent men wanting large estates, and the strong driving the weak from their holdings as a result;

The communities of the Mediterranean coasts of France, subject to classical influences since the foundation of Massilia in 600 BC, adopted elements of classical architecture into their temple building. At Roquepertuse in Provence the columns of the temple porch were carved with niches to hold several human heads. The cult of the severed head was widespread among the Celts. They believed the head was the seat of power.

❧

to prevent them building houses designed to keep out the heat and cold; to prevent people becoming greedy for money, a thing that gives rise to divisions and strife; and to keep the ordinary people contented and quiet by letting each man see that he is just as well off as the most powerful members of the tribe.

The greatest glory for a German tribe is to lay waste as much land as   23
possible around its own territory and keep it uninhabited. They consider it a mark of valour to have driven their neighbours from their land so that no one dares to settle near them; they think too that this will give them greater security because it removes the risk of sudden invasion.

Whenever a tribe is involved in a war, either offensive or defensive, officers are chosen to have command in that campaign and are given the power of life and death. In times of peace there is no central magistracy; the chiefs of the various districts and cantons administer justice and settle disputes among their own people.

No disgrace attaches to armed robbery, provided it is committed outside the frontiers of the tribe; indeed, the Germans claim that it is good training for the young men and stops them becoming lazy. When one of the chiefs announces at an assembly that he is going to lead a raid, and calls for volunteers to go with him, those who agree with the raid and approve of the man proposing it stand up, and, applauded by the whole gathering, promise him their help. If any of these men then fail to go with him, they are regarded as deserters and traitors and no one ever trusts them again in anything.

The Germans think it sacrilegious to wrong a guest; anyone who has come to a house of theirs for any reason is shielded from injury and treated as sacrosanct; such guests are welcomed to any man's home and given a share of the food there.

24   There was once a time when the Gauls were more warlike than the Germans. They actually invaded German territory and sent colonists across the Rhine because there was not enough land in Gaul for its large population. And so the Volcae Tectosages seized and settled in the most fertile district of Germany, namely the part near the Hercynian forest – which, I observe, was known to Eratosthenes and other Greeks, who called it Orcynia. The Volcae Tectosages remain in that area to this day, and have a very high reputation for justice and prowess in war. At the present time they endure the same life of want and poverty as the Germans, eating the same kind of food and wearing the same kind of clothes.

The Gauls, on the other hand, through living near the Roman provinces and being familiar with goods that come in from overseas, are well supplied with both luxuries and necessities. They have gradually become accustomed to defeat, and having fought and lost so many battles they do not even pretend to compete with the Germans in valour.

25   The Hercynian forest, mentioned above, is so wide that it would take a man travelling light nine days to cross it; the Germans are unable to describe its width in any other way, for they have no measurements of distance. The forest starts on the frontiers of the Helvetii, the Nemetes, and the Raurici, and runs straight along the line of the Danube to the country of the Dacians and the Anartes. At this point it turns away from the river northeastwards, and is of such enormous length that it touches the territories of many different peoples. No one in western Germany would claim to have reached the eastern edge of the forest even after travelling for 60 days, or to have discovered where it ends.

It is known that there are in the forest many kinds of wild animals not seen elsewhere; some of these seem worth mentioning because they are very different from those found in other parts of the world.

26   There is an ox shaped like a deer; projecting from the middle of its forehead between the ears is a single horn that is straighter and sticks up higher than those of the animals we know, and at the top spreads out like a man's hand or the branches of a tree. The male and female are alike, with horns of the same shape and size.

27   There are also creatures called elks. These resemble goats in their shape and dappled skins, but are slightly larger than goats and have only stumpy horns. Their legs have no joints or knuckles, and they do not lie down to rest; if they fall down by accident, they cannot get up or even raise themselves. When they want to sleep they use trees; they support themselves against these, and in this way, by leaning over just a little, they get some rest. When

hunters have noticed their tracks and so discovered their usual retreats, they undermine the roots of all the trees in that area, or cut the trunks nearly through so that they only look as if they were still standing firm. When the creatures lean against them as usual, their weight is too much for the weakened trunks; the trees fall down and the elks with them.

There is a third species called the aurochs. These creatures are slightly   28 smaller than the elephant, and resemble the bull in appearance, colour and shape. They are very strong and can move very swiftly, attacking any man or beast they catch sight of. The Germans are very keen to trap these animals and kill them. Their young men are toughened by this arduous sport, and hunting the aurochs is good training for them. Those who kill the largest number of these animals, and take back the horns to show in public as proof of their achievement, win great glory. But it is impossible to domesticate or tame the aurochs, even if caught quite young. Their horns are much bigger than those of our oxen and quite different in shape and appearance. They are much sought after by the Germans, who put silver round the rims and use them as drinking cups at their grandest banquets.

3 Ambiorix and the Sugambri

When I learned from the Ubian scouts that the Suebi had retreated into their   29 forests, I decided not to advance any farther. I was afraid that we should run out of grain because, as I have just explained, no German tribes pay much attention to agriculture.

However, so that the natives should still feel I could well return, and in order to prevent their reinforcements arriving too quickly, I withdrew my army and broke down the last two hundred feet of the bridge where it touched the Ubian bank of the Rhine. At the Gallic end I constructed a tower four storeys high, posted a garrison of 12 cohorts to protect the bridge, and fortified the position with strong defence works. I left young Gaius Volcacius Tullus in command of the position and its garrison.

When the crops were beginning to ripen, I myself set off to make war on Ambiorix. I marched through the forest of the Ardennes, which is the largest in the whole of Gaul, stretching from the frontier of the Treveri on the bank of the Rhine to that of the Nervii, and more than 500 miles long. I sent Lucius Minucius Basilus on ahead with all the cavalry, to see if he could gain some advantage by travelling quickly and exploiting any chance that arose. I warned him not to allow any fires in his camp, to avoid giving the enemy advance warning of my approach, and told him I should be following directly.

Basilus carried out these orders and completed his march more quickly   30 than anyone thought possible. He took the natives by surprise and captured a number of them in the fields; acting on information these people gave him, he marched to the place where Ambiorix himself and a few cavalrymen were said to be.

Luck plays a great part in all things, but particularly in war. Basilus was very lucky in catching Ambiorix completely off his guard and unprepared, and in appearing on the scene before there was any report or even rumour that he was on his way. But by a great stroke of luck, too, Ambiorix himself escaped with his life, even when he had lost all the military equipment he had with him, including his horses and wheeled vehicles.

But escape he did. For the house where he stayed was in a wood, as is usual with the houses of the Gauls, who generally look for sites near woods and rivers to avoid the heat; because they were fighting in a confined space, his followers and friends managed to hold out against the attack of our cavalry for a short time. While they were fighting, one of Ambiorix's men put him on a horse and so he got away, his flight concealed by the wood. Thus it was largely luck that had put him in danger, and luck that saved him.

31   Ambiorix did not mobilize his forces, but it is not clear why: either it was part of his policy, because he thought it unwise to fight; or perhaps he thought he had not time, because the sudden arrival of the Roman cavalry had taken him by surprise, and he felt sure the main body of our army was coming up close behind. At any rate, he sent out messengers through the countryside, with orders for every man to look out for himself.

Some of the people fled into the forest of the Ardennes, others into the continuous belt of marshes. Those who lived nearest to the sea hid in islands that are cut off from the mainland by the high tide. Many left their own country and entrusted themselves and all their possessions to utter strangers. Catuvolcus, who was king of half of the Eburones and had joined Ambiorix in the conspiracy, was now old and weak, unable to endure the hardships of war or flight. He solemnly cursed Ambiorix for instigating the conspiracy, and then poisoned himself with yew, a tree which is very common in Gaul and in Germany.

32   The Segni and Condrusi, who live between the Eburones and the Treveri but are of German origin and so count as Germans, sent envoys to me to beg me not to regard them as enemies, and not to assume that all the Germans on the Gallic side of the Rhine were in league against me. They had never contemplated making war on the Romans, they said, and had sent no help to Ambiorix. I checked their statements by questioning prisoners, and then ordered them to bring back to me any fugitives of the Eburones who had gone to them. I told them that if they did this, I would not harm their land.

I then split my forces into three divisions and took all the heavy baggage to Aduatuca, a fortress roughly in the middle of the territory of the Eburones, where Sabinus and Cotta had had their winter quarters.

There were several reasons why I chose this place, but the most important was that last year's fortifications were still intact, which meant that the

Caesar makes much of the river Rhine as a boundary. To him, and to his audience, the river was indeed a symbolic boundary between the known and the unknown. His crossing of the river in 55 BC had enormous emotional appeal. But to say that the Rhine was the divide between the Celts (or Gauls) and the Germans was little more than a convenient generalization. If one accepts that an ethnic distinction of this kind has some validity, then it is more realistic to assume that a broad band of hybridization extended on both sides of the river. Indeed Caesar mentions the Germanic antecedents of the Belgic tribes. Place-name evidence has also shown there to be many Celtic names north of the Rhine.

soldiers would be spared the labour of building new ones. To guard the heavy baggage there I left the Fourteenth legion, one of the three recently formed that I had brought from Italy. I put Quintus Tullius Cicero in charge of the legion and the camp, and gave him 200 cavalry as well.

Having divided up the army, I ordered Titus Labienus to set out with three   33
legions towards the coast, into the region bordering on the territory of the Menapii. I sent Gaius Trebonius, also with three legions, to lay waste the country on the frontiers of the Aduatuci. I myself took the remaining three legions and decided to proceed to the river Scheldt, which flows into the Meuse, and to the western edge of the Ardennes. I had heard that Ambiorix had set out for that area with a few cavalrymen.

As I was leaving, I promised I would return in seven days; I knew that an issue of grain would be due on that date for the legion left behind to guard the baggage. I urged Labienus and Trebonius to return by that date, if they could do so without danger to Roman interests, so that they could take part in further discussions and examine the tactics of the enemy before resuming the campaign.

As I have already said, there was no regular enemy force assembled, no   34
oppidum, and no garrison to offer armed resistance. The population was scattered in all directions, and each man had settled wherever a remote valley or a place in the woods or an impenetrable marsh offered some hope of protection or safety.

These hiding places were known to the people living nearby, and it required great care to ensure the safety of our troops – not in protecting the army as a whole, for when the troops were kept together there was no danger to them from an enemy that was scattered and panic-stricken, but in keeping individual soldiers safe, though this of course was relevant to the security of the army as a whole. Their eagerness to get plunder caused many individual soldiers to venture too far, and the woodland, with its ill-defined and half-concealed paths, made it impossible for men to advance in close formation.

If I wanted the business finished off and the criminals rooted out and killed, I had to divide my troops into a number of small detachments and send them out in different directions. If I wanted to follow the established practice of the Roman army and keep the companies in regular formation, then the terrain itself acted as a protection for the enemy, who were, as individuals, quite bold enough to lay an ambush and surround any of our men who strayed from the main body of our army.

Many objects of Celtic inspiration found their way north of the Rhine into Germany and beyond. One, of great archaeological significance, is the silver cauldron found dismantled and buried in a bog at Gundestrup in Denmark. Presumably it was an offering to the gods in anticipation or repayment for some act of favour. The panel illustrated here is of particular interest since it shows infantry and cavalry troops armed as the Celts would have been. The men carry shields and swords and wear helmets with crests in the form of animals and birds, while at the end are three warriors blowing boars'-headed war trumpets. All these details are mentioned in the writing of the classical authors as typical of the Celts at war.

Considering these difficulties, I took every precaution that could be taken. Even though the troops were burning with desire for revenge, I thought it better to let go the opportunity of inflicting damage on the enemy if it could be done only at the cost of losing some of my own men. I sent messengers out to the neighbouring tribes, and by offering them the prospect of booty, called on them to join me in pillaging the Eburones. My intention was to put Gauls rather than Roman legionaries at risk in the forest, and, at the same time, to overwhelm the Eburones with a huge force of men, and so wipe out that tribe and its very name, as a punishment for the great crime it had committed. Large numbers of Gauls quickly assembled from all sides.

35   Every part of the territory of the Eburones was now being plundered, and it was getting close to the day on which I had intended to return to the legion that had been left guarding the baggage. At this point there was another example of the significant part played in war by luck, and the important consequences it can have.

I have already explained that the enemy had scattered, panic-stricken. There was therefore no body of troops to give us even the slightest cause for alarm. But news reached the Germans across the Rhine that the Eburones were being pillaged and that everyone else was being invited to join in the plunder. A force of 2,000 cavalry was raised by the Sugambri, who live close to the Rhine and who, as already mentioned, had received fugitives from the Tencteri and the Usipetes.

Using boats and rafts, they crossed the river 30 miles below the place where I had left the garrison at the bridge we had built. They invaded the territory of the Eburones, captured a number of the scattered fugitives, and seized large numbers of cattle, booty much sought after by uncivilized peoples. Greed for booty led them to advance farther; they were born and bred to be fighters and bandits, and no marsh or forest was going to stop them.

They asked their prisoners where I was, and discovered that I had gone farther afield and that the whole army had left the district. At this, one of the prisoners said, 'Why go after wretched, meagre booty like this, when you could be really rich now? In three hours you could be at Aduatuca, where the Roman troops have collected all their belongings. The garrison there is so small that it can't even man the wall, and no one dares set foot outside the fortifications.' When this prospect was put before them, the Germans hid the booty they had already got and set out for Aduatuca, guided by the man who had given them the information.

36   Throughout the preceding days, Cicero had followed my instructions and been most careful to keep his men inside the camp, not even allowing a single servant to go outside the fortifications. But on the seventh day, he began to doubt that I would be back on the day I had specified; he had heard that I had gone farther afield, and there was no news of my return. At the same time he was influenced by the complaints of the men; they said that this lack of action, with no one allowed to set foot outside the camp, was just like being besieged.

He did not expect anything serious to happen within three miles of his camp; there were nine legions and a large force of cavalry in the field, and the enemy had been scattered and almost wiped out. So he sent out five cohorts to get grain from the nearest fields. There was just a single hill between these fields and the camp.

With the cohorts, but as a separate detachment, were sent some 300 legionaries I had left behind in Cicero's camp because they were wounded, but who had recovered in the course of the week. A large number of camp servants was also given permission to accompany the cohorts, and they took with them a great many of the pack animals being kept in the camp.

Just at this critical moment the German cavalry appeared. They rode   37 straight on without slackening speed and tried to break into the camp by the back gate. There were woods in the way on that side, so the Germans were not seen until they came up to the camp, so close, in fact, that the merchants who had their tents at the foot of the rampart had no chance to get away.

Our men were taken completely by surprise; the suddenness of the thing threw them into confusion, and it was only with difficulty that the cohort on guard withstood the first attack.

The enemy swarmed round the other sides of the camp, trying to find a way in. Our men were barely able to hold the gates; elsewhere the fortifications and the very nature of the ground provided protection.

There was panic all over the camp: men were asking each other the reason for the uproar; no one knew where to assemble or in which direction to advance. Some of them said the camp was already captured; others claimed that the Germans had come in triumph after destroying the Roman army and its commander-in-chief. Most of them fell prey to strange, superstitious fancies caused by the place itself. They seemed to see before their eyes the disaster that had befallen Cotta and Sabinus, who, they imagined, had perished in that very fortress.

With our men panic-stricken by fears like that, the Germans were convinced that what the prisoner had told them was true, and there was no garrison inside the camp. They struggled to force their way in, urging each other not to let such a stroke of luck slip from their grasp.

Among the sick men left with the garrison was Publius Sextius Baculus,   38 who had served under me as chief centurion of his legion; I have already mentioned him in descriptions of earlier battles. Baculus had now been without food for five days. Feeling anxious about his own safety and that of his comrades, he emerged from his tent unarmed. Seeing that the enemy were close at hand and the situation critical, he seized weapons from the men nearest to him and took his stand in the gateway.

The centurions of the cohort on guard joined him, and fighting together, they held out against the enemy attack for a short time. Baculus was severely wounded and fainted, but his companions managed to drag him back to safety. This short respite enabled the rest of the troops to pull themselves together sufficiently to take up their positions on the fortifications and give the appearance, at least, of defending the camp.

Meanwhile the men who had gone out to collect grain had completed   39 their task. Now they could hear shouting coming from the camp. The cavalry hurried on ahead and discovered how dangerous the situation was. The men were terrified; there were no fortifications out there to protect them. They were raw recruits with no experience of warfare, so they simply turned to the military tribunes and centurions and waited to be told what to do. Even the bravest men among them were unnerved by this unexpected turn of events.

The Germans caught sight of the standards in the distance and left off attacking the camp. At first they thought it was the return of those legions that the prisoners told them had gone further afield. But when they saw how few men there were, they contemptuously attacked them from all sides.

40   The servants ran forward to the nearest high ground, but were quickly dislodged from there. They then rushed up to the companies that were forming around their standards, and so made the already nervous soldiers even more alarmed. Some of the troops thought they should adopt a wedge formation and make a quick breakthrough to the camp, since it was so close. Even if some of their number were surrounded and killed, they were sure the rest would be able to get through safely. Others thought they should take up position on the higher ground and all face the same risk.

The veteran soldiers, who, as already stated, had gone out with the cohorts, did not approve this alternative plan. They therefore shouted encouragement to each other and then, led by their commander Gaius Trebonius, a Roman of equestrian rank, they broke right through the middle of the enemy and got safely back into the camp without a single man lost.

The servants and cavalry followed on behind in the same charge and got through safely, thanks to the courage of the veterans. But those who had taken up position on the higher ground showed that even now they had learned nothing of the science of warfare. They could not stick to the plan they had chosen of defending themselves on the higher ground, nor could they imitate the vigour and speed they had seen serve the others so well. Instead they tried to get back into the camp, and so came down from the higher ground and put themselves in an unfavourable position.

Some of the centurions had been promoted for gallantry from the lower grades in the other legions to the higher grades in this one. They did not mean to lose the reputation for valour they had already won, and they fell fighting with the utmost bravery. The courage of these centurions forced the enemy back, and so some of our soldiers got safely into the camp, much to their own surprise. The rest were surrounded and killed by the enemy.

41   Now that the Germans could see our men in position on the fortifications, they gave up all hope of taking the camp by storm. They withdrew across the Rhine, taking with them the booty they had hidden in the woods.

But even after the enemy had gone, there was such panic among our men that when Gaius Volusenus, whom I had sent on ahead with the cavalry, arrived at the camp that night, he could not make them believe I was at hand with my army safe and sound. They were so completely in the grip of fear they seemed almost to have lost their wits. They said that the whole army had been destroyed and only the cavalry had escaped from the rout;

if the army really were intact, the Germans would never have attacked the camp.

My arrival put an end to the panic. I am well aware of how things happen 42
in war, so when I returned I had only one complaint to make: in my opinion the cohorts should not have been sent out, thus leaving their posts in the garrison, for I thought that nothing at all should have been left to chance.

I did, however, acknowledge the important part luck had played in the whole episode. It was chance that had brought the enemy to the camp so suddenly, and even more was it chance that had caused them to turn away when they were almost at the rampart and the gates of the camp. But the most remarkable thing of all was that the Germans, who had crossed the Rhine with the intention of plundering the territory of Ambiorix, had been diverted into attacking the Roman camp, and in this way had done Ambiorix as great a service as he could wish for.

I set out once more to harass the Eburones. A large force of men was 43
collected from the neighbouring tribes and sent out in all directions. Every village and every building they saw was set on fire. Cattle were taken from every part and driven off as booty. Much of the grain had been flattened by the seasonal rains, and the rest was consumed by the great numbers of animals and men, so that it seemed clear that if any of the enemy had managed to hide for the time being, they must surely die of starvation when our army was withdrawn.

With such a large force of cavalry split up and sent in every direction, it happened more than once that we took prisoners who had just seen Ambiorix in flight and would look round to see where he was, insisting that he surely could not have vanished from sight. Their hopes of catching up with him were raised, and since they thought they would win my highest favour if they succeeded, they took enormous trouble and made almost superhuman efforts.

But always it seemed they had just missed what would have crowned their efforts with success; Ambiorix would get away to some hideout in the wooded valleys, or would head for another district in some other direction under cover of night, with no more to protect him than four horsemen, the only people he dared trust with his life.

When we had laid the country waste in this way, I withdrew the army, 44
now minus the two cohorts that had been lost, to Durocortorum, a town of the Remi.

I called a Gallic council there and held an inquiry into the conspiracy of the Senones and the Carnutes. Acco, who had been the instigator of the plot, was condemned to death and executed in the ancient Roman manner. Some fled, fearing the outcome of the inquiry, and they were declared outlaws.

I then decided where the winter quarters of the various legions should be; two had their winter camps on the frontier of the Treveri, two among the Lingones, and the other six at Agedincum in the country of the Senones. I made arrangements about their grain supplies and then, since Gaul was quiet, I set out as usual for Italy to hold the assizes.

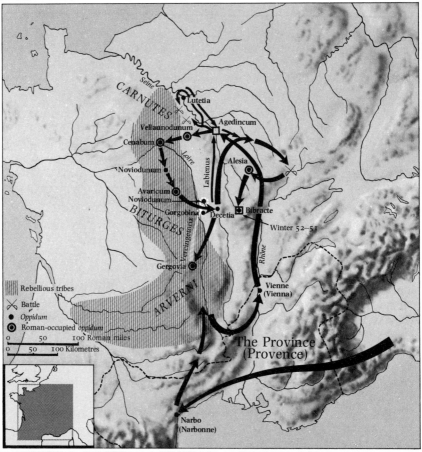

There had been rebellions against the Roman presence before but none were as serious as that which broke out in 52 BC. Significantly the rebellion was initiated by the Carnutes in whose territory it was that the annual druidic gatherings were held (VI 13) but the war leader who emerged, Vercingetorix, was a young dissident of Arvernian origin. His father, we are told, had tried to make himself king – an offence punishable by death among the more socially advanced tribes of Gaul. By this stage kingship had been abolished in favour of elected magistrates. Vercingetorix was therefore something of a social outcast who had nothing to gain from conforming – but leading a rebellion against authority had much to offer this ambitious young man. Of all the Gaulish leaders who had stood against Caesar, Vercingetorix came nearest to success.

BOOK VII · 52 BC

1 Vercingetorix's rebellion

When I arrived in Italy, I learned of the assassination of Publius Clodius and was told of the decree of the Senate ordering all Italians of military age to be sworn in. I therefore set about conscripting recruits throughout the Cisalpine province. 1

These events were quickly reported across the Alps, and the Gauls themselves added to them, inventing stories that seemed not inconsistent with the facts. They made out that I was being detained there by the troubles in Rome, which were so acute that I could not rejoin the army. The Gauls already resented being subject to the sovereignty of Rome; they now thought their chance had come, and it spurred them on to start planning more boldly and openly for war.

Meetings were arranged in remote places in the forests, and at these their leading men complained about the death of Acco, pointing out that they themselves could well suffer the same fate. They lamented the condition of their whole country and promised all kinds of rewards to any who would make the first moves in a war and be prepared to risk their own lives to set Gaul free.

The most important thing, they said, was to work out how I could be cut off from my army before their secret plans could leak out. This would be easy to do because the legions would not dare to leave their winter camps in the absence of their commander-in-chief, and he would not be able to reach them without a strong escort. Besides, they declared, it was better to be killed in battle than to fail to recover their ancient glory in war and the freedom they had inherited from their ancestors.

All these matters were discussed. The Carnutes then came forward and said they were ready to face any danger for the common cause, and offered to strike the first blow in the war. 2

They admitted that it was not then possible to exchange hostages as pledges of their good faith, for fear that should give away their intention; but they asked the others to bring all their military standards together — a most solemn ceremony according to Gallic custom — and to swear a binding oath not to desert them once they had started the war. The Carnutes were greatly praised by the others, and all those present took the oath. They fixed a date for the revolt to begin, and dissolved the assembly.

The appointed day came. The Carnutes, led by two desperate individuals called Cotuatus and Conconnetodumnus, at a given signal swooped down on Cenabum. They killed all the Roman citizens who had settled there as traders and plundered their property. One of those killed was Gaius Fufius Cita, a distinguished Roman of equestrian rank, whom I had put in charge of the grain supply. 3

News of this quickly spread to all the tribes of Gaul. For when something important or remarkable happens, the people shout the news of it to one another through the whole country; one after another they take up the report, passing it on to their neighbours. That is precisely what happened on this occasion. What had taken place at Cenabum at dawn was known in the country of the Arverni, about 160 miles away, before eight o'clock that night.

4   There the first move was made by Vercingetorix, a young Arvernian with very great power in his tribe. His father, Celtillus, had once been the most powerful man in the whole of Gaul and had been killed by his fellow tribesmen because he wanted to become king.

Vercingetorix called his dependants together and had no difficulty in rousing their passions. When it was known what Vercingetorix intended to do, there was a rush of armed men to join him. His uncle, Gobannitio, and the other leading men of the tribe, who thought that his plan should not be put into action, tried to restrain him. He was expelled from the *oppidum* of Gergovia, but that did not deter him; he raised a band of beggars and outcasts from the countryside.

Once he had recruited these, he brought over to his side all the Arvernians he approached, and by urging them to take up arms in the cause of Gallic freedom, he soon collected a large force of men. He expelled from the tribe those opponents by whom, not long before, he had been driven out himself. He was proclaimed king by his followers, and sent out deputations in every direction, calling upon the tribes to stay loyal.

He quickly won the support of the Senones, the Parisii, the Pictones, the Cadurci, the Turoni, the Aulerci, the Lemovices, the Andes, and all the other tribes on the Atlantic coast. By general consent he was given the supreme command.

Having gained this power, Vercingetorix demanded hostages from all the tribes who had joined him, and ordered each tribe to bring him a specified number of soldiers at once. He stipulated how many weapons each tribe must provide from its own resources and by what date; he paid particular attention to the provision of cavalry.

He was a man of enormous energy, but also a very strict disciplinarian: the severity of his punishments compelled any who were hesitating to obey. Anyone guilty of a serious crime was put to death at the stake or tortured to death; anyone guilty of a lesser crime was sent back home with his ears cut off or a single eye gouged out, to be a warning to others and frighten them

5   by the severity of the punishment. By these savage means he quickly got an army together.

He sent a man of great daring, a Cadurcan called Lucterius, into the territory of the Ruteni with part of his forces; he himself set out for the territory of the Bituriges.

At his approach, that tribe sent envoys to the Aedui, whose dependants they were, to ask for help to give them a better chance of resisting the enemy forces. The Aedui asked the advice of the legates I had left with the army, before sending a force of cavalry and infantry to the aid of the Bituriges.

When these troops reached the river Loire, which separates the Bituriges from the Aedui, they waited there for a few days, not daring to cross. Then they turned and went back home. To explain why they had returned in that way they told my legates that they had been afraid of treachery on the part of the Bituriges, whose plan they had discovered; this was, if they crossed the river, to cut them off from one side, while the Arverni did the same from the other. We cannot tell for certain whether they really acted for the reason they gave to the legates, or whether it was treachery that motivated them, and so it is impossible to make a definite statement on the subject. As soon as the Aedui left, the Bituriges allied themselves with the Arverni.

I was in Italy when news of these events reached me. I could tell by this 6 time that the situation in Rome had improved, thanks to the vigorous action of Gnaeus Pompeius, and so I left Italy for Transalpine Gaul.

When I got there I was faced with a very difficult problem. How was I to reach my army? If I summoned the legions to come to me in the Province, I knew they would have to fight battles on the march without me. On the other hand, I could march towards them myself; but I thought it unwise to trust my own safety even to those tribes who now seemed harmless.

Meanwhile Lucterius the Cadurcan, who had been sent to the Ruteni, 7 won that tribe over to the Arverni. Next he moved on to the Nitiobriges and the Gabali and took hostages from both tribes. Then with the large forces he had gathered together he proceeded in the direction of Narbonne, meaning to break out into the Province.

When this was reported to me, I decided that all my other plans must wait; I marched for Narbonne.

Having arrived there, I reassured its frightened people and posted garrisons among the Ruteni inside the Province, the Volcae Arecomici, the Tolosates, and around Narbonne itself – that is, in all the districts closest to the enemy. I ordered part of the force from the Province and fresh troops that I had brought from Italy to concentrate in the territory of the Helvii, which shares a boundary with the Arverni.

As a result of these measures, Lucterius was checked and then forced to 8 retire, because he thought it dangerous to enter country covered by Roman detachments. And so I set out for the territory of the Helvii.

The Cevennes mountains separate the Helvii from the Arverni. It was the hardest time of the year and snow lay thick on the mountains, blocking the passes. However, by clearing away drifts that were up to six feet deep, the soldiers opened up the route, and thanks to their sweat and toil I got through to the country of the Arverni.

We took them completely by surprise, for they were under the impression that the Cevennes provided them with protection as good as a solid wall: even individual travellers had never before managed to get through the passes at that time of year. I ordered the cavalry to range over the country as widely as possible and frighten the natives as much as they could.

Vercingetorix soon heard of this, through rumours and more reliable reports. The Arverni were terrified. They all went to him, begging him to have a thought for them and not to let their country be pillaged by the enemy,

especially since he could see that they were now the target for the entire
Roman initiative. Influenced by their pleas, Vercingetorix moved his camp
from the territory of the Bituriges closer to that of the Arverni.

9   This was what I had expected he would do, so I stayed there only two
days and then, on the pretext of collecting reinforcements and cavalry, I
went away, leaving young Brutus in command of the troops. I gave him
instructions that the cavalry should range over as wide an area as possible,
in all directions. I said I would try not to be away from the camp longer than
three days.

When these arrangements had been made, I proceeded at full speed to
Vienne, much to the surprise of my escort. There I picked up a fresh contingent of cavalry, which I had sent on there some days earlier.

Then I made my way through the territory of the Aedui into that of the
Lingones, where two legions had their winter quarters. I travelled without
stopping day or night, so that if the Aedui were plotting to kill me, my speed
would thwart their designs. When I reached the camp there, I sent word to
the other legions, and had them all concentrated in one place before news
of my arrival could reach the Arverni.

When Vercingetorix did get to know, he led his army back again into
the country of the Bituriges, and from there set off to attack Gorgobina, an
oppidum of the Boii, whom I had settled there under the protection of the
Aedui after I had defeated them in the battle with the Helvetii.

10   This move by Vercingetorix made it very difficult for me to decide what
to do next. If I kept all the legions in one place for the rest of the winter,
there was a danger that the whole of Gaul might join in the revolt, for they
would see that I was incapable of protecting my friends if a people dependent
on the Aedui were overpowered. If, on the other hand, I led the army out
from their winter quarters too early in the year, I risked getting into difficulties over supplies of grain because of the problems of transporting it.

However, it seemed better to face any difficulties rather than suffer a loss
of prestige and so lose the goodwill of all my supporters. I therefore urged
the Aedui to bring up supplies. I sent ahead to the Boii to tell them I was on
my way and to encourage them to stay loyal and put up a stout resistance
to the enemy's attack. Then, leaving two legions and the heavy baggage
of the entire army at Agedincum, I set out for the country of the Boii.

11   Next day I reached Vellaunodunum, an *oppidum* of the Senones. I decided
to attack it, so that I could have my grain supply free from the threat of an
enemy left in my rear.

In two days we had encircled the *oppidum* with our entrenchments and
on the third day a deputation was sent out to discuss surrender. I ordered
them to collect and hand over their weapons, to bring out all their pack
animals, and to give 600 hostages. I left the legate Gaius Trebonius to see
that these orders were obeyed, and being anxious to finish my journey to
Gorgobina as soon as possible, I set out myself for Cenabum in the territory
of the Carnutes.

The Carnutes had only just heard about the siege of Vellaunodunum and
they thought it would go on for some time. They were arranging for troops

to be sent in to garrison Cenabum, when I reached it, two days after leaving Vellaunodunum. We pitched camp in front of the *oppidum*, but because it was too late to act that day, we put off our attack until the next; I ordered the soldiers to make all the necessary preparations for this.

There was a bridge over the river Loire close to Cenabum, and I was afraid that the inhabitants might escape under cover of darkness, so I ordered two legions to stand by armed all night. Shortly before midnight, the people of Cenabum silently left the *oppidum* and started to cross the river. My patrols reported this to me. I had the gates of the *oppidum* set on fire, then sent inside the legions I had ordered to be ready for action.

The place was now in our hands, and because the narrowness of the bridge and roads had prevented a mass escape, all but a very few of its inhabitants were captured. I had it sacked and set on fire, and distributed the plunder among my soldiers. Then I led my army across the Loire and reached the territory of the Bituriges.

When Vercingetorix heard of my approach, he raised the siege of Gorgo-   12
bina and set out to meet me.

I had begun to attack Noviodunum, an *oppidum* of the Bituriges that was on my route. Envoys had come out from it to beg me to pardon them and spare their lives. In order to complete this campaign with the speed of action that had already brought me success, I ordered their weapons to be collected, their horses to be brought out, and hostages to be given. Some of the hostages had already been handed over and the other conditions were being supervised by centurions and a small number of soldiers, who had been sent inside the place to collect the weapons and horses.

At this point, the cavalry, which was riding in advance of Vercingetorix's marching column, appeared in the distance. As soon as the people of Noviodunum caught sight of them, and thought they now had some hope of being relieved, they raised a cheer and began to seize their weapons, shut the gates, and man the wall. The centurions inside the place could tell from this behaviour that the Gauls had changed their plan, so they drew their swords, got control of the gates, and brought all their men out safely.

I ordered our cavalry out of the camp and engaged Vercingetorix in a   13
cavalry battle. When they got into difficulties, I brought up to help them about 400 German horsemen, whom I had decided to keep with me from the beginning of the campaign. The Gauls were unable to stand up to the attack of the Germans; they were put to flight and, after heavy losses, withdrew to their main column.

With Vercingetorix's cavalry thus routed, the people of Noviodunum were panic-stricken once more. They arrested those they believed responsible for stirring up the people, and after handing these instigators over to me, surrendered themselves.

When matters there had been settled, I set off for Bourges, the largest and best fortified *oppidum* in the territory of the Bituriges and one lying in an extremely fertile part of the country. I was sure that once it had been taken, I should bring the whole tribe into submission.

2 The capture of Bourges

14 Vercingetorix had now suffered a series of setbacks, at Vellaunodunum, Cenabum, and Noviodunum. He therefore called his supporters to a council of war, and pointed out to them that the war must be waged in quite a different way from hitherto. They must direct all their efforts towards cutting the Romans off from forage and supplies.

This would not be difficult, he said, because the Gauls were strong in cavalry and the time of year was in their favour. At that season it was not possible to cut grass, so the enemy would have to send out groups of men to get fodder from barns; as these foraging parties went out, the Gallic cavalry could pick them off daily. In addition, since their lives were at stake they must forget their rights as individuals. All villages and isolated buildings must be set on fire in every direction from the Romans' line of march as far as foragers seemed likely to be able to reach.

They themselves, he claimed, had plenty of supplies because they were supported by the resources of the tribes in whose territory the war was being waged. Not so the Romans, who would either starve or have to take the great risk of venturing too far from their camp. It did not matter whether the Gauls killed them or merely stripped them of their equipment, for without that they could not continue the war.

Vercingetorix proposed that they must also set fire to any *oppida* that were not made absolutely safe by manmade fortifications or natural defences. This would prevent them being used by Gauls as refuges to escape the fighting, and also by Romans as sources of supplies and plunder. If these measures seemed harsh and difficult to bear, they would reckon it much worse to have their wives and children dragged off into slavery, and to be killed themselves: that was the inevitable fate of the vanquished.

15 This proposal was approved unanimously, and in a single day more than 20 towns of the Bituriges were set on fire. The same thing was done in the other tribes and fires could be seen in every direction. Although it grieved them all greatly to do this, they consoled themselves with the thought that victory was practically theirs and that they would quickly recover all they had lost.

There was discussion in a joint council whether Bourges should be burned or defended. The Bituriges fell down at the feet of all the other Gauls, begging not to be compelled to set fire with their own hands to what was perhaps the most beautiful town in the whole of Gaul, at once the pride and the chief protection of their people. They said they would easily defend it because of the strength of its position; it was almost completely surrounded by a river and marsh, with only one very narrow way through.

Their request was granted, though at first Vercingetorix argued against it, only later yielding to their pleas and the pity shown to them by all the others. Troops were chosen specially to defend the *oppidum*.

16 Vercingetorix then followed my march by easy stages and chose for his camp a site protected by marshes and forests, some 16 miles from Bourges. There he was hourly informed by a well-organized system of patrols of what was going on at Bourges, and gave appropriate orders.

He kept a close watch for all our parties going out for grain or fodder. When these became scattered because they were obliged to go farther afield, he would attack them and inflict heavy losses, even though we, for our part, took all precautions we could possibly think of against him, varying the times and routes of our foraging parties.

I had placed my camp on the side of the *oppidum* where there was a gap 17 in the circle formed by the river and marshes, which, as I have already mentioned, offered a narrow way in. I began to build a siege-terrace, bring up protective sheds, and construct two towers on the terrace, for the nature of the terrain made it impossible to construct a ring of fortifications around it.

All the while I kept urging the Boii and the Aedui to supply us with grain. The Aedui were not at all enthusiastic and gave little help; the Boii, a small weak tribe, had very limited resources and soon used up what they did have. So the army was in very serious difficulties over grain supplies, what with the limitations of the Boii, the negative attitude of the Aedui, and the burning of the barns. Things were so serious, in fact, that for several days the men had no grain at all and managed to avoid starvation only by bringing in cattle from distant villages.

But even so, no one uttered a word that was unworthy of the greatness of Rome or of the victories they had already won. Indeed, when I went round and spoke to the men of each legion as they worked, saying that I would raise the siege if they were finding their privations too much to bear, every man of them begged me not to.

They had now served under me, they said, for many years without ever losing their good name or anywhere abandoning a task they had once begun. They would be disgraced if they gave up the siege they had started, and they would rather endure any hardship than fail to avenge the Roman citizens who had been killed at Cenabum through the treachery of the Gauls. They made these same feelings known to the centurions and military tribunes, with requests that they should pass them on to me.

Our siege-towers had already been moved up close to the wall, when I 18 discovered from prisoners that Vercingetorix had moved his camp closer to Bourges because he had run out of fodder. He had then gone off with his cavalry, and the light-armed infantry who normally fought among the cavalry, to lay an ambush where he thought our men would go next day to forage.

When I heard this, we set out silently at midnight and reached the enemy's camp in the morning. However, their patrols quickly reported to them that I was approaching, and they drew up all their forces on some open, rising ground, having hidden their wagons and baggage in the thickest parts of the woods. When this was reported, I ordered my troops to pile their packs together and get their weapons ready for action.

The hill the Gauls were occupying sloped gently up from the base and 19 was almost entirely surrounded by a marsh, no more than 50 feet wide but forming a barrier difficult to cross. They had broken down the causeways over the marsh and now stayed on the high ground, relying on the strength of the site.

They were formed up in tribal groups and were guarding all the shallows and tracks that led to the marsh, their intention being – if the Romans attempted to force a way across – to launch an attack on them from the higher ground as they were floundering in the marshy water. One would have thought, seeing how close they were, that the Gauls were ready to fight on almost equal terms. But a glance at the disparity of the conditions would have made it clear that their display of defiance was a mere sham.

My troops were indignant that the enemy dared to stand in full view of them at such close range, and they demanded the signal to charge. But I explained how costly a victory there would be and how many brave men's lives it would inevitably claim. When I saw them so ready to face any danger to advance my glory, I said, I should be guilty of the greatest injustice if I did not consider their lives more dear than my own. Having calmed their indignation in this way, I led them back to camp the same day, and proceeded to make all the other preparations for the siege of the *oppidum*.

20   When Vercingetorix returned to his forces, he was accused of treachery on the grounds that he had moved his camp closer to the Romans, gone away taking all the cavalry with him, and left such a large army without anyone in supreme command; and when he had gone, the Romans had seized their chance and moved in quickly. All this, they alleged, could not have happened by accident, but must have been deliberately planned: Vercingetorix preferred to have the kingship of Gaul conceded to him by Caesar than bestowed on him by his own people.

To these accusations Vercingetorix replied that he had moved camp because of the shortage of fodder, and they themselves had been urging him to do something about it. He had gone closer to the Romans because he had been prompted by the advantages of the position, which needed no fortification for its defence. As for the cavalry, there ought to have been no need for them on marshy ground, whereas they had been very useful in the area to which he had taken them.

He explained that he had deliberately not handed over the supreme command to anyone when he left, in case the individual chosen might yield to pressure from the mass of the soldiers and fight a pitched battle. For their lack of resolution made it obvious to him that a pitched battle was what they all wanted because they were incapable of enduring hardship any longer. If the Romans' arrival was due to chance, then they had luck to thank for it. If it was due to information supplied by a traitor, then they should thank that person for enabling them, from their position on the hill, to see how small the Roman force was and to despise the cowardice of troops who did not dare to fight but retreated ignominiously to their camp.

'As for supreme power,' he went on, 'I have no need to get that from Caesar as a reward for treachery. I can get it through the victory that I and all the Gauls have already almost won. Take it back for yourselves, if you think that the glory I gain from it is greater than the security you get from me. So you can see I'm telling the truth, listen to what Roman soldiers have to say on the matter.'

At this point he brought forward some camp servants whom he had

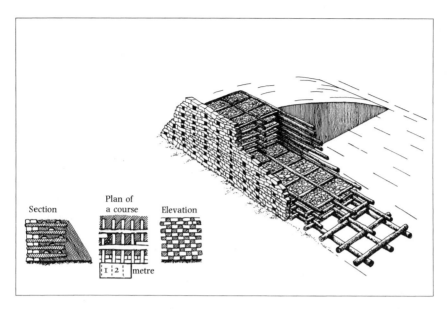

Caesar's description of the typical Celtic defensive work – the *murus gallicus* – which he encountered at Arvaricum, is of particular interest since the type has now been recognized at a number of excavated sites (e.g. at Vertault in the Côte d'Or: *above*). Although Caesar's account implies that the type of construction was developed in response to Roman warfare it embodies techniques of construction, such as the use of vertical walling and horizontal timbering, which can be traced back for 1000 years. The nailing of the timbers with large iron spikes was, however, a new development. The *murus gallicus* type of construction occurs extensively in France and Germany.

captured on a foraging expedition a few days earlier and had been torturing with starvation and chains. They had already been told in advance what their story should be when they were questioned. They said they were Roman legionaries, and that hunger and privation had made them leave the camp secretly to see if they could find any grain or cattle in the fields. The whole army was suffering in the same way; no one had enough strength left to carry on even daily work. For this reason their commander-in-chief had decided to withdraw the army in three days' time, if they made no progress with the siege of the *oppidum*.

'This', said Vercingetorix, 'is what you owe to me whom you charge with being a traitor. It is thanks to me that without shedding a drop of Gallic blood, you see this great, conquering army wasting away with hunger. And I have taken care that when it is routed and retreats in disgrace, no tribe will allow it inside its territory.'

21　　All the people shouted out together and clashed their weapons, as Gauls usually do when they want to show their approval of what a speaker has said. They declared that Vercingetorix was a superb leader and his loyalty should not be doubted: no war strategy could be better than his.

They decided to choose 10,000 men from their combined forces and send them to Bourges. They did not think their national security should rest with the Bituriges alone; if the Bituriges saved the *oppidum*, they realized it would be they who won the glory for the final victory.

22　　Our soldiers showed extraordinary courage, and the Gauls had to resort to all kinds of devices; they are a most ingenious race, very good at imitating and making use of any ideas suggested to them by others. For instance, they pulled our siege hooks away with nooses, and when they had them fast, hauled them inside with windlasses. They also undermined our siege terrace, all the more skilfully because there are extensive iron mines in their country, and so they know all about the various methods of underground working.

All along the entire wall they had built storeyed towers and had covered these with hides. At that stage they were making constant sorties, day and night, and either setting fire to our terrace or attacking our soldiers when they were at work there. As our ramp grew and the height of our towers increased day by day, they added extra storeys between the uprights of their own towers to ensure they were not overtopped by ours. They also countermined the subterranean tunnels we constructed, using sharpened stakes that had been hardened in fire, boiling pitch, and enormous rocks to prevent them being extended closer to the wall.

23　　All Gallic walls are built roughly on this plan. Wooden beams are laid

❧

The art of the Gauls, with its love of the abstract and of simple line, would have pervaded Gaulish life. Everything was a medium for decoration – sword scabbards, horse trappings, fabrics, pottery and even, among some of the more remote tribes, the human body itself, which was tatooed with blue woad. This stone head from the sanctuary of Roquepertuse, in southern France, is a brilliant example of Celtic abstraction at its most perfect.

on the ground at regular intervals of two feet along the whole length of the wall and at right angles to it. They are fastened together on the inside and covered with a thick layer of rubble; at the front large stones are used to form a facing, which fills in the spaces between the timbers. When this first course has been laid and made firm, another is added. This is set on top in such a way that although there is a two-foot space between its timbers as well, they do not touch those of the first course but are separated from them by a vertical interval of two feet. A large stone is inserted to keep every beam apart from each of its neighbours and so the timbers are held firmly in position. One course is added to another in this way and the fabric is built up until the wall reaches the required height.

The varied appearance resulting from this method of construction is not unsightly, with alternating timbers and stones running in straight rows at proper intervals from each other. It is also a very useful structure, ideally suited for the defence of towns. The stonework protects against fire and the timber against battering rams; for rams cannot pierce or shake to bits such a structure, secured as it is on the inside by continuous timbers up to 40 feet long.

Devices of this kind hampered our operations, as did the constant cold weather and continual rain. But our men worked ceaselessly and overcame all these difficulties; in 25 days they raised a siege-terrace 330 feet wide and 80 feet high, and this almost touched the wall.   24

One night, I was staying up as usual with the working parties, urging the men not to leave off their efforts even for a moment, when shortly before midnight smoke was seen rising from the terrace; the enemy had dug a tunnel underneath and set it on fire.

At the same moment a shout went up all along the wall and the Gauls came pouring out of the *oppidum* by the two gates on either side of our towers. Others began to throw burning torches and dry wood down from the wall on to the terrace, and they poured down pitch and every other kind of inflammable material.

It was hard to know where first to direct our resistance or which threatened area to relieve. But it was my practice always to keep two legions in front of the camp ready for action throughout the night, while larger numbers of men worked on the siege operations in shifts. So we were able to act quickly, some men fighting off the Gauls who had come out of the *oppidum*, while others dragged the towers back and made a gap in the terrace, and all the men still in the camp rushed out to extinguish the fire.

Throughout the rest of the night, fighting went on everywhere, and the enemy's hope of victory was being renewed all the time; they could see that the sheds that protected the men moving our towers had been burnt, making   25

❧

Aerial photography using modern infrared techniques is adding greatly to our understanding of Roman military works. Rene Goguey's photograph, taken in 1976, shows the line of Caesar's siege works at Alesia with remarkable clarity.

it difficult for our troops to advance without cover to help their fellows, whereas in their own ranks fresh men were continually relieving those who were exhausted. They thought the whole fate of Gaul depended on that very moment, and, as we looked on, there was an incident I consider so remarkable I must not leave it out.

One Gaul stood in front of the gate of the *oppidum* taking lumps of tallow and pitch that were handed to him and throwing them into the fire opposite one of our towers. He was pierced in the right side by an arrow from a catapult and fell dead. Another Gaul, standing nearby, stepped across the body and did the same job. When he too was killed in the same way by a catapult shot, a third man took his place, and then a fourth. The post was not abandoned by its defenders until the fire on the terrace had been put out, the enemy pushed back at every point, and the fighting brought to an end.

26   Having tried everything, but without success, the Gauls decided next day to escape from Bourges, at the urgent insistence of Vercingetorix. By making their attempt at dead of night they hoped to succeed without serious loss; Vercingetorix's camp was not far away and the continuous stretch of marshland would hamper the Romans' pursuit.

At night they were already getting ready to escape when suddenly the wives came running out into the open. Weeping, they flung themselves down at the feet of their menfolk, begging and praying that they should not abandon them and the children they shared to the cruelty of the enemy, since they were not by nature strong enough to join in the flight.

People facing extreme danger are usually too afraid to feel any pity, and so the men remained unpersuaded. Realizing this, their womenfolk began to shout out and make signs to our troops, betraying the planned escape. This frightened the Gauls into abandoning their intention – they were afraid that our cavalry would seize the roads before they could get away.

27   Next day one of our towers was moved forward, and the other siegeworks I had had made were brought into position. There was a heavy rainstorm, and it occurred to me that this would be a good opportunity to launch an assault, because I noticed that the guards on the wall were not quite so carefully posted as usual. I told our men to go about their work less energetically and explained to them what I wanted done.

The legions got ready for action outside the camp. They were under the cover of the protective sheds and thus concealed from enemy view. Now at last, I urged, they could taste the fruits of victory, the reward for all their labours. I offered prizes to those who would be first to climb the wall, then I gave the signal to attack.

The soldiers suddenly darted out from every point and quickly got control 28 of the wall. The Gauls had not expected this, and they panicked. They were dislodged from the wall and towers, but formed up in the marketplace and other open spaces in wedge-shaped masses, with the intention of fighting a pitched battle against attackers coming from any direction.

When they saw that no one was coming down to meet them on level ground, but instead our men were going right round them, occupying the whole circuit of the wall, they were afraid they would be cut off from all hope of escape. So they threw their weapons away and, rushing in a mass, made for the farthest parts of the *oppidum*. There some of them were killed by our troops as they were crammed together in the narrow gateways; others got out through the gates but were then killed by our cavalry.

None of our men stopped to think about booty; they were so infuriated by the massacre of Romans at Cenabum, and by the efforts they had had to make over the siege, that they spared neither the old nor the women nor the children.

Of the whole population, which had numbered some 40,000, barely 800 got through safely to Vercingetorix; these people had rushed out of the place at the very first sound of the attack. Vercingetorix took them into his camp silently, late at night. He was afraid there would be a mutiny in his camp if they came in *en masse* and so aroused the compassion of the common soldiers. He therefore stationed his friends and the tribal leaders on the road some distance from his camp with orders to sort them out and see that they were conducted to whatever part of the camp had been assigned to each tribe at the beginning of the campaign.

Next day a council of war was called. Vercingetorix encouraged his **29** people, urging them not to be too downhearted or distressed by this setback. The Romans had won, not by valour or in a fair fight, but because of some ingenuity and skill in siegecraft in which the Gauls were inexperienced.

People who expected everything to go their way in war were mistaken, he said, adding that he had never been in favour of defending Bourges, as they themselves could bear witness. The present setback had been caused by the Bituriges's lack of sense and the blind acquiescence of the others to their proposal. But, he claimed, he would soon remedy this by greater successes. By his own efforts he would win over the tribes that were not yet in agreement with their aims. Then he would create a single policy for the whole of Gaul, and had already almost brought this about. With Gaul thus united, the whole world could not stand against them.

He thought it only fair in the meantime, for the safety of them all, to set about fortifying the camp, to make it easier for them to withstand any sudden attacks the enemy might make.

This speech of his was well received by the Gauls, especially because **30** Vercingetorix himself had not lost heart after suffering so great a defeat, and had not gone into hiding to avoid being seen by his troops. He was thought to have shown particular foresight and intuition because, even before things became desperate, it had been his view first that Bourges should be burned, and later that it should be abandoned. And so, although most commanders have their authority diminished by failure, with Vercingetorix just the opposite happened – his reputation grew with every day that followed his defeat.

At the same time, through his assurances, the Gauls became optimistic about their chances of inducing the other tribes to join them. And then, for the first time, they set about building a fortified camp. They were unused to hard work, but had been so shocked by the experience of defeat that they thought they must put up with all they were told to do.

31   Vercingetorix did all he had promised, using every means he could think of to bring the other tribes into the alliance, even trying to seduce them with bribes and promises. For this job he chose men who were particularly suited and likely to succeed either because they had a subtle way with words or because they were friends of the tribes concerned.

He saw to it that those who had escaped after the sack of Bourges were given weapons and clothing. At the same time he took measures to bring his weakened forces back up to full strength; the various tribes were ordered to provide troops, each one being told the precise number to be brought to the camp and the day by which they were to arrive. He also gave orders that all archers (of whom there were very many in Gaul) should be sought out and sent to him. By these measures he quickly made good the losses at Bourges.

Meanwhile Teutomatus, king of the Nitiobriges, whose father Ollovico had been given the title 'Friend' by the Roman Senate, joined Vercingetorix, taking with him a large number of cavalry, some of them from his own tribe, others whom he had hired in Aquitania.

3 The revolt of the Aedui

32   I stayed at Bourges for several days. We found grain and other supplies in abundance there and this enabled my troops to recover from the hardships and lack of food they had suffered. Winter was now almost over. It was time for campaigning to begin, and I had decided to march against the enemy to see if I could lure them out of the marshes and forests or else blockade them where they were.

At that point leading men came from the Aedui to beg me to help them in what was a most critical time for their tribe. The situation was extremely dangerous, they said: although their long-established custom had always been to elect a single magistrate to hold sovereign power for one year, there were now two magistrates in office, each claiming to have been appointed legally. One of these was Convictolitavis, a wealthy and distinguished young man; the other was Cotus, who came from a very ancient family and was himself powerful and well connected, and whose brother Valetiacus had held the same office in the previous year.

Their whole country, they said, was now in arms; the council was split and so was the people, with each of the two claimants having his dependants to support him. If the quarrel were allowed to go on any longer, it would lead to civil war. Only my intervention and authority would prevent that happening.

33   Although I thought it would be very much against our interests to withdraw from the fighting front, still I was well aware of the serious harm that can result from disputes of that kind. The Aedui were a powerful tribe whose ties with Rome were very close; I had always fostered their interests and treated them with every distinction. So I thought my first duty should be to prevent their coming to blows with each other, in case the side that considered itself the weaker should summon help from Vercingetorix.

Aeduan law forbids those who hold the chief magistracy to leave their country, so in order not to give the impression that I had slighted their rights or their laws, I decided to go myself into their land, and summoned their whole council and the two men who were in dispute to meet me at Decetia.

Almost all the tribe assembled there, and I was told what had led to the quarrel. Apparently just a few people had been summoned to a secret assembly, held not in the proper place nor at the proper time, and Cotus's election had there been announced by his brother. However, Aeduan law forbade two members of the same family to be appointed magistrates while both were alive, or indeed to be members of the council together. I therefore made Cotus resign. Convictolitavis had been appointed according to the customs of the tribe by priests when the office was vacant, so I told him to continue in his magistracy.

Having decided the dispute in this way, I urged the Aedui to forget their quarrels and differences and, putting everything else aside, to concentrate their energies on the war we were fighting. I told them to look forward to receiving from me the rewards they deserved once Gaul had been completely conquered, and I asked them to send all their cavalry and 10,000 infantry quickly, so that I could station them at various places to guard the grain supplies.   34

I then divided my army into two parts. Four legions and part of the cavalry I gave to Labienus to take into the territory of the Senones and the Parisii; I myself took the other six and the rest of the cavalry into the territory of the Arverni, travelling along the line of the river Allier towards Gergovia.

When Vercingetorix heard of this, he broke down all the bridges over the Allier and began to march along the bank opposite us. The two armies had thus taken separate banks of the river. They pitched camp more or less opposite and in sight of each other. The Gauls posted patrols along their bank to prevent us building a bridge and so getting across the river. My position was therefore difficult; I was in danger of being barred by the river for most of the summer, as it is usually autumn before the Allier can be forded.   35

To avoid being held up there, I pitched camp in some woodland opposite one of the bridges that Vercingetorix had had destroyed, and I stayed there next day with two legions, concealed. I sent on the rest of my troops with all the baggage, as usual, but with some of the cohorts split into smaller units to give the impression that the number of legions was the same. I ordered them to cover as much ground as they could, and then, when the time of day made me think they must have reached camp, I started to rebuild the bridge on the original piles, the lower parts of which were still intact.

The work was soon finished. I took my legions across, chose a suitable site for a camp, and then recalled the rest of my troops. When Vercingetorix discovered what I had done, he went ahead by forced marches, to avoid being compelled to fight a pitched battle against his will.

After five days' marching from there I reached Gergovia. On the day of our arrival we fought a cavalry skirmish and reconnoitred the position of the town. It was situated on a very high mountain and every approach to it was difficult. I gave up any hope of taking the place by storm, and decided to do nothing about besieging it until I had arranged about our grain supply.   36

Vercingetorix for his part had pitched camp near the *oppidum* and had kept the forces from the various tribes in separate contingents positioned at short distances all around his headquarters. They occupied all the heights of that mountain ridge, from which they could be seen. The sight they presented was terrifying.

Every day at dawn Vercingetorix ordered those tribal chiefs he had chosen as his councillors, to come to him to pass on information or to make arrangements. Hardly a day was allowed to go by without cavalry being sent into action, with archers included among them, to test the spirit and courage of each man among his forces.

Opposite the *oppidum* was a hill rising from the very foot of the mountain. It had strong natural defences, being steep on all sides. If our men could get control of it, it seemed likely that we should be able to cut the Gauls off from most of their water supply and from foraging at will; but they held the place with a garrison, though not a very strong one.

I set out from camp at dead of night and gained control of that hill, dislodging the garrison before help could arrive from the *oppidum*. I stationed two legions on it and connected this smaller camp with the larger one by means of a double trench 12 feet wide, so that men could come and go, even one at a time, free from the threat of any sudden enemy attack.

37 While these operations were taking place at Gergovia, the Aeduan Convictolitavis, whom I had confirmed in his magistracy, as I have described above, was approached by the Arverni and bribed to enter negotiations with some young men of his tribe, led by Litaviccus and his brothers, members of a very distinguished family.

He shared the money with them and urged them to remember that they were free men, born to rule. The Aedui were the one tribe preventing what would otherwise be certain victory for the Gauls. Since it was their influence that prevailed on the other tribes to stay out of the alliance, when once they changed their allegiance to the Gallic side, the Romans would have no foothold in Gaul.

He admitted he was under a certain obligation to me, but suggested that I had really done nothing more for him than see him win his claim, when it was in any case a perfectly just one; besides, he thought their nation's freedom was more important than that. Why, he went on, should the Aedui turn to Caesar to interpret Aeduan rights and laws? The Romans did not seek their help in questions of Roman law.

These words of their chief magistrate, and the money he gave them, quickly won the young men over, and they offered to lead the enterprise. However, there was some question about how to put it into practice, since they were not confident the tribe could be induced to go to war without a very good reason.

It was decided that Litaviccus should be put in command of the 10,000 men who were to be sent to serve me in the war; while he organized their march, his brothers were to hurry on ahead to me. They decided, too, how the rest of their plan should be carried out.

38 Litaviccus took command of the troops. When they were about 30 miles

from Gergovia he suddenly called a meeting of the soldiers and addressed them, with tears in his eyes.

'Where are we going, soldiers?' he said. 'All our cavalry, all our men of rank have perished. Eporedorix and Viridomarus, two of our leading men, have been accused of treason and put to death by the Romans without a trial. Let these men who were there, and who escaped from the massacre, tell you about it. Grief for my brothers and all my other relatives who have been killed makes it impossible for me to describe what happened myself.'

Then some men were brought forward. Litaviccus had already told them what they were to say, and they gave the troops the same tale he had told. The Aeduan cavalry had been killed, they said, because they were alleged to have entered negotiations with the Arverni; they themselves had hidden among the mass of soldiers and had escaped while the massacre was still going on.

The Aedui shouted out in anger. They begged Litaviccus to consider what was best for them. 'Oh, yes,' he said, 'if you think it needs consideration, instead of marching straight to Gergovia and joining the Arverni! Does any of us doubt that the Romans, having committed such an abominable crime, are even now on their way to kill us too? So, if we have any spirit left in us, let us avenge the shameful death that our fellow Aeduans suffered, by killing these robbers we have here.'

With that he pointed to some Roman citizens, who, relying on Litaviccus's protection, were with the Aeduan troops. The large quantity of grain and other provisions they had with them he plundered; the men themselves he had cruelly tortured to death.

He then sent messengers out into every part of Aeduan territory and, by using the same false story about the massacre of the cavalry and the nobles, roused the people, urging them to avenge the wrongs they had suffered, by acting as he had done.

Eporedorix and Viridomarus had come with the cavalry contingent sent **39** by their tribe in response to my particular summons. Eporedorix was a young man from one of the noblest Aeduan families and was very powerful in his country. Viridomarus was the same age as Eporedorix and just as influential, but he was not of such a distinguished family; Diviciacus had recommended him to me, and I had raised him, though his origins were humble, to a position of great honour. These two were rivals for power and in the recent dispute about the supreme magistracy, Eporedorix had put all his weight behind Convictolitavis, while Viridomarus was equally committed to supporting Cotus.

Eporedorix now heard of Litaviccus's enterprise, and came, in the middle of the night, to tell me of it. He begged me not to allow his tribe to lose the friendship of the Roman people just because of the misguided plans of some of its young men. In his opinion that would be the inevitable result if all those thousands of men joined Vercingetorix, for neither the men's relatives nor the tribe as a whole could disregard their safety or think it a matter of slight importance.

I was extremely disturbed by this news, because I had always treated the **40**

Aedui with particular consideration. Without a moment's hesitation I took four legions ready for action, together with all the cavalry I had, and left the camp.

In such circumstances there was no time to reduce the size of the camp; everything seemed to depend on speed of action: I left the legate Gaius Fabius with two legions to guard the camp. I ordered the brothers of Litaviccus to be arrested, but discovered that they had fled to the enemy a short time before.

I urged my men not to resent the laborious march the crisis made inevitable. They all responded with great enthusiasm, and after advancing 25 miles, we sighted the Aeduan column.

I sent forward cavalry to slow down their march and hinder their progress, but issued strict instructions to them all that they were to kill no one. I told Eporedorix and Viridomarus, whom the Aedui believed killed, to move about among the cavalry and speak to their own people. They were recognized, and the deceit of Litaviccus became plain; the Aedui began to stretch out their hands to indicate surrender, and threw down their weapons, begging for their lives.

Litaviccus fled to Gergovia with his dependants; according to Gallic custom it is a crime for such people to desert their patrons even when the
41 situation is desperate. I sent messengers to the Aeduan authorities to tell them that although, according to the rights of war, I should have been perfectly justified in putting their men to death, I had instead spared them as an act of kindness.

4 The attack on Gergovia

I gave my army three hours of the night to rest before starting towards Gergovia. We were almost halfway there when some horsemen, sent by Fabius, met us and described the great danger that had threatened them. They explained that the enemy had attacked our camp in full force and then had repeatedly sent in fresh troops to relieve those who were weary. In this way they wore our men out; for the size of the camp meant that the same troops had to stay on the rampart with no relief, and they became exhausted with the continual exertion this involved.

Many of our soldiers, they said, had been wounded by the hail of arrows and every other kind of missile, but the artillery had been very useful in helping them hold out. As the Gauls had now withdrawn, Fabius was blocking up all the gates except two, and adding breastworks to the rampart, in readiness for meeting a similar attack the next day. When I heard this, I summoned a supreme effort from my men, and succeeded in reaching the camp before dawn.

42 While this was happening at Gergovia, the Aedui received the first messages from Litaviccus. They did not allow themselves time to check the truth of his reports, but accepted idle rumour as established fact. Some of them were influenced by greed, others by anger and that impetuousness which is the most marked characteristic of their race.

They plundered Roman citizens of their property, killing some and dragging others off into slavery. Convictolitavis helped the movement along, goading the people on to frenzy, so that once they had committed serious crime they would be too ashamed to return to their senses.

One of my military tribunes, Marcus Aristius, who was on his way to join his legion, was induced to leave the *oppidum* of Cabillonum by the promise of safe conduct. Roman merchants, who had settled there, were forced to leave with him. As soon as they set off, the Aedui attacked them and robbed them of all their baggage. The Romans fought back, but the Gauls surrounded and attacked them throughout the day and night, calling more of their people to arms after many had been killed on both sides.

Meanwhile they received news that all their army was in my power. **43** At this they came running to Aristius, claiming that their government was not responsible for what had happened. They ordered an inquiry into the theft of the property, confiscated the goods of Litaviccus and his brothers, and sent envoys to me to excuse themselves.

Their aim in doing this was to get their own people back. But they were implicated in the crime and much taken with the idea of the profits to be had from the plunder. Many of them had been party to it, and they were terrified at the prospect of being punished. So they set about making secret plans for war, and sent deputations to win support from the other tribes.

I knew all about this, but still I spoke with their envoys as mildly as I could, telling them that I did not judge their tribe too harshly merely because of the ignorance and irresponsible actions of the ordinary people; nor had my goodwill towards them been affected.

I was expecting the disturbance in Gaul to spread, and wanted to avoid having hostile tribes all around me. I began to plan how I could leave the neighbourhood of Gergovia and once more concentrate all my troops. But I was anxious that my departure should not appear to be caused by my fear of revolt and so resemble flight.

While I was thinking about this problem, there occurred what seemed to **44** be an opportunity of fighting a successful action. I had gone to the smaller camp to inspect the defence works, when I noticed that a hill the enemy controlled was completely deserted; on previous days there had been so many men on it the ground was scarcely visible.

I was surprised, and questioned some of the deserters, who now came to to me in great numbers every day. Their answers all confirmed what I had already discovered myself from my patrols: the top of this hill was almost level, but it was wooded and narrow where it gave access to the farther side of the *oppidum*; the enemy were very anxious about the safety of this hill, being convinced that if the Romans, who controlled one hill, got control of this one too, the Gauls would clearly be almost walled in, unable to get out and prevented from foraging. Vercingetorix had withdrawn all men available in order to fortify this ridge.

When I discovered this, I sent several cavalry squadrons there about **45** midnight, with instructions to range over the whole district making rather more noise and disturbance than usual.

At dawn I ordered a large number of pack horses and mules to be brought out of the camp. They were to have their pack saddles removed, and their drivers were told to put on helmets and ride round on the higher ground giving the appearance of being regular cavalry. I sent with them a few cavalrymen, who were to range over a wider area and make sure they were seen.

They were all told to make a long detour and converge on the same place. All this could be seen, at a distance, from Gergovia, since that *oppidum* commanded a view of the camp, but it was too far away for the enemy to make out with any certainty what was going on.

I sent one legion along the same ridge and when it had advanced a little way, had it halt lower down the hill, concealed in a wood. The Gauls became more suspicious that something was afoot, and transferred all their forces there to work on fortifying the hill. When I could see that their camps were empty, I had my men cover up the crests of their helmets and hide the standards. Then I moved them from the larger camp to the smaller one, in small groups to avoid being noticed from the *oppidum*.

I explained to the legates in charge of the various legions what I wanted done, warning them particularly to keep tight control of their men and prevent them from advancing too far in their eagerness to fight or in hope of plunder. I explained what a disadvantage the slope of the ground was for us; speed of action was the only way to counter this; it was a question of making a surprise attack, not fighting a regular battle. After that, I gave the signal for attack. I sent the Aedui up the hill at the same time, but by a different route, on the right.

46 From the point on level ground at which the ascent began, the distance to the wall of the *oppidum* was just over a mile, or would have been if the path had been straight. But the distance to be covered on foot was greater because of the zigzags necessary to ease the gradient. About halfway up and following the contour of the hill, the Gauls had built a six-foot wall out of huge stones, to hamper our attack. All the slope below this had been left unoccupied, but the upper part of the hill, right up to the wall of the *oppidum*, had been covered with encampments, placed very close together.

When the signal was given, our troops quickly moved up to this wall, climbed over it, and captured three of the encampments. These were taken at such speed that Teutomatus, king of the Nitiobriges, was surprised in his tent, as he was taking his midday rest. He just managed to escape from groups of soldiers looking for plunder, and got away, naked to the waist and riding a wounded horse.

47 Having achieved my purpose, I ordered the recall to be sounded. The Tenth legion, which was with me, halted at once. The soldiers of the other legions did not hear the trumpet call, because they were on the far side of quite a wide ravine; however, their legates and military tribunes, acting in accordance with my instructions, tried to keep them in check. But the soldiers were elated at the prospect of a quick victory, by the enemy's flight, and by memories of their own success in earlier engagements. Nothing seemed to them too difficult for their valour to achieve, and they went on with their pursuit right up to the wall and gates of Gergovia itself.

Then shouts went up from every part of the town. Those who were some distance away from the action were terrified by the sudden uproar; they thought the enemy was already inside the gates and so rushed out of the *oppidum*. The wives began to throw clothing and silver down from the walls. Leaning over, with bared breasts and outstretched hands, they called on the Roman soldiers to spare them and not to kill women and children, as they had done at Bourges. Some of the women were lowered by hand from the wall and gave themselves up to the soldiers.

Lucius Fabius was a centurion in the Eighth legion; that day he had been heard by his men to say that he was inspired by the rewards that had been won at Bourges and so was not going to let anyone climb the wall before he did. Now he got three men from his company to hoist him up, climbed the wall and then in turn pulled each of them up on to it.

Meanwhile those Gauls who had gathered on the other side of the *oppidum* **48** to help with the fortifications, as described above, heard the sound of shouting first, and then were roused by a series of reports reaching them that Gergovia was in our hands. Sending their cavalry on ahead, they hurried there in a great throng.

Each man as he arrived took up position close up to the wall, adding to the numbers of their fighting men. When a great crowd of them had gathered, the women, who just a short time before were stretching out their hands to the Roman soldiers from the wall, began to call upon their own menfolk and in Gallic fashion showed their dishevelled hair and brought their children out for the men to see.

Both numbers and position were against us now, and it was not easy for our men to hold out. They were already exhausted by their rapid climb and by the length of time they had been in action, whereas their opponents were fresh, having just come on the scene.

I could see that we were fighting on unfavourable ground and that the **49** enemy forces were being strengthened. I was anxious about the safety of my men, and so sent orders to the legate Titus Sextius, whom I had left to guard the smaller camp, to get his cohorts out of camp quickly and draw them up at the foot of the hill on the enemy's right flank. If he saw our men dislodged from their position, he would be a threat to the enemy and restrict their pursuit. I myself advanced with my legion a little way from the position it had taken up, and waited there to see how the battle would turn out.

There was fierce fighting at close quarters; the Gauls relied on their **50** superior position and numbers, our men on their own valour. Suddenly the Aedui, whom I had sent by another route on the right to create a diversion, appeared on our right flank. The weapons of these Aedui were like those of the other Gauls, and this terrified our men. Even though it was obvious that their right shoulders were uncovered, the usual sign to show they were friends, the troops thought that this had been done by the enemy to trick them. At that moment too, the centurion Lucius Fabius and the men who had climbed the wall with him were surrounded and killed, and flung down from the wall.

Marcus Petronius, a centurion in the same legion, tried to break down the gates but was overpowered by the throng. He had already been wounded many times. Realizing there was no hope left for him, he shouted to the men of his company who had followed him, 'I can't save both myself and you. But at least I'll do what I can to help you get away alive. I got you into this because I was looking for glory. Take this chance! Look after yourselves!'

As he said this he charged into the middle of the enemy, killed two, and drove the rest back a short way from the gate. His comrades tried to help him. 'It's no use your trying to save me,' he said, 'I've already lost too much blood, and my strength is gone. So get away, while there's a chance. Get back to the legion!' Soon after this he fell, fighting. His action had saved his men.

51   Our men were being hard pressed from every side, and were eventually driven down from their position, with the loss of 46 centurions. However, the Tenth legion, which had been drawn up in support on rather more favourable ground, prevented the Gauls from pursuing them too ruthlessly. This legion was in turn supported by cohorts from the Thirteenth, which had been brought out of the smaller camp by the legate Titus Sextius and had occupied higher ground.

As soon as the legions reached level ground, they halted, turning about to face the enemy. Vercingetorix withdrew his forces from the foot of the hill and led them back inside their fortifications. That day we lost almost 700 men.

52   Next day I called a meeting of the troops. I reprimanded them for their rashness and overeagerness, in having decided for themselves where they should advance and what action they should take. They had failed to halt when the recall was sounded, and they had disobeyed the orders of their military tribunes and legates.

I pointed out the possible effects of having to fight when the enemy had the advantage of position, and explained what had prompted my own action at Bourges, when, although I had caught the enemy without their leader and cavalry, I had let almost certain victory go to avoid suffering even the smallest losses by fighting on unfavourable ground.

I admired their bravery in not allowing the fortifications of the camp, the height of the hill, or the *oppidum* wall to stop them. But equally I blamed their lack of control, and the highhandedness apparent in their assumption that they knew more about winning victories and about the results of military actions than their commander-in-chief. I looked for discipline and self-control

53 in a soldier just as much as valour and bravery. After this harangue, I concluded by encouraging the men not to be upset by what had recently happened. They must not imagine that it was caused by any valour on the part of the Gauls; it was the unfavourable ground that had been responsible for our reverse.

My views about withdrawing from Gergovia remained unchanged, so I led the legions out of camp and drew them up in battle formation in a suitable position. Even so, Vercingetorix came down into the plain. There was a cavalry skirmish in which we came off better, and then I took my army back into camp.

The same thing happened the next day too. Then, thinking that enough had been done to deflate the conceit of the Gauls and to strengthen the morale of my own troops, I moved camp and marched into the territory of the Aedui. The enemy did not pursue us even then. On the third day we reached the river Allier, and when we had repaired a bridge, I led my army across.

There I was greeted by the Aeduans Viridomarus and Eporedorix, and 54 learned from them that Litaviccus had set out with all the cavalry to try to win over the Aeduans. It was essential, they said, for them to get there before him to keep the tribe loyal to us.

Even though I had by this time much clear evidence of the treachery of the Aedui, and thought that if these two men went off to them, the revolt would break out all the sooner, I still decided to let them go, so that I should not appear to be insulting them, or give the impression that I was afraid.

As they were leaving I briefly outlined what I had done for the Aedui, reminding them of the degraded condition they had been in when I received them into alliance, how they had been kept inside their *oppida*, deprived of their lands, stripped of all their forces, obliged to pay tribute and to meet the most humiliating demands for hostages. I recalled the prosperity and importance I had given them, so that they had not only regained their former power but seemed to have achieved greater prestige and influence than ever before. I then let the two Aeduans go, telling them to pass on this reminder to their tribe.

The Aeduan *oppidum* of Noviodunum occupied a good defensive position 55 on the banks of the river Loire. I had collected in it all the hostages from the various Gallic tribes, the stores of grain, the public funds, and a great deal of my own luggage and that of my troops. I had also sent to it large numbers of horses that had been brought in Italy and Spain for this campaign.

When Eporedorix and Viridomarus reached Noviodunum, they heard news of what was happening in their tribe: Litaviccus had been received by the Aedui at Bibracte, their most important *oppidum*; the chief magistrate Convictolitavis and most of their tribal council had met him there, and envoys had been sent officially to Vercingetorix to make a treaty of peace and friendship with him.

They thought this was a chance not to be missed. So they killed the guards at Noviodunum and those who had gathered there as traders. They shared the money and horses between them, and had all the hostages from the various states taken to the magistrate at Bibracte. They did not think they could possibly hold the *oppidum*, so they set it on fire, to prevent its being of any use to us. They carried away by boat all the grain they could in the time and the rest they burned or dumped in the river.

They then began to collect troops from the neighbouring districts, posting garrisons and guards along the banks of the Loire and making displays of their cavalry all over the area. Their aim was to intimidate the people there and to see if they could cut us off from our grain supply, or bring us to such a state of privation that we could be forced to withdraw into the Province. They were greatly encouraged in this hope because the Loire was so swollen with melting snow it seemed absolutely impossible to ford.

56 I learned what had happened and decided I must act quickly. We might have to build bridges, and if, while doing so, we had to deal with an attack, it would be better to build them before the enemy could bring up larger forces.

I could always change my whole plan of campaign and withdraw into the Province, but I did not think I should adopt that course, however serious the threat. I thought it was out of the question because of the disgrace and humiliation involved, and because, in any case, there would be difficulties too in getting across the barrier of the Cevennes. More important, I was extremely anxious about Labienus and the legions I had sent with him. Therefore marching by day and night and so covering much greater distances than usual, we reached the Loire before anyone thought possible.

The cavalry discovered a ford that would serve in such an emergency, when all that was necessary was for the men to keep their arms and shoulders above the water to hold up their weapons. Cavalry were positioned at intervals in the water to break the force of the current.

The enemy were unnerved by the sudden sight of us, and I was able to lead the army safely across. We found grain and a good supply of cattle in the fields, and with these I made good the inadequacies in our supplies before setting out to march into the territory of the Senones.

5 Labienus at Paris

57 While I was thus engaged, Labienus had left the draft that had recently arrived from Italy at Agedincum to protect the baggage. He himself had then set out with his four legions for Paris, an *oppidum* of the Parisii, situated on an island in the river Seine.

When the enemy heard of his arrival there, large forces from the neighbouring tribes assembled. The supreme command was given to an Aulercan called Camulogenus, who although extremely old was called to this honour because of his outstanding knowledge of warfare. He observed that there was an unbroken stretch of marshes, draining into the Seine and making that whole area almost impassable, and it was there that he took up position, meaning to prevent our men getting across.

58 Labienus first tried to bring up protective sheds, and then to stabilize the marshy land with hurdles and piles of earth in order to make a causeway across it. He found this too difficult, however. So he quietly left the camp soon after midnight, and marching along the same route as he had come, reached Metiosedum, an *oppidum* of the Senones situated, like Paris, on an island in the Seine.

He seized about 50 ships, quickly lashed them together and using them as a bridge sent troops across to the island. Most of the inhabitants of the place had been called to the war; those who had remained behind were terrified by this unexpected turn of events, and so he gained control of Metiosedum without a struggle.

He rebuilt the bridge, which the enemy had broken down a few days earlier, took his army across, and began to march down river to Paris. The Gauls, informed of this by fugitives from Metiosedum, ordered Paris to be set on fire and its bridges to be destroyed. They then left the marshes, moved towards the banks of the Seine, and established camp opposite Paris, in a position facing Labienus.

By this time it was known that I had withdrawn from Gergovia, and **59** now rumours were going around concerning the revolt of the Aedui and the success of the rebellion in Gaul. In conversation with our own native troops, Gauls were confidently asserting that my march to the Loire had been stopped, and famine had forced me to withdraw into the Province. When the Bellovaci, who had already set their minds on revolt, heard of the Aeduan rebellion, they began to mobilize their forces, openly making preparations for war.

Labienus saw that the situation had now changed dramatically. He realized that he must make significant alterations to his plans. He no longer contemplated making conquests or inflicting damage on the enemy in the field, but was concerned merely to get his army back to Agedincum intact. For on the one side he was threatendd by the Bellovaci, considered to be the toughest tribe in Gaul, and on the other Camulogenus was established, with a well-equipped army ready for action. His own present position was such that his legions were cut off from their reserves and baggage by a great river. Suddenly confronted by such formidable difficulties, Labienus saw that he must look to courage and resolution to save them.

Towards evening he called a council of war, at which he urged his officers **60** to pay scrupulous attention to his orders and their efficient execution. He put a Roman of equestrian rank in charge of each of the ships he had brought from Metiosedum, with orders to sail silently downstream at about ten o'clock at night for a distance of four miles, and then wait for him there.

He told the five cohorts that he considered would be least reliable in open battle to remain behind to guard the camp, ordering the other five cohorts of that same legion to set out and march upstream at midnight, taking all the baggage with them and making as much noise as they could. He also got together some smaller craft, which he sent in the same direction, with instructions that they should be rowed with much splashing of oars. Soon afterwards he himself quietly left the camp with three legions and marched downstream to the place where he had ordered the ships to put in.

A great storm suddenly blew up, and so their arrival there took by surprise **61** the patrols the enemy had posted all along the river. They were overpowered by our men. The legions and the cavalry were quickly sent across the river under the supervision of the officers of equestrian rank in charge of that part of the operation.

Just before dawn the enemy received simultaneous reports that there was unusual commotion in the Roman camp, that a large column was marching upstream, that the sound of oars could be heard in the same direction, and that a little way downstream soldiers were being ferried across the river. These reports made the enemy think the legions were crossing at three different places, and that they were all preparing for flight because of their alarm at the revolt of the Aedui.

They therefore divided their own forces also into three sections. One of these was left on guard opposite the Roman camp; a small detachment was sent in the direction of Metiosedum with orders to advance only as far as the boats had gone; the rest of their forces they led against Labienus.

62 By dawn all our troops had been taken across, and the enemy's fighting line was in sight. Labienus urged his men to remember their record of valour and all their great successes in battle. He told them to imagine that I, under whose leadership they had so often defeated the enemy, was there in person with them. Then he gave the signal to attack.

In the first encounter, the Gauls were driven back and put to flight on the right wing, where the Seventh legion was positioned. On the left, which was held by the Twelfth legion, although the front ranks of the enemy were pierced by our weapons and killed, still the rest put up a very fierce resistance, not one of them looking as if he would ever think of running away. Camulogenus himself, their commander-in-chief, was there with his men, urging them on.

It was still not clear who would emerge victorious, when the tribunes of the Seventh legion, receiving reports about what was happening on the left wing, appeared with their men at the enemy's rear and charged. Not even then did any of the Gauls give ground. They were all, Camulogenus included, surrounded and killed.

However, the detachment that had been left on guard opposite Labienus's camp heard that battle had been joined, and went to help their fellow Gauls. They occupied a hill but were unable to hold out against the attack of our victorious troops. So they joined their comrades running away, and those who did not succeed in reaching the shelter of woodland or mountains were killed by the cavalry.

With this operation complete, Labienus returned to Agedincum, where the baggage of the entire army had been left. From there he marched with all his forces and reached me on the third day.

6 The siege of Alesia

63 When the revolt of the Aedui became known, the war was stepped up. Deputations were sent into every part of the country; they did all they could, using their influence, prestige and money, to win the other tribes over to their cause. They got hold of the hostages I had left in their keeping, and by threatening their lives they intimidated any who were hesitating to join them.

The Aedui asked Vercingetorix to come and arrange with them a joint plan of campaign. He agreed, and they then went on to demand that they should be given the supreme command. This led to an argument, and a general council of the whole of Gaul was summoned at Bibracte.

Gauls gathered there in great numbers from all over the country, and when the matter was put to a general vote, Vercingetorix was confirmed as commander-in-chief by their unanimous decision. Absent from this council were the Remi and the Lingones, who retained their alliance with us. The Treveri did not attend either, because they were too far away and were being harassed by the Germans – which, incidentally, was the reason for their taking no part at all throughout the entire war and sending no help to either side.

The Aedui bitterly resented being denied the leadership. They lamented the change in their situation and regretted having sacrificed my generous friendship. However, they had undertaken to fight and did not now dare to break with the other tribes. Eporedorix and Viridomarus, the two young men who had entertained such high hopes, took orders from Vercingetorix, much against their will.

Vercingetorix himself ordered the other tribes to provide hostages, and 64 decided on the day by which this should be done. He ordered the whole force of cavalry, numbering 15,000 men, to assemble quickly at Bibracte.

He said that he would be satisfied with the infantry he had before, because he was not going to tempt fortune by fighting a pitched battle. Since he was strong in cavalry, it would be very easy, he said, to stop the Romans getting supplies of grain and forage, always provided the Gauls themselves would not object to destroying their own grain crops and burning their buildings; they must see that by sacrificing their private property in that way they would be gaining power and freedom for ever.

After making these arrangements he ordered the Aedui and Segusiavi, who live on the frontiers of the Province, to provide 10,000 infantry. To this force he added 800 cavalry and placed them under the command of Eporedorix's brother, telling him to invade the territory of the Allobroges. In the other direction, he sent the Gabali, and those cantons of the Arverni that were nearest, into the territory of the Helvii; and the Ruteni and the Cadurci to lay waste the territory of the Volcae Arecomici.

All the same, he sent secret messages and deputations to try to win over the Allobroges, hoping they were not yet completely reconciled to us after the previous war. He offered bribes to the leaders of the Allobroges, and promised the tribe it would have control over the whole Province.

A defensive force had been devised beforehand to meet any such contin- 65 gency; it consisted of 22 cohorts, and had been raised in the Province itself by the legate Lucius Caesar. The cohorts were sent to oppose the enemy at all the points where they were threatening.

The Helvii, acting on their own initiative, joined battle with the tribes on their borders. They were defeated, and many of their tribe were killed, including their chief, Gaius Valerius Donnotaurus, the son of Caburus; as a result they were driven back within the walls of their *oppida*. The Allobroges posted many detachments of troops along the Rhône, and protected their own frontier very carefully and efficiently.

I was aware that the Gauls were superior in cavalry, and that if they blocked all the roads I had no chance of getting reinforcements from the Province or from Italy. I therefore sent across the Rhine to the German tribes I had subdued in previous years, asking them to send cavalry and the light-armed infantry who regularly went into battle with them. When these arrived, their own horses were not really suitable, and so I took the horses from my military tribunes, the other Romans of equestrian rank, and the re-enlisted veterans, and gave them those to ride.

66   While this was happening, the enemy assembled their forces, both the troops that had been in the territory of the Arverni, and the cavalry that had been levied from all over Gaul. Large numbers of their cavalry had already gathered, and I was marching along the edge of the territory of the Lingones to get to that of the Sequani so that I could send help for the Province more easily.

Vercingetorix established his forces in three camps about ten miles away from us. He summoned his cavalry officers to a council of war and told them that their hour of victory had arrived. 'The Romans are leaving Gaul,' he said, 'and fleeing to the Province. That is enough to win our freedom for the moment, but certainly not enough to ensure our peace and security for the future. The Romans will raise a greater army and return to continue the war against us.

So we must attack them now, while they are on the march and encumbered by their baggage. The infantry may come to their rescue, but if they are held up doing that, the Romans cannot continue their march. If, as I think is more likely, they abandon the baggage and concentrate on saving themselves, they will be stripped of their necessary supplies and their reputation will have gone as well.

You certainly must not feel any uneasiness about the possible reaction of the Roman cavalry. You can be quite sure that not one of them will dare so much as to step outside the column. To give you even more confidence, I shall have all our troops drawn up in front of the camps to strike terror into the enemy.'

The cavalry officers shouted out that they should swear a most solemn oath that anyone who did not ride twice through the Roman marching column should not be allowed to enter his home again, or to see his children,

67   his parents, or his wife. This proposal was approved, and they all took the oath.

Next day they divided their cavalry into three sections; two of these appeared in battle order on our two flanks, while the third began to block the way of our vanguard. When this was reported to me, I divided my cavalry into three sections as well, and ordered them to advance against the enemy.

Fighting broke out simultaneously at every point. Our column halted and the legions formed a hollow square with the baggage inside it. Wherever I saw our men in difficulties or being particularly hard pressed, I ordered infantry detachments to move up and form lines of battle. This was effective in two ways; it slowed down the enemy's pursuit and made our cavalry more confident by assuring them of support.

Eventually the German cavalry gained the top of a ridge on the right, dislodging the enemy, who fled as far as the river where Vercingetorix had taken up position with his infantry. The Germans pursued the fugitives and killed many of them, and the rest, seeing what had happened and afraid that they would be surrounded, turned and fled. They were slaughtered all over the field.

Three Aeduans of the highest rank were taken prisoner and brought to me. They were the cavalry commander Cotus, who had had the dispute with

Convictolitavis at the recent election; Cavarillus, who had been put in command of the Aeduan infantry after Litaviccus deserted us; and Eporedorix, who had led the Aeduans in their war with the Sequani, before I arrived in Gaul.

Now that all his cavalry had been routed, Vercingetorix withdrew the   **68** forces he had positioned in front of the camps, and began at once to march to Alesia, an *oppidum* of the Mandubii. He ordered that the baggage should be assembled from the camps at once and brought on after him.

I had our baggage moved to a nearby hill, left two legions to guard it, and then followed the enemy for what was left of that day. We killed about 3,000 of their rearguard. The next day we encamped near Alesia.

The Gauls were terrified by the defeat of their cavalry, on which they particularly relied. After making a thorough examination of the position of the town, I encouraged my soldiers to set about the strenuous task of constructing siege works round the place.

The actual *oppidum* of Alesia was on a hill top, its position being so high   **69** that it was clearly impregnable except by blockade. At the bottom, the hill was washed by rivers on two sides. In front of the *oppidum* was a plain about three miles long; on all other sides it was closely surrounded by hills about as high as that on which it stood. The Gallic troops had occupied the whole of the eastern slope of the hill below the wall of the *oppidum*, fortifying their position with a ditch and a six-foot wall.

The siegeworks that we were beginning to build formed a circuit of 11 miles. Camps were constructed at strategic points along it, and we built 23 redoubts there as well. Pickets were stationed in these during the daytime to guard against any sudden breakout from the *oppidum*; at night they were occupied by strong garrisons with sentries on watch.

We had started constructing our siegeworks, when a cavalry engage-   **70** ment took place on that three-mile stretch of plain that lay between the hills, as I have described above. There was hard fighting on both sides, and seeing our men in difficulties I sent up the Germans to support them, and drew up the legions in front of their camps to prevent the enemy infantry making any sudden attack. The confidence of our men increased when they knew they had the legions behind them.

The enemy were put to flight, and because there were so many of them they made things difficult for themselves, getting jammed in the narrow gateways. The Germans pursued them fiercely right up to their fortifications, and there was great slaughter. Some of them abandoned their horses and tried to get across the ditch and climb the wall.

I ordered the legions I had drawn up in front of the rampart to move forward a little way. The Gauls inside the fortifications became just as alarmed as the rest. They thought there was going to be an immediate attack on them, and so they shouted out a call to arms. Some, in terror, rushed into the *oppidum*, and to prevent the camp being left unguarded, Vercingetorix ordered the gates of the *oppidum* to be closed. After killing many of the fugitives and capturing large numbers of horses, the Germans withdrew.

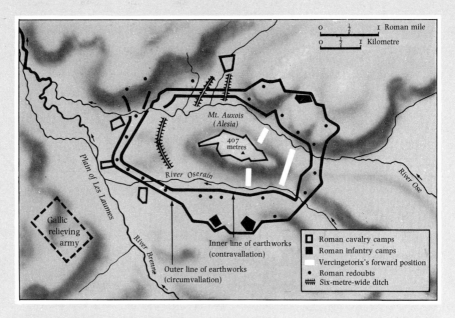

The diamond-shaped plateau of Alesia where Vercingetorix made his last stand against Caesar's army. The detailed work of French archaeologists, which began over a century ago at the instigation of the Emperor Napoleon III, has gradually brought to light evidence of Caesar's enormous complex of siege works. The inner line of earthworks kept Vercingetorix bottled up while the outer line protected Caesar's rear from the attacking relief forces.

Vercingetorix decided to send out all his cavalry by night before we could   71
complete our fortifications. As they were leaving he told them that each
man should go to his own tribe and summon to the war all fellow tribesmen of military age.

He pointed out how much they owed to him, and called on them to have
a thought for his safety; he had done so much for the freedom of Gaul, and
they should not now hand him over to the enemy to be tortured. He explained that unless they did their utmost, 80,000 picked men would perish
with him. He had worked it out that he had barely 30 days' supply of grain,
though by rationing it strictly he could hold out a little longer.

After giving them these instructions, he sent the cavalry out quietly just
before midnight, through a gap in our fortifications.

Then he ordered all the grain to be brought in to him; death would be the
punishment for any who disobeyed this order. A large quantity of cattle had
been brought in by the Mandubii, and this he distributed individually to his
men. Grain was to be doled out in small quantities at a time. All the troops
who had been posted outside the *oppidum* were taken inside. By these means
he prepared to wait for reinforcements from Gaul while still carrying on
the war.

When I was informed of this by fugitives and prisoners, I began building   72
siegeworks of the following kind. I had a trench dug 20 feet wide, with
perpendicular sides so that it was as broad at the bottom as it was at the
top. Then I moved all the other siegeworks back 400 paces from this trench.
I did this to counter certain difficulties: the area to be enclosed was very wide
and it would not be easy to man the whole circuit; the enemy might suddenly
swoop down *en masse* on our fortifications at night, or they could possibly,
during the daytime, hurl their weapons at our men while they were busy
and occupied with the work.

So, at this distance of 400 paces, I had two trenches dug, of equal depth
and each 15 feet wide. The inner one ran across the plain and the
low ground, so I filled it with water diverted from the river.

Behind these trenches, I erected a rampart and palisade 12 feet high.
To this I added a breastwork with battlements, with large forked branches
projecting at the point where the breastwork joined the rampart, to stop
the enemy if they tried to climb up. Finally, I had turrets erected at intervals
of about 80 feet along the entire circuit of our fortifications.

While these great siegeworks were being constructed, it was necessary   73
to send out parties of men in search of timber and grain, and since this took
them quite a distance from the camp, it meant that our forces available
there were under strength. Sometimes the Gauls tried to attack our works
by making violent sorties from several of the gates of the *oppidum*. I therefore decided that I must make further additions to our fortifications, so that
they could be defended by a smaller number of men.

And so tree trunks or very strong branches were cut down, and the
ends of these were stripped of bark and sharpened. Long trenches were
dug, five-feet deep, and the stakes were sunk into them with just the top
parts projecting; they were fastened at the bottom so that they could not be

pulled out. There were five rows in each trench, fastened together and interlaced, and anyone who got in among them impaled himself on the sharp points. The soldiers called them 'grave-stones'.

In front of these, pits were dug, arranged in diagonal rows to form quincunxes [∴]. They were three-feet deep and tapered gradually towards the bottom. Smooth stakes as thick as a man's thigh, with sharpened ends and hardened in the fire, were set into these pits in such a way that they projected no more than four inches above the ground. To keep them firmly in position, earth was thrown into the bottom of the pits and trodden down to a depth of one foot, the rest of the space being covered with twigs and brushwood to conceal the trap. The pits were constructed in groups; each group had eight rows, three feet apart. The soldiers called them 'lilies' because of their resemblance to that flower.

In front of these we had another device. Wood blocks a foot long were sunk completely into the ground, with iron hooks fixed in them, and scattered thickly all over the area. These the soldiers called 'goads'.

74 When these defence works were finished, I constructed another line of fortifications of the same kind, but different from the first in being directed against the enemy on the outside. This second line formed a circuit of 14 miles and followed the most level ground we could find. It was intended to prevent the garrisons in our siegeworks being surrounded, however large a force came against us.

I ordered each man to provide himself with grain and fodder to last 30 days, to avoid the danger of having to leave their camps.

75 While this was happening at Alesia, the Gauls summoned a council of their chiefs. They decided against calling up every man capable of bearing arms, as Vercingetorix had proposed. They were afraid that with such a vast number massed together, they would be unable to control their own contingents or keep them separate, or maintain grain supplies for them. Instead they decided to order each tribe to provide a fixed number of men.

The Aedui, together with their dependants the Segusiavi, the Ambivareti, the Aulerci Brannovices, and the Blannovii – 35,000; the Arverni, together with their dependants the Eleuteti, the Cadurci, the Gabali, and the Vellavii – 35,000; the Sequani, the Senones, the Bituriges, the Santoni, the Ruteni, and the Carnutes – 12,000 each; the Bellovaci and the Lemovices – 10,000 each; the Pictones, the Turoni, the Parisii, and the Helvetii – 8,000 each;

Armed with Caesar's description of the battle of Alesia, Colonel Stoffel, who led Napoleon III's expedition, set out to find the site of Vercingetorix's last stand. On Mt. Auxois, near Alise Ste.-Reine, he identified the plateau where the besieged Gauls probably camped, and in the countryside around, by field work and excavation he located Caesar's siege works. His publication, a blend of fact and interpretation based on Caesar's text, archaeological evidence and intelligent imagination, is still a standard work today.

Right: a page from Napoleon III's great book *Histoire de Jules César* giving a reconstruction of Caesar's works of circumvallation.

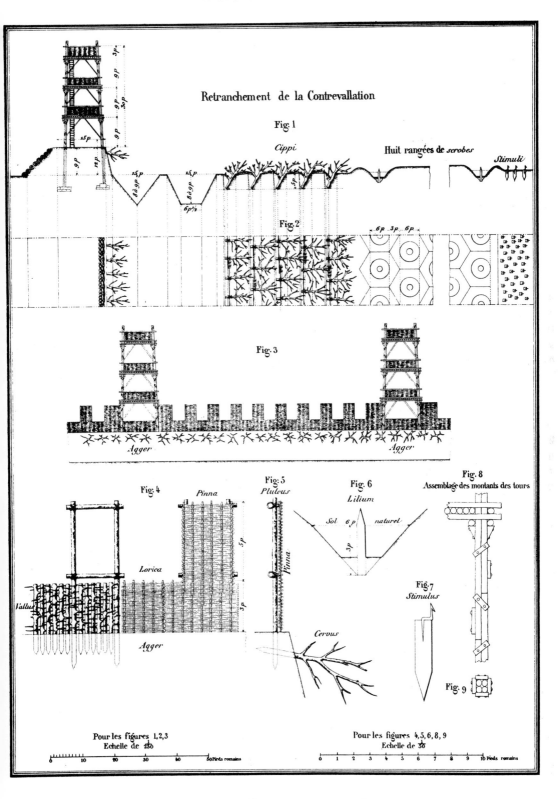

Retranchement de la Contrevallation

Fig. 1

Cippi

Huit rangées de *scrobes*

Stimuli

Fig. 2

Fig. 3

Agger

Agger

Fig. 4

Pinna

Fig. 5
Pluteus

Fig. 6
Lilium

Fig. 8
Assemblage des montants des tours

Lorica

Sol. 6 p. naturel

Fig. 7
Stimulus

Vallus

Pinna

Cervus

Fig. 9

Agger

Pour les figures 1, 2, 3
Echelle de 250

Pour les figures 4, 5, 6, 8, 9
Echelle de 36

The enormity of Caesar's circumvallation and the
technical skill with which it was designed
cannot fail to impress. Since Napoleon III's times
there have been many attempts at reconstruction.

Artist's vision of the building in progress;
(*inset*): modern full-scale reconstruction
near Beaune, Côte d'Or.

the Suessiones, the Ambiani, the Mediomatrices, the Petrocorii, the Nervii, the Morini, the Nitiobriges, and the Aulerci Cenomani – 5,000 each; the Atrebates – 4,000; the Veliocasses, the Lexovii, and the Aulerci Eburovices – 3,000 each; the Raurici and the Boii – 2,000 each; the tribes, known as Aremorican, living on the Atlantic coast and including the Curiosolites, the Redones, the Ambibarii, the Caletes, the Osismi, the Veneti, the Lemovices, and the Venelli – 30,000 altogether.

The Bellovaci did not send their full quota. They said they were going to wage war with the Romans on their own account and in their own way, and would not take orders from anyone. However, when they were asked to do so by Commius, they did send 2,000 men to join the rest, as a token of their friendship with him.

76   As I have already mentioned, I had enjoyed the useful and reliable service of Commius in earlier years in Britain. To reward him, I had ordered that his tribe should be exempt from taxation and have its independence restored; I had also put the Morini under his control. But the whole of Gaul was so united in its desire to gain freedom and recover its former military prestige that acts of kindness and memories of friendship no longer had any influence with them. All the Gauls were directing their energies and their resources to that war.

When 8,000 cavalry and about 240,000 infantry had been assembled, the whole force was reviewed in the territory of the Aedui; its numbers were checked and officers appointed. The supreme command of this force was entrusted to Commius the Atrebatian, the two Aeduans Viridomarus and Eporedorix, and the Arvernian Vercassivellaunus, who was a cousin of Vercingetorix. Representatives chosen from the various tribes were attached to these supreme commanders to act as advisers on the conduct of the campaign.

They all set off for Alesia, eager and full of confidence. Every single one of them believed that the mere sight of such an enormous force would be too much for us, especially as we should be under attack from two directions at once: the besieged Gauls would make a sortie from the *oppidum* as soon as that vast relieving force of cavalry and infantry came into view outside it.

77   However, the Gauls besieged in Alesia did not know what was going on in the country of the Aedui. The day on which they had expected relief had gone by; their grain was all used up. So they summoned a council and discussed what was to happen to them.

Various opinions were expressed: some advocated surrender, others that they should break out of the *oppidum* while they still had the strength. I think that one speech deserves to be remembered because of its extraordinary and appalling cruelty. It was made by Critognatus, an Arvernian of noble birth, held in great esteem.

'I intend to say nothing at all,' he began, 'about the view of those people who are advocating shameful submission to slavery, but making it out to be surrender. In my opinion such people should not be regarded as fellow citizens, nor allowed to come to this council. My business is with those who are in favour of breaking out.

You are all agreed that this suggestion of theirs seems to show that our ancient courage is not completely forgotten. But being unable to endure privation for a little while is not courage. It is feebleness of spirit. It is easier to find people ready to face death voluntarily than people who will put up with suffering without complaining.

Even so, I respect the authority of those who advocate this plan, and I might approve of it if I thought that it was only our lives that we should risk losing. But in making our decision, we must think about Gaul, for we have summoned the whole country to come to our aid. What spirit do you think our relatives and kinsmen will have when 80,000 of us have been killed in this one place, and they are forced to fight it out practically over our very corpses?

They have risked their own lives to save yours. Don't deprive them of your help! Don't be so foolish, reckless or feebleminded that you ruin the whole of Gaul and bring it into perpetual slavery. Do you doubt their loyalty and resolution, just because they haven't come on the appointed day?

Well? Do you think the Romans are working day after day on those outer fortifications just to amuse themselves? Since it is impossible for your fellow Gauls to get through with messages to reassure you, because every way of

The battle of Alesia was the last significant resistance to the Roman will — the death agony of the free Celtic spirit. It had involved virtually every Gaulish tribe in a disastrous defeat. The Romans had been in Gaul for seven years during which time tens of thousands of young men had been killed — there was no longer any spirit or indeed any ability to resist.

The little bronze figure of a dying (or sleeping) Gaul found at Alesia is a vivid symbol of this turning point in French history.

approach to you is blocked, you must use the Romans as witnesses that relief will reach you very soon now; it is terror of just that which is keeping the Romans working day and night on their fortifications.

What then is my advice? I suggest that we do what our ancestors did against the Cimbri and Teutoni, though that war was less important than this. They were forced into their *oppida* and threatened by starvation, just as we are. But instead of surrendering to the enemy, they kept themselves alive by eating the flesh of those they thought too old or too young to fight. And even if we had no precedent for such an action, still, since it is our liberty that's at stake, it would in my opinion be a splendid thing for us to establish the precedent for our descendants.

For what comparison is there between that war and this? The Cimbri devastated our land and did us great harm, but they did in the end leave our country and move on elsewhere. They left us our freedom, with our own rights and laws and land. But what the Romans are after is quite different. They are motivated by envy. They know that we are renowned and powerful in war. So what they want is to settle on our land among our tribes, and bind us in slavery for ever.

That has always been their reason for waging wars. You may not know what goes on in distant countries, but just look at that part of Gaul on your frontiers that has been made into a Roman province. Its laws and institutions have been changed, and the country is held in perpetual slavery, cowering under the dominion of Rome.'

78   When the various views had been put forward, it was decided that those who were too old or too young to fight, or too weak, must leave the *oppidum*. Critognatus's proposal must not be adopted until everything else had been tried. But when the time came, if there were no other way and reinforcements failed to arrive, they should put it into effect rather than surrender or submit to terms for peace.

The Mandubii, who had taken the others into their *oppidum*, were forced to leave it with their wives and children. When they came up to our fortifications, they wept and begged the soldiers to take them as slaves and give them something to eat. But I had guards posted all along the rampart with orders not to allow any of them inside our lines.

79   Meanwhile Commius and the other chief commanders arrived before Alesia with the entire relief force. They occupied a hill outside our fortifications and encamped, not more than a mile from us.

Next day they led all their cavalry out of their camp and filled the whole of that plain, which was, as I have described, three miles long. Their infantry they positioned a short distance away, concealed on higher ground.

From Alesia there was a view down over the plain, and when the Gauls inside saw the relief forces, they ran about congratulating each other; their spirits rose and they were overjoyed. They led out their forces and positioned them in front of the *oppidum*. Then they covered the nearest ditch with wattles and filled it with earth, getting themselves ready to break out and face all the dangers that would involve.

80   I posted all my infantry along both lines of our fortifications, so that if it

should prove necessary, each man would know his post and hold it. I ordered the cavalry to be brought out of camp and to join battle. From all the camps on the surrounding hilltops there was a good view down, and all the soldiers were watching intently to see which way the battle would go.

The Gauls had put archers and light-armed infantry here and there among their cavalry to help any of them who had to give ground, and to hold out against the attacks of our cavalry. Many of our men were taken by surprise and wounded by these, and had to withdraw from the fighting. The Gauls were confident that their forces were getting the better of the fight, for they could see that our men were being overwhelmed by sheer numbers.

From all sides, both those who were besieged and those who had come to relieve them shouted and yelled to encourage their men. The battle was being fought in full view of everyone, and it was impossible for any brave deed or act of cowardice to escape notice. Men on both sides were spurred on to acts of valour by their desire for glory and their fear of disgrace.

From midday almost to sunset the fighting continued, with neither side yet sure of victory. Then the Germans massed their squadrons together on one side, charged the enemy, and drove them off.

When these Gallic cavalry broke and fled, the archers among them were surrounded and killed. The same thing happened at other points; our men pursued the fleeing Gauls right up to their camp, giving them no chance of rallying. Whereupon those Gauls who had come out in front of Alesia went back inside the *oppidum*, disappointed and having practically given up hope of success.

A day went by, during which the Gauls prepared large numbers of wattles, **81** ladders, and grappling hooks. Then at midnight they quietly set out from their camp and moved towards our fortifications in the plain. They suddenly raised a shout to inform those beseiged in the *oppidum* of their approach, and then set about throwing wattles on to the trenches, driving our men off the rampart with slings and arrows and stones, and doing everything necessary to take our position by storm.

At the same time Vercingetorix, hearing the noise of the shouting, sounded the trumpet and led his forces out of the *oppidum*.

Our men moved up to the fortifications, each one taking up his allotted position, as on previous days. They kept the Gauls off with slings, large stones, bullets, and stakes, which they had put ready at intervals along the rampart.

It was impossible to see far because of the darkness, and there were heavy casualties on both sides. Many missiles were discharged by our artillery. The legates Marcus Antonius and Gaius Trebonius, who had been assigned to the defence of this sector, brought up men from the more distant redoubts and sent them in to reinforce any point where they had seen our men were under pressure.

As long as the Gauls were at a distance from our fortification, they derived **82** more advantage from the great number of missiles they were hurling. But when they came closer, the extra devices we had planted there took them by surprise. They got themselves caught up on the 'goads', or they fell into the pits and impaled themselves, or else they were pierced and killed by the siege-spears that we hurled at them from the rampart and the towers. They suffered many casualties at every point, but did not succeed anywhere in penetrating our lines of defence.

When it was almost dawn they withdrew to their original position, afraid that we would break out of our camps on the higher ground and surround them on their right flank.

As for the Gauls besieged inside the *oppidum*, they lost a considerable amount of time bringing out the equipment prepared by Vercingetorix for the sortie, and filling up the ditches farthest from them. Consequently they had not got close to our main fortifications before they heard that their fellow Gauls had retreated. So they went back into the *oppidum* without having achieved anything.

83   Having now suffered two costly defeats, the Gauls deliberated about what they should do. They called in men who knew the terrain and ascertained from them the positions of our higher camps and the state of their defences.

On the north side of Alesia there was a hill that our men had not been able to include in the circle of our siege works because its circumference was too great. They had had to build the camp there on a gentle slope, and this was slightly to our disadvantage. The legates Gaius Antistis Reginus and Gaius Caninius Rebilus held this camp with two legions.

The enemy commanders had scouts reconnoitre the position. They then chose from their entire force 60,000 men from the tribes that had the greatest reputation for valour, secretly decided what ought to be done and how it should be carried out, and fixed noon as the time for starting their attack.

The Arvernian Vercassivellaunus, one of their four chief commanders and a relative of Vercingetorix, was put in command of this force. He left camp soon after sunset and had almost completed his march before dawn. He concealed his men behind the hill, telling them to rest after that night's hard work. When he could see that it was almost midday, he marched towards that camp of ours described above. At the same time, the Gallic cavalry began to advance towards our fortifications in the plain and the rest of their forces appeared in front of their camp.

84   From the citadel of Alesia Vercingetorix could see these fellow Gauls. He therefore came out of the *oppidum*, bringing with him the wattles, poles, protective sheds, hooks, and other equipment he had prepared for the sortie. There was simultaneous fighting all along our lines and every sort of method was tried by the Gauls; they concentrated at any point where the defences seemed most vulnerable.

The extent of our fortifications meant that the troops had to be thinly spread along them, and this made it difficult for them to meet the attacks that were being made at many different points. They were greatly unsettled by the noise of shouting they could hear behind them as they fought; it made them aware that their own safety depended on what happened to others. And, of course, people are almost always more unnerved by dangers they cannot see.

85   I found a good place from which I could see what was happening at any point; where our men were in difficulties I sent up reinforcements.

Both sides knew only too well that this was the moment when a supreme effort was called for. The Gauls realized they had no hope of surviving unless they broke through our lines of defence; we knew all our hardships would be over if only we could hold out.

The difficulties were greatest at the fortifications on the hill, where, as already mentioned, Vercassivellaunus had been sent. The unfavourable downward slope of the ground was a factor seriously to our disadvantage. Some of the enemy hurled spears, others advanced on us with their shields held up to form a protective shell, and as their men became exhausted, fresh troops came up to relieve them. Their entire force threw earth against our fortifications, which allowed them to climb on to the rampart and also covered up the devices we had hidden in the ground. Our men were beginning to run out of weapons, and their stamina was failing too.

I saw what was happening and the difficulties they were experiencing, **86** so I sent Labienus and six cohorts to their relief. I told him that if it proved impossible for him to hold the position, he was to withdraw his cohorts and fight his way out. But I made it clear to him he was not to do that unless absolutely necessary.

I went to other parts of the line in person, and urged the men there not to give in under the pressure. I told them that the fruits of all their previous battles depended on that day, and on that very hour.

The Gauls inside the *oppidum* now gave up hope of getting through our fortifications on the plain because of their scale. Instead, they climbed up and attempted to attack the steep slopes, bringing up the equipment they had prepared. With a hail of missiles they dislodged the defenders from the towers. They then filled the ditches with earth and wattles, and tore down the rampart and breastwork with hooks.

First I sent some cohorts with young Brutus, then others with the legate **87** Gaius Fabius. Finally, when the fighting was getting fiercer, I went in person, taking fresh troops to relieve them. Battle was renewed, and the Gauls were driven back.

I then hurried to the point where I had sent Labienus, taking four cohorts from the nearest redoubt; I ordered some of the cavalry to follow me, and told others to ride round the outer fortifications and attack the enemy from the rear.

Labienus realized that neither ramparts nor trenches were proving capable of checking the Gauls' violent attacks. Fortunately, he had been able to collect together 11 cohorts, drawn from the nearest redoubts, and he now sent messengers to tell me what he thought must be done. I hurried on so as to arrive in time to take part in the action.

The enemy knew who was approaching by the colour of the cloak I always **88** wore in action to mark me out; and from the higher ground where they stood, they had a view of the lower slopes and so could see the squadrons of cavalry and the cohorts I had ordered to follow me. They therefore joined battle.

A shout went up on both sides, answered by the men on the rampart and along the whole line of the fortifications. Our men dispensed with their javelins and used their swords. Suddenly our cavalry could be seen to the rear, and fresh cohorts were moving up closer. The Gauls turned tail, but our cavalry cut off their flight.

There was great slaughter. Sedulius, the military commander and chief of the Lemovices, was killed; the Arvernian Vercassivellaunus was captured alive in the rout; 74 of their war standards were brought in to me; out of all that great army only a few got safely back to camp.

The Gauls in the *oppidum* could see the slaughter and the rout of their countrymen; they gave up all hope of being saved and took their men back inside from the fortifications.

When news of our victory reached them, the Gallic relief force immediately fled from their camp. But for the fact that our men were exhausted by their exertions throughout the entire day and their constant efforts to relieve the threatened points, the Gauls' entire army could have been wiped out. Cavalry, which I sent out, caught up with the enemy rearguard about midnight and killed or captured great numbers of them. The survivors fled, making off to their various tribes.

89   Next day Vercingetorix called a council. He pointed out that he had undertaken the war not for any personal reasons but for the freedom of Gaul. Since he must now yield to fortune, he was putting his fate in their hands. They must decide whether they wanted to kill him, and so make amends to the Romans, or hand him over to them alive.

Envoys were sent to me to discuss this. I ordered that their weapons should be surrendered and their tribal chiefs brought before me. I took my place on the fortifications in front of the camp and the chiefs were brought to me there. Vercingetorix was surrendered, and the weapons were laid down before me. I kept the Aeduan and Arvernian prisoners back, hoping to use them to regain the loyalty of their tribes. The rest I distributed as booty among the entire army, giving one prisoner to each of my men.

90   When this business had been settled, I set off for the territory of the Aedui, and received the submission of that tribe. While I was there, the Arverni sent envoys to me, promising to obey any orders I gave them. I told them to provide a large number of hostages. I then sent the legions into winter quarters. I restored to the Aedui and the Arverni about 20,000 prisoners.

I told Titus Labienus to take two legions and some cavalry and set out for the country of the Sequani; I sent Marcus Sempronius Rutilus to serve under him. I stationed the legate Gaius Fabius and Lucius Minucius Basilus with two legions in the territory of the Remi, to prevent them suffering harm at the hands of their neighbours the Bellovaci. I sent Gaius Antistius Reginus into the country of the Ambivareti, Titus Sextius to the Bituriges, and Gaius Caninius Rebilus to the Ruteni, each with one legion. I stationed Quintus Tullius Cicero and Publius Sulpicius in Aeduan territory near the river Saône, at Cabillonum and Matisco, to organize the grain supply. I myself decided to winter at Bibracte.

When dispatches made these successes known at Rome a public thanksgiving of 20 days was decreed.

BOOK VIII · 51–50 BC

Author's Preface

You have constantly asked me, Balbus, to undertake this task, and I have until now each time refused your requests. I realize it must have seemed that my reluctance was due to laziness rather than to the difficulties inherent in the undertaking. However, I have now taken it on, and very difficult it has proved to be.

I have continued the commentaries our friend Caesar wrote of his achievements in Gaul, since there is no continuity between these earlier writings and his later ones. His latest work goes only as far as the operations in Alexandria and no further; I have completed it, continuing the account up to Caesar's death, not as far as the end of civil strife, for there is no end yet in sight.

I hope that those who read my work will realize how reluctant I have been to take it on, for if they do, I may stand a better chance of avoiding the charge of stupidity and arrogance for having intruded myself into the middle of Caesar's writings. For everyone agrees that other writers' most elaborate literary efforts are surpassed by the elegant prose of Caesar's *Commentaries*. They were published merely to provide future historians with information about those great events, but have met with such universal admiration that, so far from giving the historians an opportunity, they seem to have robbed them of it.

That is something you and I may marvel at more than others do, for while other people can appreciate the skill and precision of the work, we know as well how easily and quickly he produced it. Caesar was endowed not only with a talent for writing the most elegant prose, but also with a perfect knowledge of how to explain his plans and ideas.

As for me, it so happened that I did not even take part in the Alexandrian and African campaigns; and although I know something about them from what Caesar told me, it is one thing to be enthralled because the events being described are new and astonishing, but quite another to listen with the intention of writing an objective account of them. However, while I am listing all these reasons why I should not be compared with Caesar, I am, of course, thereby laying myself open to a charge of presumption, in imagining that anyone would even think of comparing me with him. Farewell.

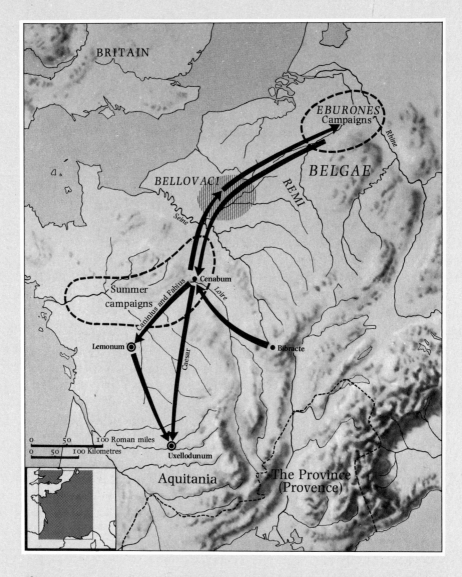

The opening words of the eighth book 'The whole of Gaul was now conquered' were true to a point. Gaul was now completely under Roman control but there were still pockets of discontent with which Caesar and his generals had to contend. In the north, among the Belgae, the Bellovaci had begun to make a nuisance of themselves by threatening the clients of Rome's traditional allies the Remi. Caesar did not miss the excuse to interfere: his show of strength dealt a final blow to latent Belgic resistance. Finally he turned south, crossing the Loire into western France. Until now he had been content to leave the submission of the area in the hands of his generals but he must have felt his personal intervention was necessary to make the final arrangements. Such resistance as there was, was comparatively insignificant: only Uxellodunum held out for a brief period. After visiting Aquitania he marched into Provence for a few days but felt impelled to return to northern Gaul, where he spent the winter putting the final touches to his political settlement. Apart from the Bellovacian revolt his last year in Gaul had been largely uneventful: by the end of it he could return to Italy content in the knowledge that his conquests and achievements would survive.

1 Winter operations

The whole of Gaul was now conquered. As the fighting had been going on   1
without a break since the summer of the previous year, Caesar wanted to
allow his soldiers time to rest in their winter quarters to recover their strength
after all their great efforts. But it was reported that several tribes at once
were plotting together, making plans to renew hostilities.

The likely explanation given for this was that all the Gauls realized that
however large an army they might concentrate in one place, they still
could not stand up to us; but if several tribes all started hostilities in different
places at the same time, the Roman army would not have enough allies,
enough time or enough manpower to deal with all of them at once. So they
thought no tribe should refuse its share of the sacrifice, if by thwarting the
enemy in that way they would enable the rest to win back their liberty.

Caesar wanted to prevent this idea of the Gauls' getting firmly established.   2
He left the quaestor Marcus Antonius in charge of the winter camp, and
with a cavalry escort set out from Bibracte himself on the last day of December
to join the Thirteenth legion, which he had stationed in the territory of the
Bituriges not far from that of the Aedui. To reinforce it he brought in the
Eleventh legion, which was the nearest.

Leaving behind two cohorts from each legion to guard the baggage, he
led the rest of the force into the most fertile part of the country of the Bituriges.
This tribe had extensive territory and a number of *oppida*; a single legion in
winter quarters there had not been able to prevent them plotting and making
preparations for war.

Caesar's arrival was unexpected; they were unprepared and scattered,   3
with the inevitable result that our cavalry came upon them as they were
working in their fields without any thought of danger, and overwhelmed
them before they could take refuge in their *oppida*.

Before the attack, Caesar had given orders that nothing was to be set on
fire; this was to ensure adequate supplies of grain and fodder if he chose to
advance farther, and to avoid giving the alarm. So the Bituriges did not
even have the usual warning of an invasion, smoke rising from burning
buildings.

When many thousands of their people had been taken prisoner, the
Bituriges became panic-stricken. Those who had managed to escape our
first onset had fled to the neighbouring tribes, relying on personal ties of
hospitality there, or on the fact that these neighbouring tribes were in
league with them against Rome.

But it was in vain. By means of forced marches Caesar turned up everywhere; no tribe had time to think of anyone's safety but their own. By the
speed of his action Caesar was able to keep friendly tribes loyal and to frighten
the waverers into accepting terms for peace.

The Bituriges saw that because of Caesar's clemency it was still possible for
them to regain his friendship; the neighbouring tribes had delivered up
hostages and been taken back into his protection without suffering any
punishment. Anticipating that they would be treated under the same
terms, they also submitted.

4   The soldiers had worked very hard and put up with a great deal. During those winter days they had enthusiastically persevered in their efforts, marching over very difficult tracks in unbearable cold. As a reward for their hard work and endurance, he promised them gratuities in lieu of booty – 200 sesterces for each soldier and 2,000 for each centurion. He then sent the legions back into their winter quarters, and returned to Bibracte himself 40 days after he had set out.

    While he was occupied with his judicial business there, the Bituriges sent envoys to him to ask for his help against the Carnutes, who they complained had attacked them. When he heard this, although he had been only 18 days in his winter quarters at Bibracte, he brought the Fourteenth and Sixth legions from their winter camps on the Saône, where they had been stationed to secure the grain supply, as was mentioned in the previous book. With these two legions he set out to punish the Carnutes.

5   When the enemy received word that our army was on the way, they remembered the fate of the other tribes. The Carnutes abandoned their villages and *oppida*, where they were living in wretched hovels that had been hastily erected to meet the need for shelter against the winter weather; for in their recent defeat they had lost several of their *oppida*. They scattered and fled.

    Caesar did not want to expose his soldiers to the extremely bitter weather conditions prevalent at that time of the year, and so he camped at Cenabum, an *oppidum* of the Carnutes. Some of the soldiers were billeted in houses belonging to the Gauls, others in shelters hastily thatched over to cover the tents.

    But the cavalry and auxiliary infantry were sent out in every direction the enemy was reported to have taken. This policy proved successful, for our men generally came back bringing large quantities of booty.

    The Carnutes suffered greatly from the severity of the winter; they were also terrified by the danger that threatened them. They had been driven from their homes and did not dare to stay long in any one place; but they could find no shelter or protection in the forests in such bitter weather. They scattered, and a great many of them perished; the rest were dispersed among the neighbouring tribes.

6   It was the most difficult time of the year for campaigning. Caesar therefore thought it was enough merely to disperse the enemy forces that were concentrating, for that would prevent war breaking out. He felt reasonably certain that no large-scale war could flare up before the summer campaigning season. So he left Gaius Trebonius in command of the two legions he had brought with him, and stationed them in winter quarters at Cenabum.

2 The Bellovacan campaign

There was another problem for Caesar to deal with. The Remi were constantly sending deputations to him reporting that the Bellovaci, who had the best reputation in war of all the Gauls and even of all the Belgae, were combining with neighbouring tribes, mobilizing and concentrating their forces under the leadership of the Bellovacan Correus and the Atrebatian

Commius. They intended, so it was said, to make a concerted attack on the territory of the Suessiones, who had been made dependants of the Remi.

The Remi were allies who had served Rome well, and Caesar considered that his honour, as well as his interests, demanded that they should not come to any harm. So he once again called out the Eleventh legion from its winter quarters, wrote to Gaius Fabius telling him to take his two legions into the territory of the Suessiones, and sent for one of the two legions under the command of Titus Labienus.

In this way he shared out among the legions in turn the work involved in campaigning, in so far, that is, as the situation of the various winter camps and the strategy of the war allowed. Caesar himself worked unceasingly.

When these forces had assembled, he set out against the Bellovaci, camped 7 in their territory, and sent out squadrons of cavalry in all directions to bring in prisoners from whom he could find out what the enemy's plans were. The cavalry carried out their instructions, and reported that only a few people had been found in the houses, and that these had not stayed behind to work their fields but had been sent back to act as spies; the whole country had been thoroughly evacuated.

Caesar asked these prisoners where the main force of the Bellovaci was and what their plans were. He discovered that all the Bellovaci capable of bearing arms, together with the Ambiani, the Aulerci, the Caleti, the Velio-casses, and the Atrebates, had gathered in one place. For their camp they had chosen some high ground in a wood surrounded by a marsh; they had taken all their property into more distant forests.

There were several chiefs leading the revolt, but the one who had greatest influence over the people was Correus, because they knew he loathed the name of Rome. A few days earlier Commius the Atrebatian had left this camp and gone to get help from the German tribes; they were not far away, and their manpower was unlimited.

But the Bellovaci had decided, with the unanimous approval of the chiefs and the eager agreement of the people, that if Caesar was coming with three legions, as reported, they would offer battle. Their aim was to avoid being forced to fight later on against the whole Roman army, when conditions would be harder and less favourable to them. If, on the other hand, he brought more than three legions, they would stay in the position they had chosen, and resort to ambush as a means of preventing the Romans getting grain, forage (which at that time of the year was scarce and to be found only here and there), and other supplies.

When he questioned more prisoners, Caesar found their story was the 8 same. He considered the enemy's plan of campaign a most sensible one, and very different from the recklessness that is the usual characteristic of native peoples. So he decided to concentrate all his efforts on bringing the enemy to battle quickly, by making them think his own force was small and therefore to be despised.

He had three veteran legions of outstanding fighting ability, the Seventh, Eighth, and Ninth; he also had the Eleventh, a legion made up of picked younger men and now in its eighth year of service. The men of this legion showed great promise, but had not yet served as long or gained the same reputation for valour as the others had. And so he summoned a council of war, at which he passed on to them all the information he had received, encouraging the men to be of good heart.

In the hope of being able to lure the enemy out to fight by making it seem that he had only three legions, he organized his marching column like this: the Seventh, Eighth, and Ninth legions were to march in front, then the entire baggage train, which was quite small, as is usual for a quick expeditionary force, and the Eleventh legion would bring up the rear. This meant that the enemy would only be able to see a force of the size they had declared they were prepared to take on.

This marching order almost amounted to the hollow-square battle formation. Caesar brought his army into enemy view before the Gauls
9   expected it, and the sight that suddenly met them was of legions advancing steadily, drawn up as if for action.

The Gauls' plans, as reported to Caesar, were full of confidence. But whether because of the risk involved in fighting an engagement, or because of the suddenness of our arrival, or because they were waiting to see what we would do, they merely drew up their forces in front of their camp without coming down from the higher ground.

It had been Caesar's intention to join battle, but, surprised at the great size of the enemy army, he established camp opposite theirs, with a deep, though not very wide, valley between them. The camp's fortifications consisted of a rampart 12 feet high, with a breastwork of proportionate height built on top; two ditches were dug, 15 feet wide and with perpendicular sides; three-storeyed towers were erected at frequent intervals and linked by floored galleries protected at the front by wicker breastworks.

The aim was to protect the camp against enemy attacks by the double ditch, and also by a double line of defenders: one line, on the galleries, would be less vulnerable because they were high up, and thus able to hurl their missiles more confidently and make them go farther; the other line, posted actually on the rampart and so closer to the enemy, would be protected by the galleries from weapons falling down on them. The gateways were fitted with doors and higher towers.

10 Caesar had two motives in building these fortifications. He hoped their very size would make the Gauls think he was afraid and so increase their confidence; and he saw that with such fortifications the camp could be defended by just a small force, when it was necessary for the rest to go quite far afield to get fodder and grain.

Meanwhile, there were frequent skirmishes between small groups from each side who ran forward on to the marshy ground between the two camps. Sometimes our Gallic and German auxiliaries crossed the marsh in vigorous pursuit of the enemy; sometimes the Gauls in their turn would cross it and drive our men some way back. We had to fetch fodder from buildings scattered here and there over the country, so it inevitably happened during our daily foraging expeditions that parties of our men because isolated and surrounded in difficult places.

The losses of baggage animals and slaves that we suffered in this way were not in themselves significant. But they encouraged the natives in foolish hopes, especially since Commius, who, as I have mentioned, had gone to summon help from the Germans, had come back with some cavalry. There were no more than 500 of these Germans, but the natives set great store by their arrival.

Several days went by, Caesar noticed that the enemy were keeping to their 11 camp, which, protected by the marsh and by its naturally strong position, could not be stormed without heavy casualties. He saw too that it would be impossible to invest it with siegeworks unless he had a larger army.

He therefore wrote to Trebonius telling him to summon the Thirteenth legion, which was wintering with the legate Titus Sextius in the country of the Bituriges, as quickly as he could. With the three legions he would then have, he was to set out to join Caesar by forced marches.

Meanwhile Caesar himself made use of the large numbers of cavalry he had called up from the Remi, the Lingones, and the other tribes; he sent them in turns to escort the foraging parties and guard them against sudden enemy attacks. They performed this duty day after day, and as it became 12 routine, so the men became less vigilant. This is not unusual when the same pattern of action goes on for any length of time.

The Bellovaci discovered where our cavalry escorts were posted each day, and laid an ambush of picked infantry in a wooded spot. Next day they sent some cavalry to the same place, to lure our men into the ambush and then attack them when they were surrounded.

The Remi happened to be the unlucky ones whose turn of duty it was that day. When they suddenly caught sight of the enemy cavalry, they pursued them too eagerly; they were aware of their own superior numbers, and this led them to despise the small enemy force.

As a result they found themselves surrounded on every side by the infantry. This so alarmed them that they retreated more hastily than is usual in a cavalry engagement, with the loss of their commander Vertiscus, the chief of their tribe. He was so old he could hardly ride a horse, but in true Gallic fashion he had not used his age as an excuse for refusing the command, insisting rather on being present in the actual fighting.

The enemy were excited and spurred on by this success of theirs in which the commander and chief of the Remi had been killed; for our men it was a setback that taught them to reconnoitre more carefully before posting patrols, and to be more restrained when pursuing a retreating enemy.

Meanwhile not a day went by without fighting taking place in full view of 13 both camps, at places where there were fords and tracks across the marsh.

In one of these engagements the whole of the German infantry force, brought by Caesar from across the Rhine to fight among the cavalry, resolutely crossed the marsh, killed the few men who put up any resistance to them, and then determinedly pursued the rest of the enemy force. This struck terror not only in those who were being attacked at close quarters or wounded by missiles at long range, but also in those who were, as usual, posted in reserve some way off. They all disgraced themselves by fleeing, often abandoning even positions of advantage they had taken up on higher ground. They kept on running until they reached their camp, and some fled even beyond that, too ashamed, no doubt, to face their comrades.

The peril these men had been in thoroughly unnerved their whole army; it was difficult to tell which was greater, their arrogance at some slight success or their fright after a minor reverse.

14   For several days the Bellovaci stayed in their camp. But when their leaders heard that the legate Gaius Trebonius and his legions were close at hand, they became afraid they would be besieged as Vercingetorix had been at Alesia. So they sent away by night all those who were too old or too weak to fight and those who had no weapons, and at the same time they sent off the rest of their baggage.

Even when the Gauls are supposed to be travelling light they are usually accompanied by large numbers of wagons, so now there was disorder and confusion as the column was being formed up, and it was not yet ready to move when daylight came. They therefore drew up a force of armed men in front of their camp, to prevent the Romans starting to pursue their baggage train before it had got some distance on its way.

Caesar thought he ought not to attack these troops while they were on the defensive, because that would involve advancing up a steep hill. But he thought he should move his legions far enough forward to threaten the enemy and make it impossible for them to leave their position without running the risk of being attacked. He could see that the marsh that lay between the two camps was difficult to cross, and so could hinder any rapid pursuit.

He noticed, however, that a ridge on the other side of the marsh reached almost as far as the enemy camp, being separated from it only by a narrow valley. So he had causeways laid over the marsh, took his legions across, and quickly reached the level ground on top of the ridge, which was protected on two sides by steep slopes. Once there, he drew up his legions and advanced to the edge of the ridge before halting in battle formation, in a place from which the massed formations of the enemy would be within range of his artillery.

15   The natural strength of their position made the Gauls confident, and they were willing to fight if the Romans should try to come up to the hill. But they could not disperse their forces and gradually send them off in different directions, in case their men should be unsettled by being split up in that way. So they stayed where they were, drawn up for battle.

When Caesar realized they were not going to move, he measured out the ground for a camp, and keeping 20 cohorts ready for action, ordered the rest of his men to set about building fortifications. When these were complete, he had the legions take up position ready for battle in front of the rampart, and placed cavalry patrols at various points with their horses ready bridled.

The Bellovaci saw that the Romans were ready to pursue them if they moved. On the other hand, they saw they would be at risk if they spent the night where they were, or even stayed there any longer. So they devised the following plan for getting away.

They usually had great quantities of sticks and bundles of straw in their camp. These they now passed from hand to hand and put down in front of their battle line. At the end of the day, when the word was given, they set fire to them all at once. A sheet of flame suddenly hid their entire force from the Romans, and as soon as this had happened, the Gauls fled, running away as hard as they could.

It was impossible for Caesar actually to see them withdrawing, because the flames were in the way. However, he suspected they had adopted the plan in order to get away. So he moved his legions forward and sent out squadrons of cavalry to pursue the Gauls. He himself advanced more cautiously because he was afraid of an ambush; the enemy could still be holding firm in their original position, trying to lure our men on to unfavourable ground. **16**

The cavalry were afraid of penetrating the dense barrier of smoke and flame. Those who were eager enough to advance into it could hardly see the heads of the horses they were riding. Fearing a trap, they did nothing to stop the Bellovaci getting away.

The flight of the enemy had been prompted by fear, but was carried out with such ingenuity that they suffered no losses. They moved on some ten miles before pitching camp in a very strong position, from which they kept on sending out parties of infantry and cavalry to lay ambushes. In this way they inflicted serious damage on the Roman foraging parties.

These attacks were becoming more frequent, when Caesar discovered from a prisoner that Correus, the leader of the Bellovaci, had chosen from his whole army 6,000 of his bravest infantry and 1,000 cavalry, intending to put them in an ambush at a place where he suspected that the Romans would be sending parties of men, for abundant grain and fodder was available there. On learning of this plan, Caesar sent the cavalry on ahead as usual to escort the foraging parties, with some light-armed auxiliaries among the cavalry ranks. He also brought out an unusually large legionary force; these legions, under his personal command, approached as near to the place as possible. **17**

The enemy had taken up position ready for the ambush. The place they had chosen for it was a plain no more than a square mile in area, enclosed on all sides either by woods or by a river that was almost impossible to cross. They had surrounded this plain with a cordon of men, hidden in ambush. **18**

However, because they knew what the enemy plan was, our men were mentally and physically ready for the fight. Knowing that the legions were coming up behind them, they were ready for any attack and so rode on to the plain, squadron by squadron.

Correus believed that their arrival gave him his chance to strike. He came out into view, with just a few of his men first, and charged the nearest squadrons. Our men stood up to this charge resolutely, not crowding together as often happens in cavalry engagements because of a certain nervousness; when this happens, many of the casualties that occur are caused simply by the very numbers of horsemen packed together.

The cavalry squadrons took up positions some distance from each other **19**

An artist's impression of the dense barrier of
smoke and flame employed by the Bellovaci to
escape pursuit by Caesar's cavalry. These
ingenious tactics enabled the Gauls to retreat
some ten miles without loss.

and small groups of men took turns in the fighting, thus preventing their comrades being outflanked. While Correus was actually engaged in the fighting, the rest of his cavalry burst out of the woods. There was fierce fighting in various parts of the field, and for quite a while the battle was evenly balanced.

Then gradually the main force of the enemy infantry emerged from the woods in battle formation, and forced our cavalry to give ground. The light-armed infantry, which as I have mentioned had been sent ahead of the legions, quickly went to support our cavalry. They took their places among our squadrons and put up a determined resistance.

For some time the fighting continued, neither side gaining the upper hand. But eventually the battle took the course that theory might have predicted. When they were first attacked by those lying in ambush, our men had held out. They had kept their heads and sustained no casualties, and that very fact now gave them the advantage.

Meanwhile the legions were getting nearer. Messengers kept on arriving, and both sides heard at the same time that the commander-in-chief was at hand with his troops drawn up in battle order. At this news our men fought with the utmost keenness, confident of the support of the cohorts; if the battle dragged on, they were afraid they would have to share the glory of victory with the legions.

The enemy's morale collapsed, and they tried to escape by different routes. But it was no use; they themselves were now trapped by those very obstacles by which they had intended to ensnare the Romans. However, defeated, demoralized, and dismayed by the loss of the greater part of their force, they fled — some making for the woods, others the river — only to be cut down in their flight by our men, who eagerly pursued them.

Correus meanwhile was in no way broken by this disaster. It did not make him leave off fighting and seek shelter in the woods, or surrender when offered the chance to do so. He fought on with great courage, wounding many, and in the end he provoked our victorious troops to such anger that they shot him down.

That is how the battle went. The fighting was only just over when Caesar 20 arrived. He thought that when the Gauls received news of this great defeat they would abandon their camp, which was said to be no more than about eight miles from the scene of the slaughter. He was aware that there was a river in his way, but got his army across and moved forward.

Meanwhile a few of the fugitives suddenly reached the Bellovaci and the other tribes; they were wounded but, thanks to the woods, they had managed to avoid being killed.

Everything had gone wrong for the Bellovaci: they had heard of the defeat, Correus had been killed, they had lost their cavalry and the best of their infantry, and now they thought the Romans were on their way. They hurriedly sounded the trumpet and summoned a council, at which the cry was that envoys and hostages should be sent to Caesar. When this plan 21 was approved by all, Commius the Atrebatian fled to the Germans, from whom he had borrowed reinforcements for that campaign.

The rest sent off envoys at once to Caesar, begging him to be satisfied with the punishment his enemies had already suffered. If it were in his power to inflict such a punishment upon an enemy who had not fought a battle and so had not suffered casualties, his clemency and humanity would surely never allow him to carry it out. As it was, the strength of the Bellovaci had been broken in that cavalry engagement; many thousands of their best infantry had perished, hardly any had escaped to tell the story of the massacre. But great as the disaster had been, they had gained something from that battle; Correus, who stirred up the people and was responsible for the war, had been killed. While he lived, they said, the council in their tribe had always had less power than the ignorant masses.

22   Such was the plea of the envoys. In reply, Caesar reminded them that in the previous year the Bellovaci had joined the other Gallic tribes in making war on him, and of all these tribes it was they, the Bellovaci, who had remained most stubbornly hostile, refusing to be brought to their senses even when the other tribes surrendered. He knew perfectly well that it was very easy to blame the dead for their misdeeds; but the fact was that no individual, with just the feeble support of the common people, could be strong enough to start a war and carry it on if the tribal chiefs were against the idea, the tribal council objected, and all sound patriots were opposed to it. However, he would be satisfied with the punishment they had brought upon themselves.

23   That night the envoys took back Caesar's answer and got the hostages that had been demanded. The other tribes had been waiting to see what happened to the Bellovaci, but now their envoys came hurrying in. They gave hostages and did as they were ordered.

The only exception was Commius, who was afraid of entrusting his life to anyone. In the previous year, when Caesar was holding the assizes in northern Italy, Titus Labienus had discovered that Commius was intriguing with the tribes and plotting against Caesar. Labienus decided that to put down such a traitor would not count as treachery. However, he did not imagine that Commius would come to the camp if summoned and he did not want to put him on his guard by trying that. So he sent Gaius Volusenus Quadratus to arrange a sham interview and see to it that Commius was killed during the course of it. Volusenus was given some centurions specially picked for the job.

At the interview, Volusenus gave the agreed signal by grasping Commius' hand. However, the centurion chosen for the job either lost his nerve because he was not used to such work or was thwarted by the quick intervention of Commius's friends. Whatever the reason, he failed to kill his man, though with the first blow of his sword he did inflict a severe head wound. Swords were drawn on both sides, but the main concern of all was to get away, not to fight; our men because they thought Commius was mortally wounded, the Gauls because they realized it had all been a trap and they were afraid there was more to it than they could see. After that, it was said Commius resolved never again to come into the presence of any Roman.

3 The siege of Uxellodunum

All the most warlike tribes had now been conquered, and Caesar could see   24
there was no longer any tribe capable of organizing war to resist him. But he
saw, too, that many of the Gauls were moving out of their *oppida* and leaving
their fields to avoid having to live under Roman rule. So he decided to distribute his army in various parts of the country.

He kept his quaestor Marcus Antonius and the Twelfth legion with him.
The legate Gaius Fabius was sent with 25 cohorts to the opposite side of
Gaul, because Caesar had heard that some of the tribes there were in arms,
and he did not think the two legions the legate Gaius Caninius Rebilus had
in that area were strong enough to deal with the situation. Titus Labienus
was summoned to join Caesar, but the Fifteenth legion, which had been in
winter quarters with Labienus, was sent to north Italy to protect the colonies
of Roman citizens there, and to ensure that they did not suffer the sort of
damage the people of Trieste had suffered from a barbarian raid the previous
summer, when they had been surprised and overwhelmed by a sudden
attack of Illyrian brigands.

Caesar himself set out to plunder and lay waste the territory of Ambiorix.
This chief was on the run, in terror. Caesar had given up hope of being able
to force him into submission, and had decided that in order to protect his
own prestige, the next best thing was to strip the country of inhabitants,
buildings, and cattle so completely that if any of Ambiorix's people were
lucky enough to survive, they would hate their chief for bringing such
disasters on them and so make it impossible for him ever to return. Detach-   25
ments of legionary or auxiliary troops were sent out all over Ambiorix's
territory, killing, burning, and pillaging; everything was destroyed and
great numbers of the people were either killed or taken prisoner.

Caesar sent Labienus with two legions into the territory of the Treveri.
These people were very close to Germany and therefore constantly involved
in warfare. They were very like the Germans in their way of life and in their
ferocity, and never did as they were ordered unless forced to by an army.

Meanwhile the legate Gaius Caninius received letters and messages from   26
Duratius, who had always remained loyal to Rome though some of his tribe
had rebelled. The information thus reaching Caninius was that a large
enemy force had assembled in the territory of the Pictones. He therefore
marched towards the *oppidum* of Lemonum. When he was getting near, he
received more exact reports from prisoners: Duratius was shut up inside
and being attacked by an army of many thousands led by Dumnacus, chief
of the Andes.

As Caninius's legions were under strength he dared not risk battle, and
so he established camp in a strong position. When Dumnacus heard of
Caninius's approach, he turned all his forces to face the Roman legions and
set about attacking their camp. He spent several days doing this, and his
force suffered heavy losses. However, he failed to break the defences at any
point, and so returned to resume the siege of Lemonum.

During this time the legate Gaius Fabius had been receiving the sub-   27
mission of several tribes and taking hostages from them as guarantees. A

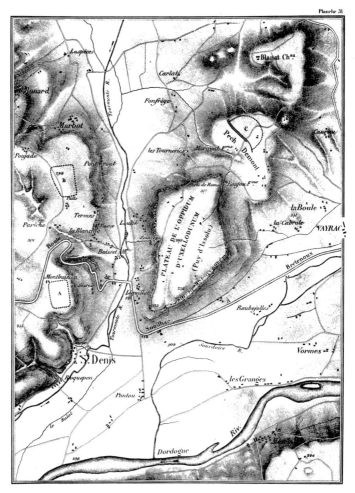

Napoleon III believed that the Puy d'Issolu overlooking the river Dordogne was the site of the native stronghold of Uxellodunum – the last native fortress to hold out against Caesar's armies. The plan above is based on this identification.

dispatch from Caninius reached him reporting what was going on in the country of the Pictones. Fabius acted immediately, setting out to help Duratius.

When Dumnacus heard that Fabius was on his way, he gave up hope. He could not possibly succeed if compelled to withstand a Roman attack from outside and at the same time watch out for a counter-attack from the enemy inside the *oppidum*. So he suddenly withdrew his forces, thinking that he would only be really safe if he took his army across the river Loire, which was too wide to be crossed except by bridge.

Fabius had not yet come within sight of the enemy or joined up with Caninius. But from information he was given by people who knew the country, he concluded that the terrified Gauls would head for precisely the place they *were* heading for. So he marched with his troops towards the same bridge, telling his cavalry to go on ahead of the legions' marching column, but not too far ahead; they must be able to get back to the main column and the camp without putting too much strain on their horses.

Our cavalry carried out their instructions, caught up with Dumnacus's marching column and attacked it. The Gauls tried to run away, panic-stricken and hampered by the packs they were carrying, but our men attacked them as they went, killing many of them and taking a great deal of booty. After this successful operation they made their way back to camp.

The next night Fabius sent his cavalry ahead, ready to engage the enemy   28
and slow up the whole column until he could catch up with it himself. The cavalry commander Quintus Atius Varus, a man of exceptional courage and intelligence, emphasized to his men that Fabius's instructions must be strictly followed.

He caught up with the enemy column and posted some of his squadrons separately in suitable positions, attacking the enemy with the rest. Their whole column halted so that their infantry could support the cavalry against ours, and with the infantry there backing them up, the Gallic cavalry fought with greater confidence.

The battle was fiercely contested. Our men despised an enemy they had beaten the day before, and fought valiantly against the Gallic infantry, aware that the legions were coming up behind. They were ashamed to give ground, and extremely anxious to finish off the battle on their own, without the legions' help. The enemy, on the other hand, believing, from the previous day's experience, that our troops would receive no reinforcements, thought they had a chance of wiping out our cavalry.

The struggle was hard fought and went on for some time. Dumnacus was   29
drawing up his infantry in battle formation, so that they could give support to the cavalry squadrons in turn as the need arose, when suddenly the massed ranks of our legions came into view.

At the sight of them the Gauls were absolutely dismayed; their cavalry and their infantry were thrown into a panic and their whole baggage train into complete confusion. They ran about in all directions, shouting and yelling, trying to get away.

Our cavalry, who shortly before had been battling bravely against enemy resistance, were carried away with the joy of victory. Loud shouts went up on all sides as they swarmed around the fleeing enemy, and they went on pursuing and killing them as long as their horses had any wind left and they themselves had strength enough in their arms to wield their swords.

In this engagement more than 12,000 Gauls were killed; some of them still had their weapons in their hands, others had thrown them down in their panic. The whole of their baggage train was captured.

There was a Senonian, Drappes, who from the start of Vercingetorix's   30
rebellion had been intercepting Roman baggage trains and supply convoys. For this purpose he had used bands of criminals assembled from all sides, and including slaves to whom he had promised their freedom, exiles whom he had summoned from various tribes, and bandits to whom he had offered refuge.

After the rout, it became known that this Drappes was making for the Province with a force of no more than two thousand, got together from the fugitives, and that he had been joined in the enterprise by the Cadurcan Lucterius, who, as we know from the previous book of the *Commentaries*, had wanted to invade the Province at the start of the Gallic revolt. The legate Caninius hurried in pursuit with two legions, for it would be a very great disgrace if the Province suffered any damage or its people were alarmed by the brigandage of these desperadoes.

31 Gaius Fabius, with the rest of the army, set out for the territory of the Carnutes and the other tribes whose forces he knew to have suffered badly in the battle with Dumnacus. He felt sure that after their recent defeat they would be less recalcitrant; but if they were given any breathing space, it was possible that at Dumnacus's instigation they might be roused to revolt.

As it turned out, Fabius was very successful in bringing these tribes quickly back to allegiance. The Carnutes now gave hostages and surrendered; even under frequent harassment, they had never previously asked for terms. The others, the so-called Aremorican tribes, who live in the extreme west of Gaul on the Atlantic coast, followed their lead; as soon as Fabius arrived with his legions they complied with his demands at once. Dumnacus was driven out of his own country and was forced to wander, alone and always in hiding, making for the remotest part of Gaul.

32 As for Drappes and Lucterius, they heard that Caninius and his legions were close at hand. They realized that they risked certain destruction if they tried to invade the Province with an army in close pursuit behind them. They saw too that their chance of ranging all over the country indulging in acts of brigandage was gone.

So they halted in the territory of the Cadurci, where Lucterius had once enjoyed great power over his fellow-countrymen in the days before the defeat of Vercingetorix; he always favoured revolutionary policies and so had great influence among those native people. Uxellodunum, which had been a dependency of his, was an *oppidum* of great natural strength, and Lucterius now occupied it with his own forces and those of Drappes, securing the support of its inhabitants.

33 Caninius was quickly on the scene. He observed that the *oppidum* was protected on all sides by precipitous rocks and would be difficult for armed men to climb up to even if there was no one to defend it. However, he saw that the people had great quantities of baggage, and that if they tried to get it away secretly they would be at the mercy not only of his cavalry but of his legions as well. So he divided his cohorts into three detachments and built three camps on very high ground. From these he set about gradually constructing a rampart round the *oppidum*, in so far as his limited manpower allowed.

34 Those inside could not forget the terrible events at Alesia, and when they saw what Caninius was doing they feared they would suffer the same fate if they too were besieged. Lucterius had been through that former siege, and now he more than anyone else warned that they must organize their grain supply. It was unanimously decided that part of their force should be

left in the *oppidum* while Drappes and Lucterius set out with a body of light-armed men to bring in grain.

The plan was approved, and the next night Drappes and Lucterius set off, leaving 2,000 armed men behind in the *oppidum* and taking the rest with them. They spent a few days in the territory of the Cadurci and succeeded in getting large quantities of grain there. This was because some of the people were eager to help and readily gave them grain, while others were unable to prevent them taking what they wanted.

They also made a number of night attacks on our redoubts, which led Caninius to postpone completing the entrenchments round the *oppidum*; if he did complete them, he would have to leave part unguarded or else man a larger number of posts, with the result that each of them would be less well guarded.

Having thus secured a large supply of grain, Drappes and Lucterius took 35 up a position no more than ten miles from the *oppidum*, intending from there to carry in the grain a little at a time. They divided the responsibility for this between them: while Drappes with some of their force stayed behind to guard the camp, Lucterius led the convoy of pack animals towards the *oppidum*. He posted pickets at various places there and, shortly before dawn, began bringing in the grain along narrow tracks through the woods.

However, the sentries on duty at the Roman camp heard the noise. Scouts were sent out and returned with reports of what was going on. Caninius took from the nearest redoubts the cohorts who were ready armed there, and quickly attacked the grain convoy just as day was breaking.

Lucterius's men were taken by surprise. They panicked and scattered, fleeing towards their own pickets. When our men saw this and found themselves up against armed men, they were spurred on to fight all the more fiercely, and allowed not one of the enemy force to be taken alive. Lucterius managed to escape from the scene with a few men. He did not, however, get back to the camp.

After this success, Caninius discovered from some prisoners that part of 36 the enemy army was encamped with Drappes no more than 12 miles away. He confirmed this report by questioning several individuals. It seemed to him that with one of their two leaders put to flight, the rest of the enemy would be unnerved and easily overwhelmed.

He thought it was a great stroke of luck that after the slaughter of the other force no one had managed to get back to the enemy camp to tell Drappes about the defeat they had suffered. But although he saw no danger in making the attempt, he sent on ahead towards the enemy camp all his cavalry, together with the German infantry, who were so very fleet of foot. He then divided one of his legions between the three camps, before setting out with the other one, lightly armed and ready for action.

When he had come quite close to the enemy position, he received the following information from the scouts he had sent on ahead: in typical Gallic fashion, Drappes had left the higher ground and camped on the bank of the river; the Germans and the Roman cavalry had swooped down on them all and attacked, taking them completely by surprise.

At this Caninius led up his legion, armed and in battle order. Thus, once the signal was given, they quickly occupied all the surrounding higher ground. When this happened, the Germans and the cavalry could see the standards of the legions and they fought harder than ever. Wasting no time, the cohorts charged down from every side. They killed or captured every Gaul there and took a great deal of booty. Drappes himself was taken prisoner in that engagement.

37   The operation had been a complete success, achieved almost without a single casualty. Caninius had destroyed the enemy force outside the *oppidum*, and now returned to besieging those inside. It had been fear of the enemy outside Uxellodunum that had earlier prevented him dividing his troops between a number of guard posts, and completing his ring of fortifications; now he ordered siegeworks to be constructed everywhere. Next day Gaius Fabius arrived there with his forces and took over a part of the siegeworks.

38   Meanwhile Caesar had left his quaestor Marcus Antonius with 15 cohorts in the territory of the Bellovaci, to see that the Belgae did not have any chance of planning further revolt. He himself visited the other tribes, demanding from them additional hostages and trying to alleviate the fear and anxiety he sensed among them all.

He visited the Carnutes, among whom the revolt had first begun, as Caesar explains in the previous book. He found that they were particularly alarmed because they were very much aware of what they had done. Caesar wanted to free this tribe from its fear as soon as possible, and so he demanded that Gutruatus, who had been an instigator of the revolt and chiefly responsible for the massacre at Cenabum, should be handed over for punishment.

This man would not trust himself even to his own countrymen. However, everyone joined in a thorough search for him and he was found and brought to the Roman camp. The soldiers, who held Gutruatus responsible for all the dangers they had been through and all the losses they had suffered, crowded round Caesar demanding that the Gaul be severely dealt with. And so, against his own natural inclination, Caesar was forced to execute him. He was flogged to death and his corpse beheaded.

39   While Caesar was among the Carnutes, he had received frequent dispatches from Caninius, informing him what had been done about Drappes and Lucterius, and how resolutely the people of Uxellodunum were holding out.

Although he regarded the numbers involved as insignificant, still he thought their obstinacy called for severe punishment. Otherwise all the Gauls might think that their own failure to stand up to the Romans had been due not to lack of strength, but lack of perseverance. Other tribes might follow the example of Uxellodunum and exploit any strong positions they held in an attempt to regain their freedom. He realized that all the Gauls knew he had just one summer left before his command expired; if they could hold out for that length of time, they would have nothing more to fear. And so he left the legate Quintus Calenus with two legions to follow at normal marching speed, while he himself took all the cavalry and hurried with all possible speed to join Caninius.

His arrival at Uxellodunum surprised everyone. He found the *oppidum*   **40**
completely enclosed by the siegeworks; escape from the blockade was
simply impossible. However, when he had learned from deserters that the
inhabitants had a very large stock of grain, he set about trying to cut off
their water supply.

The deep valley that almost entirely surrounded the hill on which stood
Uxellodunum, with its steep cliffs, had a river running through it. It was
impossible to divert this river because of the nature of the ground; it flowed
at the very foot of the mountain, so low down that ditches could not be dug
to drain it off in any direction. For anyone in the *oppidum*, however, the way
down to the river was so steep and difficult that if our men tried to prevent
them, the people inside could not get to the river, or make the difficult climb
back up again, without the risk of being wounded or killed.

Caesar was well aware of their difficulty. So he posted archers and slingers
at various points, and also placed artillery in certain positions facing the
easiest ways down. By this means he cut off access to the river water for the
Gauls inside the *oppidum*.

After that, the besieged had all to go to one place to get water. It was   **41**
right at the foot of the wall of the *oppidum* on the side where, for about 300
feet, there was a gap in the river's circuit. A great spring of water gushed out
there. All the Romans wanted to cut the Gauls off from this spring, but only
Caesar could see the way to do it.

Opposite the place, he started to push protective sheds up the hill, and to
build a ramp. This was hard work, and also involved continual fighting.
The Gauls kept running down from the higher ground and engaging our
men from long range, without any risk to themselves, but inflicting many
casualties on our men as they resolutely worked their way up. However,
our soldiers were not deterred; they pushed the protective sheds up the hill,
and by hard work and effort overcame the difficulties of the terrain.

At the same time, they dug tunnels towards the head of the spring and the
streams that fed it. They could carry out this operation without any risk
because it could be done without the enemy suspecting it.

The ramp was raised to a height of 60 feet, and a tower of ten storeys was
erected on it. The tower was not intended to reach the level of the walls, for
no siegeworks could possibly have done that. The aim was that it should
dominate the spring. When missiles from artillery mounted in this tower
were aimed at the approach to the spring, it became impossible for the Gauls
to get water safely. Consequently, not only cattle and pack animals but also
the great mass of the people of Uxellodunum were weakened by thirst.

For the besieged this was a disaster. They were terrified. They filled casks   **42**
with tallow, pitch, and pieces of wood, set them on fire and then rolled them
down on our siegeworks. At the same time, they engaged us in very fierce
fighting, so that our men would be too much occupied in hand-to-hand
combat to be able to put out the flames. In no time at all a great blaze flared
up in the actual siegeworks, for everything that was sent rolling down that
steep slope landed against the sheds and the ramp, setting fire to whatever
stopped its fall.

The triumphal arch that the Romans erected at the approach to Orange (Vaucluse) (*left*) symbolized Rome's conquest of Gaul. Erected in the first century BC, after Caesar's campaigns, it was adorned with sculptures of Gaulish battle scenes and armour. Another triumphal arch was erected at Carpentras (Vaucluse). One of the scenes (*right*) shows native prisoners chained together. Monuments of this kind would have been a constant reminder to the local population of the power of Rome.

As for our men, faced with a hazardous form of fighting on ground that was against them, they met all the difficulties with magnificent courage. The action was taking place on high ground, in full view of our army, and there was a great deal of shouting from both sides. So each man, hoping to have his courage witnessed and acknowledged by all those watching, made himself as conspicuous as he could in facing the flames and the weapons that the enemy hurled.

43   When Caesar saw that many of his men were being wounded, he ordered the cohorts to climb up the rocks on every side of the *oppidum*, and by shouting loudly all around it, create the impression they were getting control of the walls. This ruse terrified the people inside, who could not be certain what was going on in other parts of the *oppidum*.

They recalled their armed troops from attacking our siegeworks and posted them at various points along the walls. This meant the fighting stopped, and our men quickly got the blaze under control; in some places they put out the flames, in others they isolated sections of the siegeworks still burning. The besieged, however, continued offering stubborn resistance, refusing to give up even though many of their people had died of thirst.

In the end our tunnels reached the streams feeding the spring, and these were then tapped and diverted. So the spring, which had never before failed, suddenly went dry. The Gauls completely gave up hope, thinking that the spring had failed because the gods had willed it rather than because men had contrived it. So they yielded to necessity and surrendered.

44   Caesar was aware that his clemency was well known to all, and so he was not afraid of being considered cruel by nature if on this occasion he took severe measures. He realized there would never be a successful outcome for his policies if more revolts of the same kind broke out in different parts of the country. So he decided he had to deter the rest of the Gauls by inflicting an exemplary punishment in this case. All those who had carried weapons had their hands cut off, but their lives were spared so that everyone might see how evildoers were punished.

I have already mentioned that Drappes had been taken prisoner by Caninius. Either he was unable to endure the degradation of being kept in chains, or else he was afraid of a worse punishment to come. Whatever the reason, he refused to eat and so died within a few days. Lucterius, as I have already mentioned, had escaped from the fighting outside Uxellodunum. He had been constantly on the move, trusting his life to many different people because he thought it would be dangerous to stay anywhere for very long. He knew well enough that he had earned Caesar's certain enmity. Now he had come into the power of Epasnactus, an Arvernian who was very loyal to Rome. This man had no hesitation at all in putting Lucterius in chains and bringing him to Caesar.

4 Mopping up

45   Meanwhile Labienus had been in the country of the Treveri and had fought a successful cavalry engagement there, killing many of the Treveri themselves and also many Germans, who never refused help to anyone against the Romans. He took the chiefs of the Treveri alive, and with them an Aeduan chief called Surus, a man of noble birth, a distinguished soldier and the only Aeduan who was still in arms.

When Caesar heard of Labienus's success, he realized things were going **46** well in every part of Gaul. It seemed to him that now, as a result of several years' campaigning, Gaul had been defeated and subdued.

However, he had never himself visited Aquitania, though he had to a certain extent conquered it through the agency of Publius Crassus. He now therefore set out with two legions for that part of Gaul, intending to spend the last part of the campaigning season there. His operations in Aquitania were completed with the same speed and success as elsewhere. All the tribes there sent envoys to him and gave hostages.

After that, he himself set out for Narbonne with a cavalry escort, leaving his legates to organize the dispersal of the army to their winter quarters. Four legions were stationed in Belgium with the legates Marcus Antonius, Gaius Trebonius, and Publius Vatinius; two were sent to the territory of the Aedui, whom Caesar knew to be the most important tribe in Gaul; two were posted in the territory of the Turones on their border with the Carnutes, to secure all that part of the country that reached the Atlantic coast; the remaining two were stationed in the territory of the Lemovices, not far from the Arverni. This dispersal of the legions meant that no part of Gaul was left without Roman troops.

Caesar stayed in the Province for a few days, rapidly visiting all the assize towns, settling political disputes, and distributing rewards to those who deserved them. He had an excellent opportunity of finding out what individuals' attitudes had been during the general revolt of Gaul, which he had been able to withstand thanks to the loyalty and support of the Province. When this business was completed, he went back to join the legions in Belgium and spent the winter at Nemetocenna.

While he was there he heard that Commius the Atrebatian had been **47** engaged in an action against some Roman cavalry. When Antonius had reached his winter camp, the Atrebates had been quiet. But Commius, ever since the occasion mentioned above, when he had been wounded, had always been ready to get involved in any intrigues that his fellow tribesmen might start, so that if their aims turned to war, they would have someone to lead and inspire them. While the Atrebates as a whole were obedient to Rome, Commius and his band of horsemen were supporting themselves by brigandage. They planted ambushes along the roads and intercepted several of the convoys on their way to the Roman winter camps.

Gaius Volusenus Quadratus, who had been assigned to Antonius as **48** commander of cavalry, was with him in his winter camp, and so was sent by him to pursue Commius's horsemen. Volusenus was the ideal person for the job; for as well as being a man of outstanding valour, he also loathed Commius and so was all the more ready to carry out Antonius's orders. He laid ambushes at various places, made frequent attacks on Commius's men, and fought successful engagements with them.

Eventually there was a particularly fierce encounter. Volusenus, being very eager to capture Commius himself, pursued him too closely and with only a few men. Commius for his part fled as hard as he could, thus drawing Volusenus farther afield. Then, in his personal hatred for the Roman, he suddenly called on his men to show their loyalty by helping him, and not allowing the wounds so treacherously inflicted on him to go unavenged. With that, he turned his horse round and recklessly charged alone at Volusenus.

His companions all followed his example. Our small force was put to flight with the Gauls in pursuit. Commius put his spurs to his horse and caught up with Volusenus. Lowering his lance he drove it with all his might clean through Volusenus's thigh. Seeing their commander wounded, our men did not hesitate to retaliate. They turned their horses about and drove off the pursuers. When that happened, a number of the Gauls were knocked down and wounded by the violence of the charge; some were trampled underfoot in the rout, others were taken prisoner. That was a fate Commius, their leader, managed to escape by the swiftness of his horse.

Although it was the Roman cavalry that had the better of the encounter, their commander Volusenus was carried back to camp so seriously wounded it seemed he would die. As for Commius, either because his injury had been avenged, or because he had lost most of his followers, he now sent envoys to Antonius, and gave hostages to guarantee that he would live where he was told to live and do what he was told to do. He made only one request – that as a concession to his personal fear, he should not be required to come into the presence of any Roman. Antonius thought the fear was justified. He granted Commius's request and accepted the hostages.

I know that Caesar wrote one book of his *Commentaries* for each year of his campaigns. However, I have not considered it necessary for me to do so because in the following year, when Lucius Paulus and Gaius Marcellus were consuls, Caesar did not conduct any large-scale operations in Gaul. But so that everyone may know where Caesar and the army were during that time, I have decided that a short appendix ought to be written and added to this commentary.

49   While he was wintering in Belgium, Caesar had a single aim in view, namely, to keep the tribes loyal and avoid giving any of them the hope of rebellion or a pretext for it. The last thing he wanted was to be faced with the necessity of fighting a campaign just before his departure from Gaul. He was anxious that there should be no war left when it came to the moment for withdrawing his army; for if there were, the whole of Gaul would be only too glad to join in, once the threat of retaliation had been removed.

So he addressed the authorities of the various tribes in complimentary terms and gave their leading men rich presents; he did not impose any fresh burdens on them. Gaul was exhausted by so many defeats. Caesar was able to keep it peaceful by making the terms of subjection more tolerable.

5 Towards the civil war

Caesar did not follow his usual practice when the time in winter quarters
50   was over, but set out instead for Italy, travelling as rapidly as possible. His

intention was to visit in person the towns and colonies from whom he had canvassed support for the candidature of his quaestor Marcus Antonius, who was standing for a priesthood.

He made the journey gladly: he readily gave his support to Antonius, who was a close friend, and whom he had sent on ahead some time before to start his election campaign; but he was also keen to thwart the small but powerful clique who aimed to get Antonius defeated in the election because they were eager to undermine Caesar's own influence when he returned from his province.

In fact, Caesar was still travelling and had not yet reached Italy when he heard that Antonius had been elected augur. However, he thought he still had a good reason for visiting the towns and colonies. He meant to thank them for having turned out in great numbers to support Antonius's candidature, and at the same time he wanted to canvass support for himself when he stood for the consulship in the following year.

His enemies were insolently boasting that Lucius Lentulus and Gaius Marcellus had been elected consuls in order to deprive Caesar of any office or position of prestige, and that Servius Galba had been robbed of the consulship even though he had been more popular and had won more votes, because he had close connections with Caesar, having been one of his legates as well as his friend.

Caesar's arrival was greeted with extraordinary honour and affection in **51** all the towns and colonies. It was the first time he had visited them since the great war against the whole of Gaul. The people did everything they could possibly think of to decorate the gates, the streets, and all the places where he would be passing. All the inhabitants went out to meet him, taking their children too. Sacrifices were offered everywhere, and in the market places and temples there were couches set out for the statues of the gods as at their ritual banquets. From this one could get a foretaste of the joy there would be when he celebrated the triumph that had been so long awaited. Those who had wealth used it lavishly to honour Caesar; those who had not, made up for it by their enthusiasm.

Caesar passed rapidly through the whole of northern Italy before return- **52** ing as quickly as he could to the army at Nemetocenna. He ordered all the legions to leave their winter camps for the territory of the Treveri. He went there too, and held a review of the army. He put Titus Labienus in command of the Cisalpine province, hoping in this way to win greater support for him there when he stood for election to the consulship. Caesar himself undertook only as many marches as he thought necessary and sufficient to keep his troops fit by being on the move.

While he was there, he heard frequent reports that his enemies were making overtures to Labienus. He was also informed that it was the aim of a small clique to get a decree passed in the Senate depriving him of part of his army. However, he did not believe any of the reports about Labienus, and could not be persuaded to take any measures against the possibility of such a decree being passed. His view was that his position would easily be safeguarded, if the senators were allowed to vote freely.

Gaius Curio, a tribune of the people, had undertaken to speak for Caesar and defend his position, and had often made the following proposal to the Senate: if the thought of Caesar's military strength alarmed anyone, then both Caesar and Pompeius should resign their commands and disband their armies – for the military domination of Pompeius certainly did greatly alarm the city. When that happened the state would be free and independent. It was not merely a proposal that Curio was making; he also set about trying to get the Senate to vote on it. But the consuls and the friends of Pompeius blocked this, and their delaying tactics prevented it coming to anything.

53 This was an important indication of the attitude of the Senate as a whole, and in keeping with the way it had behaved earlier. In the previous year Marcellus, while making an attack on Caesar's standing and reputation, had put forward a motion about his provinces, but the motion had been premature and so contravened the law passed by Pompeius and Crassus. The matter was debated, and Marcellus had called for a division; he wanted to gain for himself all the political advantage that would result from attacking Caesar. A crowded Senate had rejected the motion. But this had not discouraged Caesar's enemies. On the contrary, it had made them realize they must find still stronger grounds for compelling the Senate to approve the measures they themselves had resolved upon.

54 The Senate then passed a decree ordering both Pompeius and Caesar to send one legion each for the Parthian war. It was obvious that both legions were being taken from only one man, Caesar. Pompeius had recruited the First legion, which he had sent to Caesar, from Caesar's own province, and it was this legion that he now offered as if it were one of his own.

The intentions of Caesar's enemies were now absolutely clear. However, he sent the First legion back to Pompeius and ordered the Fifteenth, which he had had in north Italy, to be handed over on his own account, in accordance with the Senate's decree. In its place he sent the Thirteenth legion to Italy to man the garrisons from which the Fifteenth had been withdrawn.

He arranged the dispersal of his army into winter quarters himself. He stationed Gaius Trebonius with four legions in Belgium, and sent the same number into the territory of the Aedui under Gaius Fabius. He thought this disposition of the legions would ensure the security of Gaul: the restraining presence of a Roman army would be felt among the Belgae, who were the most warlike of the Gauls, and among the Aedui, who were the most influential. Caesar himself then set out for Italy.

55 When he arrived, he discovered that the two legions he had sent back, and which, according to the decree of the Senate, ought to have been taken for the Parthian war, had instead, through the intervention of the consul Gaius Marcellus, been handed over to Pompeius and kept in Italy. After that, no one could possibly doubt what plans were being made against Caesar. But he decided that he must endure it all as long as there was any hope left that he could reach a settlement by constitutional means rather than make war.

FURTHER READING

Adcock, Frank *Caesar as a Man of Letters* Cambridge University Press (1956); Richard West (Philadelphia 1956)

Badian, Ernst *Roman Imperialism in the Late Republic* Blackwell (Oxford 1968); Cornell University Press (1968)

Brogan, Olwen *Roman Gaul* Bell (London 1953); Harvard University Press (1953)

Cunliffe, Barry *The Celtic World* Bodley Head (London 1979); McGraw-Hill (New York 1979)

Gelzer, Matthias *Caesar: Politician and Statesman* Blackwell (Oxford 1968); Harvard University Press (1968)

Grant, Michael *The Army of the Caesar's* Weidenfeld (London 1974); Scribner's (New York 1974)

Holmes, T. Rice *Caesar's Conquest of Gaul* Macmillan (London 1899)

Le Gall, Joel *Alesia* Fayard (Paris 1963)

Nash, Daphne 'The growth of urban society in France' in Cunliffe, Barry & Rowley, Trevor (eds) *Oppida: the Beginnings of Urbanization in Barbarian Europe* British Archaeological Reports (Oxford 1976)

Piggott, Stuart *The Druids* Thames & Hudson (London 1968); Praeger (New York 1968)

Powell, T. G. E. *The Celts* Thames & Hudson (London 1958); Praeger (New York 1958)

Webster, Graham *The Roman Imperial Army* A. & C. Black (London 1969); Funk & Wagnalls (New York 1970)

Wells, C. M. *The German Policy of Augustus: an Examination of the Archaeological Evidence* Oxford University Press (London & New York 1972)

Wheeler, R. E. M. *Hill-Forts of Northern France* Society of Antiquaries (London 1957)

Greece and Rome Vol IV. 1 (March 1957, various essays) Oxford University Press

NOTES ON THE ILLUSTRATIONS

Figures in **bold** refer to colour plates

jacket Sarcophagus depicting battle between Gauls and Romans. *Lauros Giraudon*

endpaper Map: Gaul in Caesar's time. *Tom Stalker-Miller*

frontispiece Bust of Julius Caesar from Vatican Museum. *Mansell Collection*

16 Campaign map 58 BC. *Tom Stalker-Miller*

18 Coins: (left) Julius Caesar. *Weidenfeld and Nicolson Archives*; (right) Dumnorix. *British Museum*

21 Marble relief from altar of Domitius Ahenobarbus (115–100 BC), showing Roman soldiers. *Lauros Giraudon*

27 Roman soldier with short javelin from Magonza Museum. *Alinari*

32 Temple of Saturn, Rome. *Ronald Sheridan*

33 Gaulish warrior from Vachères. *Ronald Sheridan*

41 Bronze calendar from Coligny, near Bourg, Ain. *Musée de la Civilization Gallo-Romaine*

42 Campaign map 57 BC. *Tom Stalker-Miller*

44 Diagram: Le Petit Celland, Normandy. *Tom Stalker-Miller*

46 Coins of the Remi. Centre: *Weidenfeld and Nicolson Archives*; rest: *Bibliothéque Nationale, Paris*

48 Gold torcs from Ipswich, Suffolk. *British Museum*

49 Coins: Suessiones (above left), Nervii (above right), Veneti (below left), Commius (below right). *British Museum*

52 Sarcophagus depicting battle between Gauls and Romans. *Mansell Collection*

58 Campaign map 56 BC. *Tom Stalker-Miller*

61 Map: Hengistbury and La Tène pottery trade routes. *Tom Stalker-Miller*
Drawing: Anchor found at Bulbury hillfort, Dorset. *Jeremy Ford*

63 Map: tribal areas and cliff castle at Pointe de Longmarc'h. *Tom Stalker-Miller*
Cliff castle at Pointe de Longmarc'h. *Thames and Hudson*

67 Drawing: Hillfort at Fécamp, Normandy. *Tom Stalker-Miller*

71 Drawing: Pot from Saint-Pol-de-Leon, Brittany. *Jeremy Ford.*

73 Campaign map 55 BC. *Tom Stalker-Miller*

79 Artist's impression: Crossing the Rhine bridge. *Ron Bowen*
Drawing: Construction of Rhine bridge. *Jeremy Ford*

88 Campaign map 54 BC (spring and summer). *Tom Stalker-Miller*

91 Diagram: Structure of Roman legion. *Jeremy Ford*

93 Denarius of L. Hostilius Saserna. *Ashmolean Museum*

95 Iron slave chain from Bigbury hillfort, Kent. *Manchester Museum*
Iron fire dogs from Lords Bridge, Cambridgeshire. *Cambridge Museum of Archaeology and Ethnology*

99 Campaign map 54 BC (autumn and winter). *Tom Stalker-Miller*

101 Roman campaign camps at Folleville in the Somme valley. Diagram: *Tom Stalker-Miller*; aerial view: *Roger Agache*

103 Artist's impression: legions of Cotta and Sabinus ambushed. *Ron Bowen*

114 Campaign map 53 BC. *Tom Stalker-Miller*

120 Diagram: Structure of Celtic society. *Jeremy Ford*

122 Bronze head, probably a god, from Garancières-en-Beauce. *Musée de Chartres. Jean Roubier*
Celtic boar-god from Euffigneix. *Lauros Giraudon*

125 Columns of the temple porch at Roquepertuse, Provence. *Musée Boily, Marseilles*

128 The river Rhine. *Spectrum Colour Library*

129 The Gundestrup Cauldron. *Nationalmuseet, Copenhagen*

134 Coin of Vercingetorix. *Bibliothéque Nationale, Paris*
Campaign map 52 BC. *Tom Stalker-Miller*

143 *Murus gallicus. Musée des Antiquities Nationales, Saint-Germain-en-Laye*. Diagram: *Jeremy Ford*

144 Stone head from the sanctuary of Roquepertuse, Provence. *Musée Boily Marseilles. Lauros Giraudon*

145 Infrared aerial photograph of Alesia. *René Goguey*

164 Diagram of Alesia. *Tom Stalker-Miller*
Aerial view of Alesia. *René Goguey*

167 Diagrams: Details of Roman works at Alesia. *Napoleon III's Histoire de Jules César*

168 Artist's impression of Romans building siegeworks at Alesia. *Ron Bowen*

169 Reconstruction of Alesia. *Musée Archeologique de Dijon*

171 Bronze figure of dying (or sleeping) Gaul. *Lauros Giraudon*

178 Campaign map 51–50 BC. *Tom Stalker-Miller*

186 Artist's impression of Belovacci retreating. *Ron Bowen*

190 Map showing the Puy d'Issolu as site of Uxellodunum. *Napoleon III's Histoire de Jules César*

196 Left: Triumphal Roman arch at the approach to the city of Orange (Vaucluse). *Mansell Collection*
Right: Detail from Roman triumphal arch at Carpentras (Vaucluse), showing chained prisoners. *Jean Roubier*

GLOSSARY/INDEX

References to the translation are according to the conventional numbered paragraphs into which the Latin text is divided for purposes of reference. They have no ancient authority, but are standard in all modern texts.

Roman citizens' names have either two or three elements: *praenomen* (personal name) and *nomen gentilicium* (family name), with the optional addition of a *cognomen* (third name), which may either be unique to an individual, as a sort of nickname, or else identify a branch of his family. Most Romans in the narrative, like Caesar himself, have the third name, and may be called either by that or by the family name. But the index is arranged according to family names, with cross-references where necessary.

205